Paris under Siege, 1870–1871:
From the Goncourt Journal

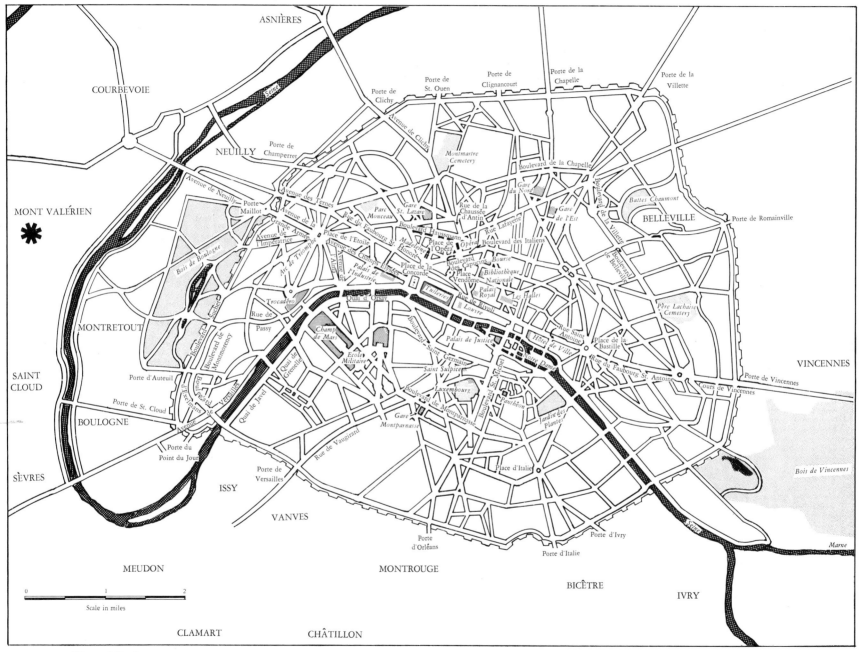

Map of Paris

Paris under Siege, 1870–1871: From the Goncourt Journal

Edited and translated by
GEORGE J. BECKER

With a historical introduction by
PAUL H. BEIK

Cornell University Press / ITHACA AND LONDON

First published 1969

Standard Book Number 8014-0532-7

Library of Congress Catalog Card Number 78-87013

PRINTED IN THE UNITED STATES OF AMERICA
BY THE VAIL-BALLOU PRESS, INC.

Acknowledgments

The text of the Goncourt *Journal* here translated is that
of the "integral" edition published by Fasquelle-Flammarion
in the 1950's. It is used with their permission and that of the
Oxford University Press, holder of English translation rights.
The complete journal from June 20, 1870, to June 20, 1871,
is given here, except for the nine passages not relevant to the
public events described. (These omissions are indicated in
the text by five dots, paragraphed.)

The illustrations, which come from the collection in the
Houghton Library, are reproduced by permission of the
Harvard University Libraries. I owe a particular debt of
gratitude to Professor Simone Smith of Swarthmore College,
who has checked my translation and often saved me from
error. Any errors which remain are the result of my own
folly or intransigence. In addition to writing the historical
introduction, Professor Paul H. Beik of Swarthmore College
has provided the "Chronology" and has been generous with
his knowledge and encouragement, without which this book
would never have reached the public.

GEORGE J. BECKER

Swarthmore, Pennsylvania
April 1969

Contents

Illustrations

Paris under Siege, 1870–1871:

From the Goncourt Journal

The Brothers Goncourt

by George J. Becker

When Jules de Goncourt died on June 20, 1870, his elder brother Edmond, aged forty-eight, felt that life was over for him too. At one point during the last agonizing weeks of Jules' illness he had even tried to steel himself to killing his brother and committing suicide. Discovering himself incapable of this, in the numbness of his grief he took consolation in the belief that his own precarious health did not leave him long to live. He did in fact live on for twenty-six years, and, something he had thought impossible, in his solitary state he produced novels, plays, and books on art, and above all continued the incomparable *Journal*.

It is by this latter work, and by the Goncourt Academy, rather than by their other writings that the two brothers are remembered today. Ironically, since in continuing the *Journal* and publishing a considerable portion of it Edmond always thought of it as a monument to his dead brother, it has turned out rather to be a monument to the survivor. For in spite—or because—of a certain dash and effervescence which disappear with Jules' death, Edmond is revealed, especially in the portion here translated, to be the observer and diarist *par excellence*. What the *Journal* gives us is a sharp, almost daily record covering a period of nearly forty-five years, from

December 2, 1851, until a few days before Edmond's death in July 1896. This record ranges widely over events and experiences of the time, but its being and its center are Paris, Paris as a changing physical and social environment, Paris as the lively forum of the arts. What we find recorded above all is a sense of movement, the volatility of emerging modern life, set down not by an ardent apologist but rather by a man who was for the most part hostile to change but who was so scrupulous an observer that he could not avoid presenting the salient characteristics of his time, by a man whose sensibility was so responsive to the minutiae of everyday life that he was bound to record that which gave his times definition even while deploring it.

Thinking back over the years when he and his brother wrote in collaboration, Edmond provided a moving preface to the three volumes of the *Journal* published in 1887:

This journal is the confession we made every evening; the confession of two lives which were inseparable in pleasure, work, and pain, twin sensibilities, twin minds receiving from their contact with men and things impressions so similar, so identical, so homogeneous that this confession may be considered the expansion of a single *me*, of a single *I*. . . .

Our effort . . . was to attempt to make our contemporaries live again for posterity in animated likeness, to make them live again through the lively stenography of conversation, the physical surprise of a gesture, those nothings of passion by which a personality is revealed, through that *je ne sais quoi* which gives the intensity of life—in short, by the notation of a bit of that fever which is characteristic of the heady atmosphere of Paris.

And in this work which sought above all to *give life* from a memory that was still warm, in this work hastily set down and not always reread—without concern for faulty syntax or words without a passport—we have always preferred the phrase and the expression which least blunted or *academicized* the liveliness of our sensations and the vigor of our ideas.

This journal was begun on December 2, 1851, the day our first book was put on sale, which was also the day of the coup d'état.

The entire manuscript was, so to speak, written by my brother, under our joint dictation, which was the way we worked in these memoirs.

At my brother's death, considering that our literary work was finished, I resolved to seal up the journal at the entry for January 20, 1870, the last lines traced by his hand. But then I was impelled by the bitter desire to recount to myself the last months and the death of the beloved, and almost immediately the tragic events of the siege and the Commune impelled me to continue this journal, which is still from time to time the confidant of my thoughts.

As the years went on, Edmond followed the first three volumes of selected passages by six more, in this way keeping himself deliciously in hot water, since contemporaries never knew in what terms they might have been impaled by his pen, or rather the author let it be known that such impaling was possible, though in fact he carefully edited material so as to avoid affront to all but the most sensitive natures. The complete manuscript was left, with his other literary effects, to the Goncourt Academy with the direction that it be published in its entirety twenty years after his death, that is, in 1916. World War I made it necessary to defer publication. After the war it was further delayed on the grounds that the sensibilities and reputations of people still living or of their families should be spared. Another war intervened, and it was not until 1955 that the first of the twenty-two volumes of the integral text appeared from the presses of the Imprimérie Nationale de Monaco. The passages appearing for the first time in this unexpurgated edition are not earth-shaking. There are a number of scatological sketches which are no doubt memorable to the collector, but they are second-hand accounts, perhaps even invented to give pleasure to Edmond, who was known to savor such things, and they have no documentary importance. The chief addition is a considerable amount of material about Princess Mathilde Bonaparte, who provided a friendship, or association, that was one of the major centers of the Goncourts' lives. In her salon the brothers met a level of society not ordinarily open to men of letters, though Sainte-Beuve, Gautier, and Flaubert also had entrée to her circle.

It may well be that the events of 1870–1871 saved Edmond de Goncourt for literature. Bereft as he was, he was forced to new interests and responses at precisely the moment when events provided them, even necessitated them. Personalities were on the whole reduced in importance. The events were dominant, and they were largely public and anonymous. They speak for themselves; they impress themselves upon the reader as they impressed themselves upon the diarist's own sensibility. This portion of the *Journal* is not concerned with events outside of Paris and barely speculates about them. It is a vivid record of what one man felt it was like to live for nearly nine months under the siege, under the brief Prussian occupation, and under the threat of the Commune, and it gives the lie to Arnold Bennett's fictional account in *The Old Wives' Tale*, which shows Parisians largely untouched by what was happening around them. Edmond roamed everywhere by train, by omnibus, on foot. Although his house on the Boulevard Montmorency opposite the Auteuil railroad station is even by today's standards well out from the center of Paris, distance did not deter him, and when Prussian shells forced the curtailment of train and omnibus service far short of Auteuil, he thought nothing of walking home through the snowy night.

As he reports, the siege of Paris was something of a joke for two months (actually the gates of Paris were not finally closed until November 27), but in December the joke turned to severe privation, and by the time of the capitulation on January 28, suffering was acute. There came a period of even more bitter psychological suffering during the token occupation of the Prussians at the beginning of March. One of the recurrent ideas of the *Journal* is a rising sense of outrage and hatred toward the enemy. As early as the September 6 entry there is mention of the necessity of revenge, that *revanche* which festered in French hearts until in 1919 the slate was wiped clean with the restoration of Alsace and Lorraine and the ritual repetition of humiliation at Versailles in the Hall of Mirrors. The greatest personal anxiety was experienced during the days of the Commune, when the Versailles forces, mounting an attack from the west, shelled the same targets which the Germans had shelled in January. (Each time Edmond's house was in the line of fire.) Yet once the crisis was over, life returned to normal with remarkable speed, at least on the level from which the diarist looked out upon the world. Flaubert came down from Rouen for dinner and talked about his next book. Edmond himself began to think about a new novel and gradually settled down to a way of life that did not vary greatly during the twenty-five years remaining to him. Princess Mathilde came back from temporary exile in Belgium. The Magny dinners involving Flaubert, Zola, Turgenev, and Henry James among others, were instituted. With the fading of the "gas-lit empire" France entered into what today is nostalgically called "la belle époque."

Other portions of the *Journal* are rarely as stirring or significant as what is presented here, particularly since the diarist never again immersed himself so completely in public happenings. But as important in such a record as the events set down is the emergent picture of the diarist himself, in which his limitations are no doubt as noteworthy as his special genius or virtue. What are we to say of Edmond de Goncourt as he reveals himself?

Above all, there are the vanity and sensitivity peculiar to the man of letters, which particularize both this man and the literary milieu in which he lived. Paris more than any other literary capital is a world of remarkable density disturbed by a remarkable intensity of literary and artistic tempests. In the last forty years of the century the new literature and the new painting were being created before the avid eyes of a public more volatile and articulate than any previous one. Novels, plays, and expositions of paintings were themselves public events of first importance. Novelists, playwrights, and painters, as wells as actresses and courtesans, were celebrities. Coteries came into being, bringing intrigue and pitched battles. There was a tremendous jockeying for position, a tremendous effort at advertisement—what the French call *réclame*—the goal of which was immediate celebrity and enduring fame. Dangling somewhere in the sky was the grand prize of election to the French Academy, with its patent of so-called immortality.

In all this frenetic striving Edmond de Goncourt always came off second best. Although he opened up the top floor of his house—his *Grenier*—for Sunday afternoon gatherings, he felt that the disciples whom Zola gathered around himself at Médan were perhaps more loyal and more distinguished. Although his novels were frequently received with esteem, they never sold in the numbers that those of Zola and Daudet did. Although numerous plays were drawn from his novels, they were greeted with indifference if not with embattled hostility. Although he had hoped at long last to impress his contemporaries by the *Journal*, Taine and others received it with cries of outrage; some threatened lawsuits; and one person dispatched an anonymous envelope containing soiled toilet paper. While Edmond felt that *Germinie Lacerteux*, written with his brother in 1865, was really the revolutionary archetype of realistic fiction, it was Zola who became the acknowledged master of the new school. While he felt that by birth, breeding, and literary achievement he should be elected to the French Academy, he was never urged to offer his candidacy and had to seek his revenge in the creation of the Académie Goncourt for a group of ten, which has turned out to be even less distinguished than the academy of the forty immortals.

Such are the important currents and crosscurrents that run through his later years. Hope, disappointment, and recrimination make up too much of the burden of those pages. Happily there was one crowning public testimonial of success. Through the good offices of Zola and Daudet in particular a great public dinner was arranged for February 1895 on the occasion of Edmond's receiving the cross of an officer of the Legion of Honor. Even this occasion was beset by typical difficulties. The dinner had to be postponed because of the death of Vacquerie, one of the members of the committee in charge of it. Edmond's outburst in the *Journal* on February 21 is typical of him: "What! Because of the death of a gentleman whom I met only once in my life, at a dinner given by the *Echo de Paris*, my dinner cannot take place two days after his death! But during this season of *influenza* who can tell whether a second member of the committee will not die before the week is up. Ah! if it had only been a reactionary instead of a republican!"

The banquet did take place on Friday March 1 and was full of gaiety and adulation. There was a congratulatory telegram from Georg Brandes hailing Goncourt as the *maître initiateur*. A Haarlem tulip-grower asked to be allowed to name a new daffodil after him. "Then the minister [Raymond Poincaré] began to talk, delivering a speech such as has never been pronounced before by a minister decorating a man of letters." Next Heredia proposed a toast to celebrate the golden anniversary of Edmond's wedding with literature. There followed speeches by Clemenceau, Céard, Zola, and Daudet. To all this, deeply moved, Goncourt replied: "I am incapable of saying ten words to ten people. And you are much more numerous, gentlemen. I can thus only thank you, in a few brief words, for your affectionate sympathy and say to you that this evening which I owe to you repays me for many of the hard passages and sufferings of my literary career." At eleven when the party broke up Edmond modestly decided to go home rather than continue the evening with some of the convivial groups. He was ravenously hungry, having barely touched his dinner. Hoping that there was something left of the chocolate and cakes with which he had told his servants to regale themselves, he went home, only to find that everything had been consumed. He went to bed hungry.

The last volume of the *Journal* published in his lifetime ends with the year 1895. The final entry describes an exposition at the Bing galleries which brings out the old man's crotchets, for he hates the furniture which he sees there and exclaims:

Is it really possible that we could be *denationalized*, morally conquered by a vanquishment worse than that of the war, in this day when there is no longer place in France for anything but Muscovite, Scandinavian, Italian, and soon no doubt Portuguese, literature, in this day when there seems to be place in France only for Anglo-Saxon or Dutch furniture!

As he left the exposition he found himself muttering aloud in the street: "A delirium, a delirium of ugliness!" A young man came up to him and asked: "Were you speaking to me, sir?"

A proper question with an easy answer: The *Journal* had been a conversation at large for more than forty-four years. With all his crotchets and limitations, Edmond de Goncourt is still speaking to us.

The Terrible Year

by Paul H. Beik

In the Paris of today one may walk from the Opéra to the Bourse along the Rue du 4 Septembre, named for the day in 1870 when the Second Empire fell. The Franco-Prussian War had begun in July and had gone badly for the French, but the shocking news of Emperor Napoleon III's capture at Sedan was decisive. A crowd of perhaps 200,000 people gathered in the Place de la Concorde adjoining the park of the Tuileries Palace, where Empress Eugénie was in residence with the four-year-old heir to the throne, and eventually forced its way across the bridge over the Seine to the Palais Bourbon, the meeting place of the Legislative Corps. When the guards of the building failed to check this flow of humanity, the legislature was dispersed and a republic was proclaimed, France's Third, for which a provisional Government of National Defense was shortly organized in a manner calculated to preoccupy and pacify the crowds. The crowds then marched along the quays of the Seine to the Hôtel de Ville, the Paris city hall, about a mile to the east, where they heard the announcement of a new group of ministers.

These events—war, defeat, the fall of the Empire—were only the first of what Victor Hugo was to call *l'Année terrible*, the Terrible Year. It was also to bring a second war, that of the Republic against the Prussians, a four-month siege of Paris, the proclaiming of the German Empire in the Hall of Mirrors at Versailles, the fall of Paris, a divisive national election, a humiliating peace, and a civil war culminating in a bloody invasion of the capital by French armies following a second siege. The year was rich in collective experiences as well as individual folly and some personal successes. For France it marked a passage to the last quarter of the nineteenth century, to a moderate republic, a new colonial empire, the Russian alliance, and a slow convalescence from the trauma of the Paris Commune, making possible further efforts to integrate the lower classes into the national community. Not all of the aspects of the Terrible Year can be described in a brief introduction, but some perspective on events may be provided by placing them in their political and geographical setting.

Paris and the Siege

The Paris of the siege that began in late September 1870 was a city of 1,825,000 according to the census of 1866, but what with natural growth and the anticipatory influx of available troops, which more than compensated for the exodus of well-to-do families as the Germans approached, there may have been 2,000,000 people within the walls. These fortifications, surprising for the nineteenth century, had been urged upon King Louis Philippe in 1840 by Adolphe Thiers, the tiny, dynamic historian-politician who was to play a leading role in the events of the Terrible Year. They consisted of a wall thirty feet high around the entire city, with protruding bastions, a ten-foot moat on the outer side, and a railroad on the inner side that could transport troops from one point to another along the forty-mile circumference. Beyond the wall were sixteen forts, carefully placed so that their heavy guns commanded a wide belt of territory approaching the various *portes*, the gateways into the city. The fortifications were still formidable in spite of improvements in artillery since the 1840's that made it possible, from such heights as Meudon and Châtillon, to bombard some of the forts and even some of the city—the Left Bank in particular (the area south of the Seine). To besiege this immensity, and to cut off food supplies, the 147,000 Prussians had to spread out over a circumference of about fifty miles, but for the siege to succeed it was imperative that the French forces from outside the capital be prevented from concentrating against the dispersed Prussians and that sorties, drives from within (for Paris contained nearly half a million armed men), be checked. Like a wrestler dominating a larger opponent, the Prussian forces had to maintain holds at key points; that is why the defeat and immobilization of Marshal MacMahon's French army at Sedan and of Marshal Bazaine's at Metz, which was surrendered on October 27, assumed such importance.

In the fall and winter of 1870 much depended on the French will to resist, the strength of which was somewhat unevenly distributed among leaders and social groupings. The Government of National Defense in Paris consisted largely of republican deputies from the Legislative Corps of the Empire who, on September 4, had succeeded in getting themselves accepted by the crowds at the Hôtel de Ville and in excluding more militant figures such as the Jacobin radical Charles Delescluze and the socialist Louis-Auguste Blanqui. The president of the National Defense Government was General Louis Trochu, military commander of Paris, who was politically moderate and extremely distrustful of the 384,000 members of the National Guard. He preferred to rely on the

72,000 regulars in the city and was in any case pessimistic about doing more than putting up an honorable show of resistance. Other members of the government were for the most part moderate republicans such as Jules Favre, vice-president and foreign minister, who consulted Bismarck about a possible armistice on the eve of the siege until he heard Bismarck's terms, and who later encouraged a similar mission by Adolphe Thiers, who definitely believed that the war should be stopped before France's losses multipled. It is impossible either to measure or to ignore altogether the element of political and social caution in the attitudes of these men. They are not to be compared with Marshal Bazaine, whose surrender at Metz was clearly facilitated by his lack of sympathy for the republic, but neither were they as militant as their young colleague, the republican radical Léon Gambetta, minister of the interior, who did his utmost to continue the war. There is no doubt that the Parisians in general, cut off from the rest of the country and soon forced to undergo unusual tension and hardships, were largely militant patriots who identified the nation with the republic (a people's government) and the republic with justice and equality. They were proud of their position in the front lines and less inclined than their government, which consistently misled them concerning the true situation, to count the war's costs and worry about the arming of the lower classes. There is no doubt that the existence of a National Guard of poorly trained citizen-soldiers who elected their officers, had little to do, and received thirty sous (one franc fifty centimes) per day (which most of them needed, owing to the economic dislocations of the siege) brought about a serious and perhaps hazardous situation not unlike that caused by the National Workshops of 1848.

The Fall of Paris

Before the Germans surrounded Paris, the government sent a delegation to Tours, on the Loire somewhat more than a hundred miles southwest of the capital, to establish relations with the rest of France. On October 7, after the siege had begun, Léon Gambetta escaped from Paris in a balloon launched from the heights of Montmartre, where the Basilica of Sacré Coeur now stands; a few days later he took charge of the Tours delegation and began to recruit volunteers. By the end of October the Army of the Loire was in being, but by that time Marshal Bazaine had surrendered Metz, liberating its Prussian besiegers to interfere with Gambetta's efforts. Through the fall and early winter Gambetta tried desperately to approach Paris in order to unite with a force from inside the capital and thereby to achieve superiority over the Prussian besiegers. For a while the French held Orléans, at the bend of the Loire closest to Paris, but coordination with the capital was dependent on carrier pigeons, and inside the city General Trochu remained pessimistic and slow to act. By December 1870 the Army of the Loire had been broken in two and the Tours delegation had been forced to retreat to Bordeaux, far in the southwest. It was there that Gambetta received a telegram from Paris, dated January 28, announcing that the city had been surrendered and that it along with the rest of France was to elect a National Assembly to consider making peace. Gambetta was indignant, but when his agents in the provinces informed him of a grass-roots desire for peace and social stability, he did not oppose the elections, which were held on February 8, 1871.

To Paris siege and winter had brought hunger, cold, overconsumption of alcohol, disease (19,200 deaths from sickness for January 1871, compared with 4,900 for August 1870), political clubs, rumors, suspicions, and a kind of tension that came to be called "siege fever"; and all these were in addition to the big-city social problems that were a legacy of the booming Second Empire, when modernization and profit-taking had advanced much more rapidly than wages. Baron Haussmann's wide boulevards, recently cut through once labyrinthine old neighborhoods, had given Paris a handsome new face, but the city was badly overcrowded, rents had risen, and an important transformation was beginning to remove poor people from their time-honored fraternization with the middle classes in common stairways and courtyards toward the segregated one-class outer ghettos that would one day grow into the city's red belt. The lower classes were still, however, mainly small retailers, artisans, and handicraftsmen, like their ancestors the sans-culottes of the Great Revolution, although among them there were now patches of factory proletarians. This amalgam held together through the siege and the Commune before splitting up in the Third Republic. During the siege self-appointed "vigilance committees" appeared in the arrondissements into which the city was divided, and capped their organization with a Central Committee. Such political activists as these belonged to two main traditions, one Jacobin in inspiration, the other socialist. The presence of armed National Guard units in even the poorest neighborhoods, coupled with radical leadership, disgust at the conduct of military operations, and indignation at rumors of peace talks, created the possibility of insurrection. On October 31, upon news of military setbacks and rumors of Thiers' peace efforts, the veteran revolutionary Louis-Auguste Blanqui and some followers took possession of the Hôtel de Ville but were chased away in the small hours of the next morning. On January 21 and 22, 1871, immediately following the last disastrous sortie organized by General Trochu on the eve of the surrender of Paris, dissident National Guardsmen again attacked the Hôtel de Ville, crying "No armistice!" and "Vive la Commune!" but were again defeated. There was still a French government in Paris and it still controlled its troops, but this stability was about to come to an end.

The National Assembly

In the French revolutionary tradition sanctified by 1789, 1792, and 1848, a National Assembly was the highest authority because it represented the sovereign people. Bismarck, in negotiating the armistice, had wanted a French National Assembly in order to make the peace treaty binding. The election on February 8, 1871, of the Bordeaux National Assembly brought an end to the Government of National Defense in Paris and its offshoot the Delegation of Tours (which had moved to Bordeaux). Hastily conducted, the election was nevertheless free, for the imperial officials were gone and new political groupings had had little time to organize. The issue was whether to make peace, and since settling for defeat was opposed by republicans, especially in the big cities, and overwhelmingly supported by the peasants and by propertied and conservative people everywhere, and since France was still 70 per cent rural (nearly 90 per cent with Paris left out of the calculation), the peace candidates won most of the seats in the Bordeaux Assembly. Their politics corresponded with their desire for peace and stability: some 400 were monarchists, a clear majority; there were no more than 220 republicans, and most of the latter were conservatives or moderates; deputies sympathetic to Gambetta and the Parisian radicals numbered only forty. This Assembly on February 17 elected Adolphe

Thiers—although he had been a critic of the Second Empire, he was still reputedly a monarchist—Chief of the Executive Power of the French Republic, with the understanding that the question of monarchy or republic would not be finally decided until the peacemaking was over and recovery had begun. Thiers went to Versailles to negotiate preliminary peace terms with Bismarck, and on March 1 the Bordeaux Assembly ratified the distasteful results: loss of Alsace and part of Lorraine; indemnity of five billion francs; triumphal procession of Prussian troops in Paris, where they would remain until the ratifications of the peace preliminaries were exchanged between the two powers.

The Germans entered Paris, a city draped in mourning, from the west on March 1 and paraded down the Champs Elysées to the Place de la Concorde. Bismarck, who had been ambassador to the court of Napoleon III, had his moment of triumph, while the young Prussian officers went as tourists to visit the Louvre. The German occupation area was cordoned off; the French National Guard kept its distance and advised the population to remain calm. To the Germans their stay was disappointingly short, for the prompt French ratification of terms obliged them to withdraw after two days, but to the Parisians it was one of a long list of blows, and, coming on top of what they had been through during the winter, it contributed to a widening abyss between Paris and the provinces.

Representing provincial common sense, conservatism, good conscience, and acceptance of the social order in existence since the Great Revolution, the Bordeaux Assembly repeatedly provoked the Parisian public. Paris had been surrendered on January 28 with only six days' food remaining, but during the siege the public had never been informed of this shortage or of other military realities. Suddenly the fight was over, the government of France was at far-off Bordeaux, and Thiers and an assembly of royalist landowners and bourgeois moderates were agreeing that the republic proclaimed by the Parisian revolution of September 4 was only provisional. Then after disturbing news from Bordeaux that National Guardsmen, in order to keep getting their one franc fifty centimes a day, would have to present certificates of poverty, came the peace terms and the German entry into the city; and finally, in a rush as the Bordeaux Assembly prepared on March 10 for adjournment, came its directive that the moratorium on payment of rents and commercial bills, in effect during the siege, be ended. (The perennial struggle of renters with landlords was thus reopened and an estimated 40,000 small businessmen were threatened with bankruptcy.) Nor was that all. The press was censored, the legendary Blanqui (who was in hiding) was sentenced to death, and the Bordeaux Assembly packed its bags for a move, not to Paris, the capital since 1789, but to Versailles, Louis XIV's creation, where Bismarck had recently resided and the King of Prussia had been crowned Emperor of Germany on January 18.

Paris *décapitalisé*, decapitalized, as people were saying, was in a state of mind compounded of exhaustion, anger, and shock; and, as René Rémond has described it, there was "mutual incomprehension and increasing animosity" in the relations between Paris and the rest of France. Between January 28 and March 18, 1871, this condition deteriorated to the verge of riot, and then was allowed to descend into civil war.

The Parisian National Guard changed character with the lifting of the siege and the provisioning of the city. Its more affluent members tended to drop out, some to reunite with families sent to the provinces before the German encirclement, others in disapproval of radicalism. The remainder, impoverished and apprehensive about rumors that the Guard would soon be abolished, became more and more active politically. On February 15 the various National Guard units in the city were federated into one organization with a Central Committee that was renewed and made into a permanent institution a month later. In the intervening period the *Fédérés,* or Federals, took part in an increasing number of demonstrations and disorders provoked by the unpleasant sequence of news items. Amid grumblings about how the upper classes would like to see them deprived of their weapons, they prepared for the arrival of the Germans on March 1 by moving some 200 cannon purchased by public subscription during the siege from depots in the western part of the city to Montmartre and other remote plebeian neighborhoods. Relations between the National Guard and the regular troops deteriorated, and, on March 8, regulars sent to take charge of the National Guard's cannon on the heights were refused access to them. By March 17, Thiers had become convinced that to maintain the respect of the great powers and the rest of France he had to demonstrate his government's control of Paris. On the night of March 17–18 he sent troops to Montmartre and the other high points with orders to seize the disputed cannon, but the coup was clumsily handled, crowds gathered, the regulars fraternized, two generals were seized and murdered; the news spread, the whole eastern half of the city was in the streets, and in the afternoon of March 18 Thiers made the fateful decision to withdraw all regular troops and government officials from Paris to Versailles. It was a move he had advised Louis Philippe to make in February 1848, and he now made it himself in the expectation that if the troops were left in Paris they would be subverted; so he abandoned the city, regrouped the regulars, added greatly to their numbers with permission from Bismarck, and waited.

The Paris Commune

Left as the sole authority in Paris, except for the mayors of the arrondissements, who tried vainly in the days that followed to mediate between the city and the National Assembly, the Central Committee of the National Guard moved into the Hôtel de Ville on the night of March 18. On the twenty-sixth, after the National Assembly at Versailles had cold-shouldered deputations from Paris, Parisian elections sponsored by the Central Committee chose a municipal council, the "Commune." This was in defiance of the National Assembly, which had refused permission for a new city government to be formed. The confrontation between the Versaillese and the Federals, France and Paris, an assembly elected by the nation and a "Commune" elected by the city, was expressed in doctrinal form by a clause in the National Guard's statutes: "The Republic, being the sole government of law and justice, cannot be subordinated to the universal suffrage that is its product." Here was an appeal to something higher than majority rule on a national scale—the right to local self-government. And emotionally the word "commune" evoked various images of liberty; for some, the charters won by medieval bourgeois from their lords; for others, the Paris Commune of the Great Revolution putting pressure on the National Convention; for moderates, de Tocqueville foreseeing and protesting against bureaucracy and asking for local management on a human scale; for socialists, Pierre-Joseph Proudhon and Michael Bakunin urging small-scale collectives. These were memories and precedents.

If one asks who were the members of the Commune's As-

sembly in the two months that it offered France a rival government to that of the Versailles Assembly, one finds a majority looking for inspiration to the Great Revolution, to the democratic current flowing from 1793; and one finds a strong minority who were part of a socialist current. Both groupings stood for reform. The first, divisible into "Jacobins," who looked to Robespierre, and "Blanquists," who looked to Blanqui, might be considered more "political," but if they gave priority to politics they were not without egalitarian social aspirations; Blanqui was a socialist, although not all of his followers may have been aware of his aims, since he had become famous for many republican conspiracies. The second or minority current was socialist in the sense of the term as understood by Proudhon and Bakunin, to whom the idea of communal autonomy was especially important, since to them the state was as oppressive to the individual as the misuse of property. The socialists took the Commune idea more seriously than did the Jacobins or Blanquists, to whom it meant decentralization but not necessarily salvation through a federation of autonomous communes; but all of the Communards, with their red flag, wanted the rest of France to follow their example. Somewhat fewer than a third of the Communal Assembly members had been manual laborers; the majority were lower-middle-class teachers, journalists, lawyers, and so on. The Commune was definitely representative of a popular movement on a large scale in Paris, but it was more of a last fling of the shopkeepers and artisans of the sans-culotte urban swarm than a proletarian rising. There were thirteen members of the French section of the International Working Men's Association, but they were Proudhonists and Bakuninists except for a single follower of Marx.

To assess the Commune's intentions by its actions may

prove misleading, for its members were preoccupied with practical problems of defense and finance. They were later criticized by Marx and others for not attacking Versailles at once, before Thiers could reorganize his armies, but the Commune was not a premeditated effort. It was an improvisation sparked by Thiers' sudden withdrawal from Paris, and in its early stages, for example at the time of the election, many Parisians did not even think of it as illegal. When a sortie against Versailles was attempted on April 3, it was a disaster, and the second siege of the city may be said to date from that attempt. This time starvation was not an issue, for Thiers was not able to blockade the north and east of the city, where the Germans were occupying the forts, but the presence of the Germans, besides being a national humiliation, was always a potential threat to the Commune. A moratorium was reestablished on commercial bills and rents, and the Commune continued to pay the National Guard, borrowing money for that purpose from the Bank of France, which they did not disturb, and from the Rothschilds. They meant to separate church and state, provide free, compulsory public education, and abolish conscription. Some of their measures were disciplinary and terroristic: they suspended newspapers from publication and made numerous arrests of suspects, as during the Great Revolution. They enacted no social legislation of significance except for the abolition of night work in bakeries and a plan, not implemented, for making workers' cooperatives out of workshops voluntarily closed by their owners. There was little time for social experiments before the Versaillese closed in, and no real unity in the government, since the Central Committee of the Guards continued to exist side by side with the Assembly of the Commune, which divided itself into committees, including an Executive Committee. On May 1 a

Committee of Public Safety was established, amid much discussion of whether this was a step forward or backward. No doubt a great many opponents of the Commune were hiding behind their shutters and awaiting rescue, particularly in the more affluent western neighborhoods. There existed wide support for the Commune, however, and it is not enough to call these people misguided nationalists whose principal motivation was anger at the peace with Prussia. The Communards were indeed nationalistic, but the values that the nation stood for had become, in their view, much more egalitarian and critical of the established nineteenth-century society than the values that the Versaillese identified with the nation. Here lay the fundamental tragedy: the conflict of two sets of convictions allowed to fuel violence. That the Parisians were advanced but not completely alone is testified to by the brief existence of Communes or insurrections in other cities—Lyon, Marseille, Toulouse, Limoges, Saint Etienne, Creusot. Many of the cities sent messages of solidarity to Paris, but their uprisings were repressed quickly, except for the one in Marseille, which held out for thirteen days.

The Paris Commune fell too, but not without a ferocious war in the streets after the National Assembly's troops, which had been bombarding the western neighborhoods, were beckoned to an unguarded gateway at the Porte de Saint Cloud on May 21 and began the conquest of the city from west to east in "bloody week," May 22 to 27. Surprised and confronted by greatly superior forces, the Commune's military organization and central direction broke down, but the lower classes resisted block by block in their home neighborhoods as in the June days of 1848, with women and children taking part and with atrocities mounting on both sides as Communards and their sympathizers were slaughtered wholesale, beyond the requirements of pacification, and as on the other side some hundreds of hostages, including the Archbishop of Paris, were murdered in reprisal. In part for tactical reasons and in part from rage and defiance many buildings were set on fire. The Tuileries Palace and the Hôtel de Ville and many lesser buildings were destroyed; the Louvre, Palais Royal, Palais de Justice, and Cathedral of Notre Dame were rescued by fire brigades. One of the last big battles was fought among the gravestones in the walled cemetery of Père Lachaise, where the outnumbered Communards died fighting or were executed in a corner that later became a shrine of the French Left, *le mur des Fédérés*. On the one side of the conflict the will to punish, on the other the will to resist, went far beyond common sense and material interest; it was like a religious war. The Versaillese lost in battle perhaps 1,000 men, the Communards 4,000, but if the roundups and executions of suspects are counted the Parisian dead numbered 17,000 to 20,000. The number arrested and tried exceeded 40,000 by the end of 1874, of whom some 13,000 were sentenced, most of them, however, to forced labor, deportation, or prison. The Reign of Terror of the Great Revolution had sentenced perhaps 17,000 to death in a year's time in all of France, but many more were killed without trials.

Like the Reign of Terror the Paris Commune has been one of the least understood and most misrepresented episodes of modern history. To the respectable and well-to-do it was incomprehensible and frightening, a revolt against necessary social relations by an ignorant populace led by hate-inspired demagogues. Although the crushing defeat and relentless prosecution of the Communards helped the Third Republic to survive by proving that it could keep order, social reform was postponed for fifteen years and the part played by the working classes in the labor movement, socialism, and politics

country because there were none ready; there was no social breakthrough within reach, no old regime near collapse; the post-1789 settlement was still viable, and although Paris could mount attacks on it, some of them prophetic, Paris was not France.

Goncourt *Journal*

1870

Tuesday, June 21, one in the morning
In the shadows falling from the curtains around his head, the light of the candle set on the night stand and flickering in the night breeze goes here and there, at times almost bringing his face to life.

It is strange: tonight, the first since his death, I no longer feel the despair of the last few days; I do not feel the grief I expected. A sweet, sad sense of peace steals over me, the result of the thought that he has been delivered from life. But wait until tomorrow.

When I get out of bed this morning, after a few hours of sleep, his face still has yesterday's expression, but with the yellow color of wax that has been exposed to heat. I make haste to imprint his adored features on my mind. I shall not see him much longer. I hear iron bumping against the stairway, the metallic sound of the handles of the coffin, which has been brought hastily because of the great heat.

That name, that name of *Jules de Goncourt*, so often linked with mine on the page of a book or a newspaper, I read it today on the copper plaque set in the oak of the coffin.

On the train, the first time that we went to Vichy. He had a liver attack that day and was asleep facing me, his head thrown back. For a second behind his living features I saw his face in death. After that day every time he was ill, every time I was anxious about him, that vision of him would come back to me when I closed my eyes.

"Come now," Pélagie[1] says, "you must eat," in order to have strength for tomorrow, for the rough day tomorrow.

Before the body of him who loved me so much, of him for whom there was nothing fine or good unless it had been done or said by Edmond, I feel myself tortured by remorse for my scoldings, my reproaches, my harshness, for all that cruel and unintelligent system by which I tried to bring him out of his apathy, tried to revive his will power! What a fool I was! If I had only known! How I would have concealed, veiled, softened everything for him; how I would have tried to give to the end of his life everything that a mother's affection and imagination would have spontaneously known how to provide!

These sad words, which were often our whole conversation, come back to me:

"What's the matter?"

"I'm discouraged."

"Why?"

"I don't know."

But he did know, he knew very well.

At noon I saw the hats of four men in black through the crack in the dining room door.

We went up to his little bedroom. They took off the covering, slipped a sheet under him, and in an instant converted his scarcely glimpsed thin body into a long bundle, with one end of the sheet turned back over his face. "Be careful," I said. "I

[1] The Biographical Notes give information about contemporaries mentioned in the *Journal*. See pages 323-334.

know that he is dead, but that makes no difference. Be careful."

Then they put him into the coffin on a bed of aromatic dust. One of the men said, "If this is too much for Monsieur, he had better leave." I remained. Another said: "Now is the time, if Monsieur wishes to put some memento into the coffin." I told the gardener: "Go cut all the roses in the garden, so that he may take them at least with him from this house he loved so much!" We threw roses in the empty space around his body and put a white one on the sheet where it was slightly upraised by his mouth. Then the form of his body was concealed under a heap of brown powder. Then they screwed down the lid. It was over. I went downstairs.

I feel as though I had suffered a complete loss of memory. Along with Banville's article I receive a letter from England, dated the day of his death, in which a publisher asks us to do a translation of our *Histoire de Marie-Antoinette.* He would have been pleased by that.

Wednesday, June 22

The weather is magnificent; the sun streams through the open window and strikes his coffin and the big bouquet of flowers at his head. Among the flowers is a magnolia blossom which he watched develop from a bud with a certain curious pleasure because it made him think of the magnolia beloved of Chateaubriand at Vallée aux Loups.

His room looks as disordered as though he were going on a trip. For the second, the quarter of a second, the lightning flash of time that it takes for thought to catch up, I have the idea—even with his coffin before me—that Jules has gone to get the carriage which every year takes us to Bar sur Seine.

My eyes rove around the little room to all the ordinary and familiar things to which his sleep bade good night and his waking said good morning. I look at the curtains of his bed, which formerly hung in the living room at Rue Saint Georges. They have the rosy tone that I used for a water color of him a good many years ago. I look at the big Vanloo drawing he helped me buy at the Boilly sale the last time we went to the auction room. I look at the big unfinished wood table at which we worked together for so long and which still has ink-stains from our book *Gavarni*.

After careful reflection I am convinced that he died from labor over form, *from agonizing over style*. I remember how after unflagging hours passed in the reworking, the recorrecting of a piece, after these efforts and expenditures of brain in search of a perfection which would make the French language do all that it was capable of and more, after these stubborn, obstinate struggles, which would sometimes give rise to the spiteful anger of impotence, I remember today the strange and utter prostration with which he would sink down on a sofa, and the prolonged smoke, at once sad and silent, which he would have afterward.

Nine o'clock

There go the church bells.

I must think about things that have to do with everyday life—thanks to send, letters to write.

Ten o'clock

In the garden I run into two undertaker's employes seated on pieces of black wood among the great church candelabra gleaming in the sun.

The coffin comes down the stairs on which, without letting him know it, I often from behind steadied his staggering steps.

Among the people waiting in the garden there is an old man whom I do not recognize. I send someone to find out his name. He sends back word that he is Ravaut. Ravaut belongs to a whole world of ancient memories. Ravaut is the aged coachman of my Villedeuil cousins, a fine fellow who almost thirty years ago made my Jules happy by taking him up beside him on the seat and putting the reins of the horses in his little hands.

In spite of all that my eyes see, all that my senses touch of this horrible reality, the idea of eternal separation cannot lodge in my brain. The pitiless *Never* cannot become a permanent part of my thoughts.

Somehow everything that is going on around me has the vagueness of things perceived as one is about to faint; in my ears there is the murmur of high waters receding in the distance. I do, however, see Gautier and Saint-Victor weeping. The religious chants undo me with their eternal and implacable *Requiescat in pace*. But, of course: after his life of labor and struggle, a peaceful rest is the least that is his due!

To go to the cemetery we take the route we so often followed to go to the Princess's; then we go along part of the outer boulevards where he and I so often gathered material for *Germinie Lacerteux* and *Manette Salomon*.[2] Clipped trees

[2] *Germinie Lacerteux* (1865), based on the shocking life of Rose, the Goncourt servant, and *Manette Salomon* (1867), which describes the artist milieu of Paris, are pioneer works in the realist tradition. *Henriette Maréchal*, mentioned below, was hissed off the stage in December 1865 in an uproar equal to that which greeted Hugo's *Hernani* a generation previously.

at the door of a cabaret remind me of a comparison in one of our books. Then I fall into a sort of exhausted somnolence, from which I am roused by a sharp turn, the turn into the cemetery.

I saw him disappear into the tomb where my father and mother are, and where there is still room for me. That was all.

When I got home, I went to bed and, covering the sheet with pictures of him, I stayed there with his image until night.

Thursday, June 23

This morning I go up to his room and sit opposite his empty bed, from which I made him get up every day, even during the intensely cold weather last winter, to take him to his shower, which was supposed to cure him. During his last months of suffering, weakness, and clumsiness, I often helped him to dress and undress on this bed.

On the night table they have left the volume by Bescherelle which was placed under the pillow in order to raise his sad head in death. The flowers with which I surrounded his agony are lying dried up in the fireplace, mixed with the blue wrappings of the candles which were lighted around his coffin; on the work table, scattered among the first letters and visiting cards, are Pélagie's prayerbooks.

Today I went to visit him after his first night passed beneath the ground.

Maria had come to see us on Tuesday, two days before the crisis. She tells me today that on Tuesday during a moment when I had gone downstairs to get some melissa cordial, Jules said to her: "Dear Maria, I am very ill, and I don't know whether you will see me again. I am very ill with an illness from which I shall not recover. All these attacks, you must realize, will end in my death."

The Princess has been good, kindly, full of sympathy; she wept on my shoulder.

At times the idea of his death is absent from my mind. This evening as I was reading an article in *Le Parisien* attacking us from a religious point of view, I found myself saying: "I must tell Jules about this."

What a devoted fellow Edouard de Béhaine has been. How completely has Marin, who came to Paris for a spree, given himself up to my sorrow, my mourning!

Bar sur Seine, Sunday, June 26

The places which were my life in other days now no longer speak to me, no longer tell me anything new. They only make me remember.

All day a strange lassitude and sleepiness. Only the food at dinner wakes me up for the evening.

In this house, where there were always two of us, I constantly catch myself thinking of him as if he were alive, or at least I forget that he is dead. There is a certain ringing of the bell which raises me out of my chair, as if it had been rung by Jules returning hastily and exclaiming to the servant as he came to the door: "Where is Edmond?"

. . . . .

July 14

The house in which he died and to which I do not want to return has been put up for sale. Today I had a very acceptable offer of a six-year lease. Well, it's illogical and unreasonable, but this offer causes me deep distress. I am tied by bonds I did not suspect to the house where I have suffered so much.

July 16

For several days in the building across the way, Catherine, an old servant of the house, has been dying, and this revives in me the agony of a few days ago.

July 18

I am not ill, but my body wants neither to walk nor to act; it finds all movement repugnant and would like to achieve the immobility of a fakir. At the same time, in the pit of my stomach I constantly have that nervous feeling of emptiness brought on by great emotion, made more intense by my anxiety over the great war which is about to break out.

July 20

Every day is an anniversary of my sorrow and grief, which begin again. Thursdays make me think of the Thursday when he had his crisis. On Fridays I think of the improvement he showed and the hope I had of keeping him. Saturdays, Sundays, and Mondays make me relive the ups and downs of hope during his last three days of life. And today is the 20th, a day which hour by hour makes me remember that for a month I have been separated from him forever.

I am sad, battered, crushed; yet I eat, I am distracted by the war. Then I wonder if a mother's grief would not be greater than mine, and such a thought hurts me.

Saturday, July 23

I would like to dream about him. My mind, occupied by thoughts of him all day, waits for him at night, calls him, solicits his sweet resurrection in the deceiving reality of dreams. But I call him up in vain; my nights are empty of him, of his memory and image.

I have heart for nothing, courage for nothing. Marin wanted to take me to the frontier, but I hesitated. I could have let my house, but I was unable to make up my mind. I no longer have the strength it takes to make a decision.

July 27

Last night I dreamed of Jules for the first time. Like me, he was in full mourning for himself, yet he was with me. We were walking along a street which vaguely resembled the Rue de Richelieu. I had the impression that we were taking our play to the director of some theatre or other. On the way we met some friends, among them Théophile Gautier. The first reaction of each of them was to offer me his condolences, a gesture suddenly broken off at the unexpected sight of my brother who, as was his habit, was walking a bit behind me in the dream. I was caught in a horrible, agonizing doubt, torn between the certainty that he was alive as attested by his presence beside me and the certainty of his death, which was brought clearly to mind at that moment by a sharp memory of the letters announcing his death which were still spread out on the table in the billiard room.

There is a little street here which is only two feet wide. On that street there is a miserable little house; through the glass of its one uncurtained window you can see a plaster head of Antinous and a colored candlestick, representing a gendarme, in which a candle is set. On the door is a piece of paper bearing these words: *For travelers of small means.* MADAME BON-DIEU.

July 30

In this town, in this house to which the two of us had been coming together for the last twenty-two years every step stirs up the past and arouses memories. This was our refuge after our mother's death and after old Rose's death; this was the place where we took our vacation every summer after the winter's labor and the volume published in the spring. In the lavender-smelling paths bordering the Seine, on the rapids negotiated by long poles, we composed the descriptions for *Charles Demailly* together. In this church we copied together the glass window of *La Promenade du Boeuf Gras*. There under the vines is the spot where we learned of the death of our dear Gavarni. Onto this bed, which has remained as it was when Jules slept there beside me, was tossed that letter from Thierry urging us to hurry back to put *Henriette Maréchal* into rehearsal.

And when I go back along the years that are gone, it is from this doorway that I see us set out in white blouses with knapsacks on our backs on our long journey through France in 1849—he with such a pretty, rosy, beardless face that in the villages through which we passed people took him for a woman whom I had abducted.

Auteuil, August 5

Days of going back and forth in this house like a soul in agony. Yes, that's the word for it.

August 6

From the Print Room in the Library I see people running down the Rue Vivienne. I start to run after them.

From top to bottom on the steps of the Bourse I see only bare heads, with hats held in air, and from every mouth there comes a mighty *Marseillaise*,[3] whose deafening bursts drown out the hum from the Exchange floor. Never have I heard

[3] The *Marseillaise* was forbidden under the Second Empire.

such enthusiasm. I walk among men pale with emotion, youngsters jumping up and down, women gesturing as though intoxicated. Capoul sings the *Marseillaise* from the top of an omnibus in the Place de la Bourse, and on the boulevard Marie Sasse sings it standing in her carriage, which is almost lifted up by the delirious crowd.

But as for that telegram announcing the defeat of the Crown Prince of Prussia and the capture of 25,000 prisoners, that telegram which, they say, is posted inside the Exchange and which everyone claims he has read with his own eyes, that telegram which by a strange hallucination some people think they actually see, saying, "See, there it is!" as they indicate a wall in the background on which there is nothing posted—that telegram I am unable to find.

Sunday, August 7

A terrifying silence. On the boulevard not a vehicle moving; in the villa not a shout expressing a child's joy; and over the horizon a Paris where noise seems to have died.

Monday, August 8

This morning in his room I read the last sad notes written by his hand.

In these great emotional crowds I feel my solitude less, and I drag myself along in them all day long, so tired that I am ready to drop, yet walking on mechanically.

Wednesday, August 10

I live the whole day in the frightful emotion of the great battle which will decide the fate of France.

I go to Saint Gratien; the Princess is in Paris in order to be closer to the news. Zeller is alone in the house so that it will not be entirely in the hands of the servants. You can already feel emptiness creeping little by little and stealthily into the imperial residence.

. . . . .

I am sad about my brother; I am sad over my country's fate. I am unable to stay home; I need to have dinner with friends, or at least with acquaintances. I go out almost at random to invite myself to dinner at Charles Edmond's. In his house at Bellevue I find, ready to sit down at the table, Berthelot and Nubar-Pasha, a European to whom his long residence in Egypt has given an almost oriental conformation of the head and in whose subtle, diplomatic mask a laugh sometimes shows the white teeth of a savage.

We talk of our reverses, of the general incapacity, of favoritism, of the corruption of men by personal power. Berthelot, whom our humiliation has made ill, is eloquent, truly eloquent in a broken voice. With the aid of innuendo Nubar gives us an idea of the graft that goes on in high government levels. He emphasizes the lack of pity of this government for the weak. He tells of the tears he shed when he was thirty-nine years old, real tears, as a result of an interview with our Minister of Foreign Affairs about French demands, which, he asserts, have produced the entire Egyptian debt. Then he asks Berthelot about the Egyptian race; he asks what curse they are under, why they are not perfectible, why the sons of the fellahin are inferior to the fellahin, why the young Egyptians, who learn more rapidly than Europeans, stop their intellectual development at fourteen, why in all the talented Egyptians, whom he has observed at close range since the time of Mohamet Ali's government, he has always noticed the lack of precision of mind.

As we gallop swiftly to Paris in his carriage, trying to get news and information, Nubar tells us that in Abyssinia when a murder has been committed, the family of the murdered man spends seven days and seven nights heaping curses on the murderer's house. He adds that the murderer almost always comes to a bad end. As I see it, the concert of curses hurled out after December 2 is having its effect today on this sad and pitiful end of a reign.

August 15, 8 o'clock

At nightfall, the time for a long smoke and the dreamy formulation of ideas, no longer to hear his original thoughts, his delightfully paradoxical words in the shadowy dusk. . . . This is the time I feel most alone.

Friday, August 19

The emotions of the last week have given the Parisian population the look of sick people. On these yellow, drawn, haggard faces you see all the ups and downs of hope through which Parisian nerves have passed since August 6.

. . . . .

August 20

Before his tomb.

He died two months ago today. Already! Yet these sixty days have seemed very long to me.

On leaving the cemetery I go to visit Feydeau; and for an hour I listen to him complain about the selfishness of his friends, his lack of money, and the impossibility of hiring a carriage to go out for a drive. Throughout this lachrymose complaining, in contrast to the immobility of the paralytic, Feydeau's pretty, smiling, carefree, scornful wife flits back and forth in a white cashmere dressing gown, disturbing us as she tidies up the room.

August 21

In the Bois de Boulogne.

To see these great trees fall under the axe, swaying like creatures wounded to death; where there had been a curtain of green, to see a field of sharp stakes shining white like a sinister harrow fills your heart with hatred for the Prussians, who are the cause of this murder of nature.

I come home every evening on the train with an old man whose name I do not know. He is an intelligent and talkative old man who seems to have lived in all levels of society and to know their secret chronicles.

Yesterday he talked about the Emperor and his marriage. His anecdote came from Morny, who said he had it straight from the Emperor. One evening, with a certain insistence and appealing to her honor as one would appeal to the honor of a man, the Emperor asked Mlle de Montijo whether she had ever had a lover. Mlle de Montijo replied: "I should deceive you, Sire, if I did not tell you that my heart has spoken several times; but I can assure you that I am still Mademoiselle de Montijo." When she had thus assured him of her virginity, the Emperor said: "Very well, Mademoiselle, you shall be Empress."

Saint-Victor said to me the other day—putting himself in a nutshell: "What times these are, when you can no longer read a book!"

44

August 22

I go to see Théophile Gautier and join him in weeping over the house which he had set up as the happy and artistic retreat for his old age.

On the boulevards you see men and women question passing faces with their eyes, turn their ears toward every mouth that speaks—disturbed, anxious, frightened.

August 23

At the Saint Lazare station I run into a group of twenty Zouaves, the remnants of a battalion that fought under Mac-Mahon. Nothing is so beautiful, nothing has so much style, nothing is so sculptural, so painterly, as these men broken in battle. They bear the imprint of a weariness in no way comparable to any other weariness; their uniforms are worn, faded, stained as if they had drunk the sun and rain for years on end.

This evening at Brébant's we go to the window, drawn by the applause of the crowd for a departing regiment as it goes by. Renan comes away quickly with a gesture of disdain as he exclaims:

"Among all those people there is not one capable of a virtuous act."

"Why do you say that?" someone shouts. "The act of devotion which makes these unnamed men, these anonymous men, these men without glory, give up their lives, what's that but a virtuous act?"

Don't talk to me about these idealists, these humanitarian sophists, in whom I feel, scarcely concealed, their unpatriotic admiration for the Prussians, that mixture of noble savage and professor of the exact sciences!

August 25

I look at this house stuffed with books, art objects, engravings, drawings, which would leave gaps in the history of French art if they were burned, and I do not have any strong desire to save these things, which were my loves, my entrails, in days gone by.

. . . . .

August 26

At the Gare de l'Est.

In the midst of boxes, baskets, bundles of old linen, hampers, bottles, mattresses, eiderdowns, all tied with heavy cord which somehow keeps together the shaking, tumbling assemblage of disparate objects, you see the bright eyes of little peasants hidden and tucked away in the recesses and open spaces.

In the foreground, with a hunting dog at her feet and a crutch at her side, an old Lorraine woman in a brown piqué bonnet from time to time takes the black grapes of her native vines from a straw basket and hands them to her grandchildren.

Saturday, August 27

Zola comes to have lunch at my house. He tells me about a series of novels he wants to write, an epic in ten volumes, *The Natural and Social History of a Family*, which he is ambitious to try and in which he will show temperaments, characteristics, vices, virtues as they are developed by environment, and are as sharply differentiated as the sunny and shady parts of a garden.

He says to me: "After the analysis of the infinitesimally small expressions of feeling carried out by Flaubert in *Ma-*

dame Bovary, after the analysis of artistic, plastic, nervous things such as you have done, after these *jewel-works*, these finely chiseled volumes, there is no room left for the young, nothing for them to do, nothing in the way of creating characters. It is only by the number of volumes, the power of their creation, that they can impress the public."

Sunday, August 28

In the Bois de Boulogne, where there never used to be anything but silk among the green trees, I see a large expanse of blue blouse: a shepherd's back near a little column of bluish smoke; and around him sheep grazing, in default of grass, on the leaves of forgotten branches. In the carriage paths great haggard, confused steers wander along in droves.

Sheep everywhere. Here on the edge of a footpath, lying on his side, is a dead ram; his head with turned-back horns is flattened out and from it drips a bit of reddish fluid, which spreads in a red stain on the sand—poor head which every passing ewe sniffs, as in a kiss.

For a moment there is pandemonium. Through all the clearings, through every hole in the greenery you see a herd of a hundred thousand headlong beasts rush for a gateway, an exit, like the avalanche in a Castiglione drawing. In the sun-struck dust on the banks of the fortifications the hurried lines of innumerable sheep look like little walls one on top of the other, which blurred vision runs together.

The pool at Auteuil is half dried up by the sheep which kneel there, drinking, in the reeds.

August 30

From the top of the Auteuil autobus as it goes down from the Trocadéro in the blinding sunlight on the great grey plain of the Champ de Mars I see a swarming of little red and blue dots: they are infantrymen.

I tumble out, and there I am among the little tents in whose triangles of shade can be glimpsed here the hilt of an officer's sword, there the tanned head of an infantryman lying in the straw by his canteen, among shining stacks of rifles, among little kitchens where the tin cooking pots bubble over bits of flame, among the handing out of leggings, among men making their toilets in the open air, in shirt sleeves of a fine rusty white color. Some soldiers are filling their canteens from bottles which a wine merchant brings around on a handcart; others are kissing a laughing woman who is selling green apples.

I am strolling through this commotion, this animation, this gaiety of French soldiers ready to go off to their deaths when the cracked voice of a little old fellow, who is bandylegged and Hoffmanesque, shouts: "Pens, pencils, writing paper!" A shout sustained on a strange note, which you might say is a *memento mori*, a kind of discreetly phrased warning, as much as to say: "If you military gentlemen were to think a bit about making your wills?"

August 31

This morning at the Point du Jour they begin demolishing houses in the military zone in the midst of a procession of refugees from the suburbs which looks like the migration of an ancient people. Bizarre corners of half-demolished houses with the remains of ill-assorted furniture. For example, a barbershop, whose gaping façade reveals the forgotten curule chair where laundry men used to get a shave on Sunday.

September 1

Yesterday the Princess asked me to dinner at her house, saying that there would be nobody there. I arrive. The curtains have been removed from the windows. The Princess seems stupefied; she keeps repeating: "I would not have believed it. If anyone had told me on August 1 what was going to happen, I would not have believed it!"

We have dinner. Around the table are old Giraud, Popelin, Soulié, Zeller, who is the new rector of the University of Strasbourg, and his daughter. Each of us gives his bit of news culled from *Le Figaro* or *Le Gaulois*. Nobody knows anything. We feel pity for the inhabitants of Strasbourg, and especially for the manuscripts. Somebody says the spire of the cathedral has fallen. To that the Princess, who has not been listening, says: "But wasn't the church solid, then?"

Nobody has the heart to smile at her naïveté.

After dinner we smoke in the small drawing room, and because the Princess complains that it smells bad, we all go for a smoke in the small reception room, except for Popelin, who, sitting solidly in his armchair in the middle of the drawing room, sends the smoke from his cigar up to the ceiling, as true master of the house. When he has finished his cigar, he installs himself in the armchair which touches the end of the canapé where the Princess usually does her knitting, showing off his white vest and tossing out from time to time cutting, contradictory, supremely scornful remarks. Poor woman! She certainly has got hold of the man who can best advertise their liaison!

When Nieuwerkerke arrives there is a curious greeting between the former and the present lover. Afterward Abbatucci comes in and rattles on without an idea and, what is worse, without any news. In that house of Napoleon's cousin, in order to get the news we have to send out for *Le Soir* and hope that Palikao's doctor may drop in during the evening.

September 2

On my way out of the Louvre I buttonhole Chennevières, who tells me that tomorrow he leaves for Brest as escort for the third shipment of paintings from the Louvre, which have been taken from their frames and rolled up and are being sent to the arsenal or the prison at Brest to save them from the Prussians. He paints me a sad and humiliating picture of this packing up, of Reiset weeping warm tears in front of *La Belle Jardinière* in the bottom of its case as though he were standing before a beloved corpse at the moment of nailing down the coffin.

In the evening after dinner we go to the Rue d'Enfer station and I see seventeen boxes which contain the *Antiope*, the finest Venetians, etc.—pictures which we thought would hang on the walls of the Louvre forever and which now are mere packages, protected against the hazards of displacement and travel only by the word *fragile*.

September 3

You are scarcely alive when you live in this great frightening unknown which surrounds and strangles you.

Things die as well as men. Chennevières told me yesterday that the stitch for Argentan lace was completely forgotten from 1815 to 1830, and that if it had not been for the long memories of two old maids who were still alive, it could not have been recovered. Even so, there is one variety of this stitch which is lost.

What an appearance Paris has this evening as the shocking news of MacMahon's defeat and the Emperor's capture circulates from group to group! Who will be able to paint the dejected faces, the heedless coming and going of feet aimlessly beating the pavement, the anxious asides of shopkeepers and

concierges on their doorsteps, the black crowds at street corners and the approaches to the municipal offices, the rush to
the newspaper kiosks, the triple lines of people reading under
every street light, and on their chairs in the living quarters
behind the shops the despairing posture of women whom you
see alone, without their men?

Then there is the rumbling clamor of the crowd, among
whom anger follows on stupefaction. Then there are large
bands running along the boulevards with flags in front of
them, repeatedly shouting: "Down with him!" "Long live
Trochu!" In short, the tumultuous and disorderly spectacle
of a nation which is going to perish if it does not save itself by
a prodigious effort, by doing the *impossible* as in the time of
the Revolution. [See Illustration 1.]

September 4

A frightening silence here, under a grey sky that makes
everything sad.

Around four o'clock this is the way the Chamber of Deputies looks on the outside. On the grey façade from which the
sun has gone, before and around the columns and on the steps,
a crowd, a world of men, whose blouses make white and blue
spots against black broadcloth. Many have branches in their
hands and green leaves on their round hats. A scattering of
Mobile Guards carry greenery on the ends of their rifles.

A hand rises above all the heads and on a column writes the
list of members of the Provisional Government in chalk in
great red letters. Somebody has already written on another
column: *The Republic has been proclaimed.* Applause,
shouts, hats thrown into the air; people climbing the pedestals
of the statues, making a group around the figure of Minerva; a
man in a blouse tranquilly smoking his pipe on the knees of

the statue of Chancellor de l'Hôpital; clusters of women hanging on the grille facing the Pont de la Concorde.

Everywhere around me I hear people greet each other feverishly with the remark: "This is it!" Above the façade a man removes the blue and white from the tricolor and leaves only the red floating in the air. On the terrace facing the Quai d'Orsay infantrymen plunder the bushes and hand green branches over the parapet to women, who snatch at them.

At the Tuileries gate, near the big pool, the gilded *N*'s are concealed under old newspapers, and wreaths of immortelles hang in the place of the departed eagles.

At the grand entry of the palace I see *Under the protection of the citizens* written in chalk on the black marble tablets. Perched on one side is a Mobile Guard, a handkerchief around his head under his kepi in the Arab fashion; on the other side a young infantryman, who holds out his shako to the crowd: "For the wounded of the French army." Men in white blouses leaning on their rifles as they stand on the pedestals of the peristyle columns shout: "Free admission to the bazaar," while the crowd rushes in, hats in the air, and an immense clamor is swallowed up in the stairway of the invaded palace. On benches next to the kitchens women are sitting with cockades stuck in their hair; and a young mother tranquilly suckles a tiny infant in white swaddling clothes.

Along the Rue de Rivoli you read on the ancient blackness of the stone: *House for rent;* and hand-written notices proclaim: *Death to thieves. Respect property.*

Sidewalks and streets are covered, are full of men and women who seem to have expanded their premises onto the sidewalk as on a holiday in the great city; a million people who have forgotten that the Prussians are at three or four days' march from Paris and who, on this warm, intoxicating

LE PORC DES TUILERIES, PAR ALFRED LEPETIT
(Dessin saisi sous l'Empire)

Adieu, mon étoile!

1. Louis-Napoleon, the swine in the Tuileries

En Vente chez Duclaux, 21.19. du Ch. d'Eau.   Dépôt chez Madre, 20, r. du Croissant.

Dans les Compagnies de Guerre.

Vous comprenez, il n'aurait qu'a venir une dame, et mon appartement sentirait le tabac; alors je fume à la fenêtre.

2. Soldierly gaiety

La Betterave, les Champignons, le Poireau.

Tout ça fait sa tête comme leurs sœurs, la carotte et la pomme de terre.

3. The high cost of vegetables

THIERS 1, ROI DES CAPITULARDS.

A LA COMMUNE

Projet de Monument destiné à remplacer la colonne Vendôme.

4. Adolphe Thiers, king of the capitulators

day, go about aimlessly, impelled by the feverish curiosity of this great historic drama which is being enacted. Troops are passing by along the length of the Rue de Rivoli, singing the *Marseillaise;* National Guards and Mobile Guards in carriages shout "Long live the Republic!" Nothing is missing, not even the carnival masks of revolutions. An open carriage conveys some men with goatees and red carnations who are holding up a huge flag, and in their midst are a drunken Algerian soldier and a tipsy woman.

It is half past five at the Hôtel de Ville. This monument of a free city, its pediments in shadow, shines in the light of the sun, which makes the clock and the two windows on either side blindingly bright. At the first-floor windows men in blouses and men in frock coats rise in tiers to the very top, the first row seated with their legs hanging out of the windows, looking like an enormous paradise of street urchins stuck in a piece of Renaissance sculpture.

The square is swarming with people. Carriages in which the curious are hoisting themselves up stand motionless. Youngsters are hanging from the ornamental street lights. And from all this throng there comes a deep, dull murmur.

Now and then little pieces of paper fall from the windows; the crowd picks them up and throws them back into the air till they look like a whirl of snowflakes overhead. These are the ballots of the May 8 plebescite with *Yes* printed on them in advance. A man of the common people says: "The ragpickers are going to have a field day!" Now and then personalities of the extreme left, whom people around me recognize by name, come out for a moment to receive the applause of the crowd; and Rochefort, who shows his thin, pale profile for a moment, is acclaimed as the future savior of France . . . poor France!

Coming back by the Rue Saint Honoré, on the sidewalks you step on bits of gilt plaster which two hours ago were the imperial arms of his former Majesty. You run into bands of people where bald-headed men try to convey with epileptic gestures what their paralyzed voices, their toneless throats can no longer shout.

I don't know why, but I have no confidence. I don't seem to discern in this screaming mob the original good fellows of the *Marseillaise*. To me, in their glee and enjoyment they seem simply to be cynical hooligans doing a job of political breakage: hooligans who have nothing on the left side of their chests to devote to great sacrifices for our country.

Yes, the Republic . . . under the circumstances I think only a Republic can save us, but a Republic to which have been called the true and exceptional talents of the land, with Gambetta added for color, not a Republic composed exclusively of all the mediocrities, of all the blockheads, young and old, from the extreme left.

This evening the flower sellers on the boulevard are selling only red carnations, and all the people of Paris reflect nothing of yesterday's defeat on their gay, laughing, hopeful faces. Is this frivolity? Or can it be heroism?

Tuesday, September 6

When I arrive at Brébant's, Renan is sitting all alone at the big table in the red room, reading a newspaper with gestures of despair.

Saint-Victor comes in and, as he drops into a chair, exclaims: "The Apocalypse! . . . The pale-colored horses."

Charles Edmond, Du Mesnil, Nefftzer, and Berthelot come in one after the other, and we eat dinner to the desolating remarks of all and sundry.

We talk of the crushing defeat, of the impossibility of defense, of the incompetence of the eleven men in the National Defense Government, of their disturbing lack of influence with the diplomatic corps and neutral governments.

We brand Prussian savagery as like that of Genseric. Renan says: "The Germans have few pleasures; they find their greatest pleasure in hatred and in the thought and execution of vengeance." And we think of all the vigorous hatred that has built up since Davout's time in Germany, adding to the hatred left by the war in the Palatinate, a hate I heard expressed in the angry words of the old woman who showed me through Heidelberg Castle a few years ago. Only yesterday, in support of this, a railroad official told me the following anecdote. Several years ago he was at Karlsruhe at the residence of the minister plenipotentiary, whom he heard caution a friend with a great reputation for gallantry: "Here, my dear fellow, you will get nowhere. While the women, to be sure, have easy morals, they don't like Frenchmen."

Someone interjects into the conversation: "Precision arms are contrary to the French temperament. Fire fast, charge with the bayonet, that's what our soldiers like. If they can't do that they are paralyzed. *Mechanization* of the individual is not for them. But that is where the Prussians are superior right now."

Renan, raising his head from his plate:

"In everything I have studied I have always been impressed by the superiority of German intelligence and work. It's not surprising that in the art of war—for it is after all an art, inferior but complicated—they have achieved the superiority which, I repeat, I have observed in everything I have studied, that I know about. . . . Yes, gentlemen, the Germans are a superior race!"

"Oh, oh!" everybody bursts out.

"Yes, greatly superior to us," Renan continues as he becomes animated. "Catholicism cretinizes the individual; all education by the Jesuits or the Christian Brothers arrests and restricts all *summative* virtue, whereas Protestantism develops it."

Berthelot's soft, sickly voice calls our minds back from sophistical generalities to menacing realities:

"Gentlemen, I wonder if you know that we are surrounded by an enormous quantity of oil which has been deposited at the gates of Paris to avoid paying the tolls and which the tax-collectors will not allow to be brought in. If the Prussians get hold of it and throw it into the Seine, they will make a river of fire that will burn both shores. That's the way the Greeks burned the Arab fleet."

"But why don't you warn Trochu?"

"Has he time?" Berthelot continues: "If they don't blow up the locks on the Marne Canal, all the Prussian heavy siege artillery will arrive under the walls of Paris as though on rollers. I believe that the locks are mined. But will anybody think of blowing them up? . . . I could keep on telling you things like that till morning."

And when I ask him if he has hopes that the committee over which he presides will come up with some new destructive device:

"Well, no. I have been given neither money nor men; and I receive 260 letters a day, which leaves me no time for experiment. It's not that there aren't things to try, to invent even, but we haven't time. . . . We haven't time to experiment on a large scale. . . . And to get something accepted, well! There's a bigwig in the artillery to whom I was talking about oil: 'Yes,' he said, 'they used it in the ninth century.' 'But,' I replied, 'in their recent war the Americans . . .' 'That's true,' he said, 'but it's dangerous to handle and we don't want to blow ourselves up.' It's always like that."

Everybody's conversation turns to the terms the King of Prussia is likely to lay down: the handing over of part of the armored fleet, a redrawing of the frontier, which someone has seen on a map belonging to Hetzel and which probably will take away several departments from France.

Nefftzer, on being questioned, replies with subtle scepticism, which he covers over with a big laugh and malicious words, the bite of which comes through his thick Alsatian accent. He talks of Gambetta, who has just sent to Strasbourg a man who fled from his post to replace a mayor who fought bravely for that city. He tells of a rumor that Duvernois made his fortune from the work on the fortifications. He tells of the graft of the military engineering officers, who would set down 300 workers on the records when only fifty were employed.

Obstinately pushing his thesis of German superiority, Renan continues to hold forth with his two neighbors when Du Mesnil breaks in: "As for the independent feeling of your German peasants, I can tell you that I have gone hunting in Baden, where they send them to pick up the game with a kick in the tail!"—"Well," Renan says, completely thrown off the track, "I prefer peasants who receive a kick in the tail to peasants like ours whom universal suffrage has made our masters. Peasants, what are they? The inferior element in civilization who imposed this government on us and made us endure it for twenty years!"

Berthelot continues his desolating revelations; at the end of them I burst out:

"Well, then, this is the end? There is nothing left for us to do but to raise up a new generation for vengeance!"

"No, no," Renan shouts, standing up all red with excitement, "no, not vengeance! Let France perish, let our country perish! The kingdoms of Duty and Reason are higher."

"No, no," shouts the whole table, "there is nothing higher than our country!"

"No," Saint-Victor shouts even louder, completely beside himself, "let's not be aesthetic, let's not be Byzantine! Screw it all, there's nothing above our country!"

Renan has gotten up and is walking around the table with uneven steps, his little arms beating the air, reciting fragments of Scripture in a loud voice, saying that it is all set down there. Then he goes up to the window, under which is the insouciant coming and going of Paris, and says to me, "There is what will save us, the softness of our population."

As we take our leave we say to one another: "Perhaps two weeks from now the Prussians will be dining at this table, sitting on our chairs."

September 7

From the Etoile barrier to Neuilly.

It had rained all night. There are drops of water in the folds of the tents and wet straw sticks out from under them, straw on which you see, inside the tents, spots of red—soldiers asleep in their overcoats.

Outside, hanging here and there to dry are socks and underdrawers, and bugles covered with verdegris; between two paving stones are little flickering fires made of rotten wood from the demolitions. Sentinels looking like hospital inmates stand guard bundled up in quilts, their heads bound with blue-checked handkerchiefs.

On their faces and in their sluggish movements all the soldiers show the discomfort of the cold night. They are not downcast, but they have a sort of passivity and resignation at once melancholy and a little stupid. They look like soldiers ready to be killed, not to go out and win; soldiers predestined to defeat by loss of morale, whose troubled minds are haunted by that great dissolver of armies, Treason. Among them there are some fine careless spirits, some gay, resistant spirits; one group cockily eating at a table made of a plank across two pieces of stovepipe; a soldier with the manner of a conqueror talking nonsense with a canteen girl of the 93rd, whose little blue-silk apron flutters over her wool skirt.

A heavy sky lowers over the fortifications, and the wind chases grey clouds above a yellow line—a sky like that De-camps puts in his pictures of battles between the Cimbri and the Teutons, a sky from which for a moment shines out the wet shining brass of a 24 artillery piece, where a youngster is monkeying with the crank.

I climb up to the ramparts. It is as though the horizon were crumbling, the trees and houses falling to earth in a great muffled noise, with panels of wall still standing like a stage set for a scene of devastation, with uncovered rafters closing in the sky, with the red corners of wine shops fallen in ruins. The only thing still standing in the greenery is the Duke of Orléans' chapel.

Disorder: people pushing on the drawbridge and in the winding road. The *ego* of men and women has already become brutal, almost ferocious. People push each other in the path of all these vehicles, all these moving vans, all these people in flight, all this procession of carts, military transports, omnibuses, and drays which are jumbled together and mired in the torn-up street.

I manage to get to the Avenue de Neuilly, grazed by wheel hubs, bumped by planks and pieces of wood carried by workmen. On either side all the way to the bridge military equipment drying at doors and windows gives the impression of an immense temple of old rags; I walk along to the dull click of rifles which soldiers are cleaning.

September 8

From the Point du Jour gate halfway to Saint Cloud, fighting to get into Paris are three or four files of vehicles of every kind and every dimension, city carriages and rustic carts; among them great hay-wagons drawn by red oxen rise up as big as houses. Hacks and carts, alternately struck by rays of the sun and bursts of rain, show, damp and shining with rain, the miserable miscellaneous furniture of the Paris suburbs in the midst of which old women sit shaking, as on their knees they hold cages where poor frightened birds flutter.

All around, big trees and houses are falling to the dull swish of branches, to the strident noise of glass breaking on the pavement. The waters of the Seine transmit the sound of bugles and batteries of drums practicing on either bank; here and there a greyish gunboat stands out surmounted by an enormous cannon.

The lawns in the park at Saint Cloud disappear under the red trousers of the infantrymen who are drilling there; you would think you were in the middle of the war to see yourself surrounded by these men spread out under the big trees, running at the double quick, kneeling, lying on the ground, and today simulating with blank cartridges the firing they will have to do tomorrow.

At the little café where less than three months ago I sat with him who is now dead, I see remnants of the dragoons pass by on their exhausted horses. They are in rags and covered with mud; their helmets are dented, their carbines shattered; stolen chickens struggle to escape from the net bags tied to their saddles.

I climb up to the earth fort being built at Montretout. Among the vines laden with black grapes I see the white necktie of old Blaisot, the dean of the print sellers; he is inspecting his little patch of vineyard and looking askance at the fort which will prevent him from building the house where he had hoped in his old age to breathe the revivifying air of the high hill, after so many hours in the stuffy air of the sales rooms.

The fort! It is still in the head of the officer of engineers who has orders to build it. You hear workmen say mockingly: "The fort will be finished in three months!" As for the 20,000 men reported to be working on it, someone tells me that in recent days there have not been more than a few hundred and today no more than a thousand. Moreover, three-fourths of them are infantrymen.

Empire or Republic, it is always the same thing! It is irritating always to hear "It's the Emperor's fault!" If the generals were incapable, if the officers were ignoramuses, if the soldiers were cowardly at times, it was not the Emperor's fault. Anyhow one man does not have that much influence on a nation, and if the French nation had not been going to pieces, the Emperor's extraordinary mediocrity would not have prevented victory. We must remember that sovereigns, whoever they are, are always a reflection of a nation and would not keep their thrones three days if they were out of harmony with its spirit.

Saturday, September 10
Catulle Mendès in a volunteer's uniform comes to shake my

hand at Peters'. He has the head of a Christ with the clap.

A young man whom I met at the spa sits next to me at dinner. He hails a man going by: "How many rifles have you left?" "About 330,000. But I'm afraid the government will take them back."

And my acquaintance tells me that the man with the rifles is a genius of sorts, a foresighted fellow who has made six million in deals that nobody else would ever think of. He bought 600,000 reject rifles out of hand at seven francs apiece and is reselling them in the Congo, to the King of Dahomey, at almost 100 francs apiece. He is also making money from the ivory and gold dust which he gets in payment. He is involved in a series of extraordinary deals, always on this scale; one day he sends 100,000 English water closets to China; another day he buys all the torn-down houses in Versailles.

Sunday, September 11

All along Boulevard Suchet, all along the road inside the fortifications, there is lively activity and large-scale movement on the part of the National Defense. All along the road they are making fascines and gabions, filling sacks of earth, hollowing out powder magazines and oil storage dumps in the trenches. In the courtyard of the former customs collectors' barracks there is the dull resonance of cannon balls falling from drays. Up above, civilians are carrying on cannon drill; down below, practice with breechloading rifles by National Guards. Bands of silent workmen pass by; the blue, white, and black blouses of Mobile Guards go by; and in the green channel of the railroad line the rapid flash of trains, of which you see only the top, covered with the red trousers, gold braid, epaulettes, and kepis of this huge military force improvised out of the civilian population. Everywhere in the midst of all this the headlong rush of little open carriages carrying curious, but slightly frightened women.

The Champ de Mars is still a camp, where soldierly gaiety has written on the grey canvas tents: *We need maids of all work*. Endless files of horses go down to the Seine to drink and stand along the quay, where rope barriers enclose artillery horses and transport for the bridge builders. [See Illustration 2.]

The Champs Elysées, which is no longer being sprinkled, is a torment of dust through which you see an armed multitude and, now and then, the gleaming helmet of a dispatch-rider standing out at the foot of the avenue against the violet sky and the white obelisk.

In the Place de la Concorde a gathering of people completely in black at the base of the Strasbourg statue. Blouse-clad men have made a human ladder and, climbing above the white stone, above the powerful and vulgar pose of hand on hip, are crowning the heroic city with branches, bouquets, flags, and republican tinsel. Down below a man in a black hat bends over in front of the gate, which is green with crowns of immortelles which have cockades stuck in them; he seems to be signing a register.

At the entrance to the Rue de Rivoli huge carts overtake me; they are carrying the four quarters of big dead steers lying on their backs covered with green serge.

The main path in the Tuileries Garden is spread with straw. On the bed of this gigantic stable, as though posing for those studies beloved of Géricault, there rise up and stretch out to the caress of the open air the white, chestnut, or dappled croups of thousands of horses. Behind them the severe line of caissons, each with its spare wheel; and farther than the eye can see under the trees, in the play of light and shadow, more horses' croups, smoke from field forges, mountains of hay and straw. What a grand, exciting spectacle this image of war is, spread out in this pleasure garden among the flowers, the orange trees, and the marble statues, on the pedestals of which sabers and issue overcoats are hung today.

This evening what insouciance, what a fine unconsciousness of the morrow, when the city may be put to fire and slaughter! The same gaiety, the same futility of words, the same light and ironic hum of conversation in restaurants and cafés. Women and men are the same frivolous beings they were before the invasion, except for a few women who are petulant because their husbands spend too long reading the paper.

At night I go back along the Tuileries and see the day's spectacle once more, now bathed in the milky light of the moon which has risen at the end of the Rue de Rivoli, its outline broken by the tall chimney on the Flora Pavilion. Under the electric brightness which makes the green foliage a glassy blue, through the trees which look like trees in mythology, in the silence of the sleeping park where you hear only the ballad of a wakeful artilleryman, all those croups in their white immobility make you think of stone horses, of a marble stud farm, taken from a Parthenon found in an ancient sacred wood.

Monday, September 12

Not only have our officers been incompetent, our soldiers have been craven. In support of what I say I have a letter from my cousin Philippe de Courmont, who was taken prisoner at Sedan, affirming that the soldiers absolutely would not fight. Can it be that the civilian population is going to show qualities that the army lacked? If that happened, the army would be forever finished in France and we would enter the revolutionary cycle under full steam.

Tuesday, September 13

This is the day of the grand review, the spectacle of a population in arms.

At the railroad station the belt-line cars are stormed by infantrymen with their round loaves of bread stuck on their bayonets. In Paris on all the streets and new boulevards of the Chaussée d'Antin district you cannot see the sidewalks because of the grey mass of living beings which covers them. A first row of Mobiles in white blouses seated on the curb with their feet in the gutter; a second row sitting or lying against the buildings. The bayonets of National Guards on their way to the Bastille go up the boulevard between a double rank of National Guards; the bayonets of Mobile Guards going to the Madeleine come down the boulevard—a two-way current, never stopping as it sparkles under the sun with flashes of steel.

From every street National Guards pour out in frock coats, in service tunics, in fatigue jackets, etc., on their lips songs that no longer have the gay or vulgar note of recent days, but in which today devotion seems to be gathering strength and enthusiasm in a mounting sentiment of heroism.

Suddenly amid the din of drums a great emotional silence; men's eyes meet each other as if giving a pledge of death. Then from this concentrated enthusiasm there arises a great shout, a full-lunged shout of "Long live France! Long live the Republic! Long live Trochu!" in salute to the rapid gallop of the general and his escort.

The parade of the National Guard begins, their rifles decked with dahlias, roses, and streamers of red ribbon—an interminable parade in which the sound of the *Marseillaise*, murmured rather than sung, lingers on behind the slow march of the men, like the sonorous, pious waves of a men's prayer.

Seeing in these ranks grey beards mingled with beardless chins and frock coats alongside blouses; seeing these fathers, some of whom hold by the hand their little daughters who have slipped into the ranks; seeing this mixture of common and middle-class people improvised into soldiers and ready to die together, you begin to wonder if there will not be one of those miracles that come to the aid of nations that have faith.

I go up Montmartre to the Moulin de la Galette; at the foot of the picturesque mill, which is garlanded with ivy running across the antique plaster heads, I find Parisian curiosity feeding on the naval battery that has been set up in the yellow sand. Men and women watch in the distance the heavy white smoke rising out of the green forests of Bondy and Montmorency, in the middle of which a burning village flames up like the fire in the chimney of a forge.

As I watch this an old woman, who still has her provincial accent, says to me: "Can it be that they are burning all that?" And I feel in her what is completely lacking in the Parisians around me, a loving attachment to nature, to trees, to everything surrounding her childhood.

I go on to La Chapelle. Nothing but rifles placed against the dirty-colored houses of the Faubourg Saint Denis; under the moldy rustic arches of the porte-cochères, nothing but rifles. Everybody who is eating or drinking at a cabaret door has a rifle between his legs. Workmen with leather aprons around their middles show their wives how a breechloader works, while a wave of men of the people in blouses who are brandishing rifles bursts out of the little door of the municipal building.

In the street the last of the belated movers hasten on, dragging handcarts, the man harnessed in front, the woman pushing from behind. Among them immense vans rise up, with barrels in front, baskets of fowl in the middle, and in the back, under a stretched covering, bedding and mattresses on which women and children are huddled together.

Next there is the green entrance of everything from the surrounding truck gardens that must be kept from the enemy, carts full of cabbages, pumpkins, leeks moving slowly under the grey sky split by a zigzag of orange. On the sidewalks and between the wheels of the vehicles a whole population of men and women moving their possessions, carrying attached to their bodies the spoils of the fields or the baroque debris of dwellings beyond the barrier. I notice a little girl who has a pair of riding boots hanging by a string over one shoulder and who carries an old gilt barometer in her free hand.

In the evening I go back to Montmartre. I climb by those stairs and ramps of an Arab city, along those strange streets which night makes almost fantastic. Of the conflagration, the reflecting sky, the flaming horizon, of everything that imagination conjures up about a forest fire, of all that the crowd trampling in the shadow near the drinking fountain tries to see, there is nothing—nothing but a line that seems to shut off sight with a sorry band of half-extinguished street lights.

September 15

On the Rue de Vannes and in the whole ragged, miserable, teeming quarter, at the front doors there are little councils of angry or despairing women talking together about the call by the municipal authorities for every able-bodied man.

In front of a house under construction the masons clean up the debris, saying that they will not work tomorrow.

On the outer boulevards you meet Mobile Guards returning with yellow issue shoes and issue bedding; and on either side, great astonished-looking steers are stabled between walls of planks.

The Senate building, with doors wide open, shows to the eyes of whoever enters its stiff and solemn furniture in red, white, and gold, like a theatre of the First Empire discovered in the desolation of an abandoned palace after a performance by Talma.

Students buzz with impatience as they wait for the evening newspapers in the Luxembourg galleries.

On the street leading to Burty's, behind the Horse Market, men in blouses read the paper in the gaslight; and the gaslights in the back rooms of wine shops show the customers doing exercises to the commands of the fat man at the counter.

At Burty's, d'Hervilly tells about seeing rabbits sold by the bushel on the Rue de Turenne; then he begins gaily and wittily to make fun of the imminent heroism and of the patriotism of his own articles. Foolery, always foolery! We are dying of that more than anything else, and I flatter myself for having been the first to say so.

All along my way as I go home at night I brush by battalions of National Guards, still in civil costume, on their way to the ramparts, escorted by wives and children marching at their sides.

Friday, September 16

Today I entertain myself by going around Paris on the belt-line railway.

It is amusing to get these glimpses, evanescent as steam, as you come out of the darkness of a tunnel and see lines of white tents, depressed roads where the cannons are passing by, river banks topped by little crenelated parapets constructed only yesterday, bars with their tables and glasses out in the sun served by volunteer barmaids, who have sewed gold braid on the bottom of their jackets and skirts—glimpses constantly interrupted and blocked by a high embankment after which comes again the eternal horizon of yellow ramparts surmounted by tiny silhouettes of National Guards.

War everywhere; everywhere soldiers and workmen toiling in their shirt sleeves; everywhere men in all sorts of costume on patrol; everywhere civilians with armbands inspecting the factories and dwellings adjacent to the fortifications. And all the time the most charming subjects for a painting. Here in a clump of trees a workshop for gabions and fascines, and the blue accent of blouses against the green and lilac of the felled trees. There, perched on a little hill between the tree trunks, an almost aerial installation of kitchen and rude beds for soldiers from the engineers.

Great emotion at the Bel Air station. With feverish gestures the employes tell me that Marshal Vaillant has just been arrested for showing the Prussians the weak points in the fortifications. They are furious that he was not shot on the spot. Always Pitt and Cobourg! In times of great danger stupidity increases to a formidable extent.

I get off at Boulevard Ornano. At the same moment a Navy battalion armed with shovels and preceded by bugles passes by and in an instant has taken over the customs officials' barracks. I have the pleasure of seeing at every window their intrepid, gravely gay faces and eyes the color of waves in the sun.

I go back up Montmartre among women dragging their feet, bent over under the weight of their spoils from the fields beyond the walls.

Well, let them come, let the cannons roar! It is going on too long! I feel like a man who has decided to have a tooth out but to whom the dentist's servant says: "Doctor is in his laboratory on the fifth floor, working on a set of false teeth which he can't leave."

Saturday, September 17

There is already panic and famine in the midst of the felling of trees in the Bois de Boulogne, where today they are going after the biggest trees and are bringing down the great oaks along the highway. I hear one woman say to another: "But I tell you, by tomorrow there won't be any more provisions in Boulogne!"

In Boulogne blinds closed on all the windows, shutters of all the shops pulled tight. The only places open are the pork butcher's, the wine merchant's, and the barber's. In the abandoned village a few moving vans, standing without horses in front of mattresses and bedding thrown out on the sidewalk, and here and there a few old women sitting in the sun by a dark entryway, obstinately remaining and wishing to die where they have lived.

In the deserted, lifeless little side streets the pigeons strut and hop on the pavement, undisturbed by any living being. In the village's apparent sleep and death the vivid flowers and the gay corners of blooming gardens in the sunlight make a strange contrast.

The road to Saint Cloud continues between rows of houses with closed blinds and closed shops, while the eye of the passer-by is intrigued by the multitude of things lost and strewn on the pavement in the precipitate rush into Paris. A tiny infant's shoe, brand new, tells me a whole story.

Saint Cloud, its houses rising up in steps under the greenery in the brightness of a beautiful day, is frightening in its silence; entering it, you feel as though you were entering a dead city under the implacable blue sky of a cholera epidemic.

In the square, usually so noisy and full of people, a few passers-by, and farther on, at the far end of streets, one or two groups talking, with despondent gestures. Here today even the stones seem to meditate like human beings in the face of great catastrophe.

In the park the remains of the yellow straw which has served as a bed for horses lies rotting around big stones blackened by the soldiers' outdoor cooking. Some children are breaking the green railing of the weighing machine, from which the seats have already been carried off.

Two or three women, who have remained alone in their stalls on the main path, shiver at the practice shots from the cannons. One of them, still young though grey-haired, is red-eyed from weeping; impelled by a grieving woman's need to talk, she says to me: "Isn't it sad, sir? I have a son who was wounded and is a prisoner in Danzig; he writes that it's very bad, that it is as cold there as in the dead of winter. I sent him forty francs, and he didn't get them; I haven't any more to send him, I haven't anything, my husband may leave this evening, and my daughter is always sick."

I go a little way into the park. Nobody, except for a Zouave washing his feet among the gigantic stone toads at La Cascade. In the distance some blouse-clad toughs go by, armed with rifles and pistols; they are out poaching, and I soon hear their shots.

It is almost deep night on the Boulevard des Italiens, where all the shops are closed except for those of Marquis, the armorer, and the gunsmith next door. In the darkness a few promenaders go by slowly, looking bored as they stop for a moment to look at the new businesses in the open air, sellers of sword canes, of water bottles, of bayonet-proof leather protectors. At a little table lit by a lamp a Jew is selling kepis and ramrods for cleaning Chassepot rifles.

There is the inevitable gathering at the corner of the Rue Drouot; in the cheerful light from the cafés at the entrance to the Passage Jouffroy, above the kepis on every head, you see stupid caricatures attacking the Emperor and Empress balancing on a string stretched between two trees.

Sunday, September 18

What especially strikes me about King William, about Bismarck, is their perfidy. This is evident in everything, in their proclamations, in their actions. It is always sly force, hypocritical victory.

This morning Pélagie could find only a sou's worth of bread at the bakeries in Auteuil.

September 19

The cannons roar all morning.

At eleven o'clock I am at the Point du Jour gate. Under the railway bridge, hanging onto the projections of the crenelated wall, which is not finished, mounted on piles of plaster and gravel, climbing on workmen's ladders, women listen anxiously for sounds from the Sèvres bridge side, while below them pass battalions of Mobiles on their way to the firing line, with difficulty forcing their way through the last of the returning dwellers from outside the walls and their loaded wheelbarrows, through squads of National Guards mixed with bands of deserters.

The people question these men. There are soldiers of the

46th with mud up to their knees, a Zouave with a scratch on his face. They say they have been cut off and seem to be trying to spread discouragement with their remarks, their frightened appearance, their cowardly expression.

In spite of this spectacle of retreat, of disorganization, of panic, some Mobiles, who are waiting for orders with something of the usual confusion of troops without officers, though they are a bit pale, have an air of decision which inspires hope. Two nervous and decidedly plucky little women next to me remark that nobody seems to be afraid.

With the martial bearing of seasoned troops a battalion of the Municipal Guard now files by; one of their officers, as he comes off the bridge and sees the Zouave with the scratch, shouts to the crowd: "Arrest that Zouave! They ran away this morning." Soon I see the Zouave taken back to battle between some Mobiles.

In a returning battalion of Mobiles one of the men has a Prussian epaulette at the end of his bayonet. Constantly on people's faces a thousand expressions of anxiety, hope, disappointment brought out by the news the new arrivals bring.

An open carriage carrying three wounded Zouaves goes by; one can see only the tops of three rifles and yellow heads in red turbans. The coachman of a coupé says he is in a hurry, and as people give way we see a man's braided sleeve and a hand resting on the pommel of a sword; a wounded officer.

The Mobiles buzz around us, feverish and impatient, asking to go to the firing line, singing the *Marseillaise*, and beginning a rolling fire with their blank cartridges which they are trying out.

From my house I become aware of a great commotion in the distance, with now and then the dull detonation of a cannon. A National Guard passes under my window driving a dray full of unpainted wooden stretchers for the wounded.

I return to the Point du Jour just as a little band of Zouaves comes back. They say they are all that is left of the corps of 2,000 men to which they belonged. Farther off a frightened Mobile is saying that there are 100,000 Prussians in the Meudon woods, that Vinoy's corps has been scattered like bird shot. He tells of a bomb bursting into twenty-two pieces near one of his comrades, of the daring and wild resolution of those men who, though there were only ten of them, attacked his battalion. In all of these accounts you discern the madness of fear, the hallucinations of panic.

At the Auteuil station a bourgeois tells me that his son, a stout fellow of twenty, has not been able to stop trembling and weeping since he helped carry some of the wounded.

A pretty little tableau at the Neuilly gate. In the pile-up of carriages and moving vans a wheelbarrow is stopped while the man pushing it gets his breath. Across the wheelbarrow is a spring mattress, on each side a heap of chairs, and in the middle innocently stretched out at full length on a quilted cover is a young girl, already good-sized, with her dress pulled up above her long stockings which encase the legs of a doe; she is sleeping weary and serene, her mouth open in a smile, showing her white teeth.

Still another band of Zouaves near the Madeleine. One of them, with a nervous laugh, tells us that there was no battle, only an immediate rout, that he did not fire a single shot. I am struck by the way these men look at you. The glance of the deserter is vague, troubled, dully evasive; it focuses on nothing, it comes to rest on nothing.

I stroll around the Place Vendôme, near the headquarters of the square, where they are continually bringing in all kinds of people who are accused of being spies. Among them I see a general and a colonel, and the crowd shouts that they are Prussian spies and ought to be shot. A little later somebody announces that they are French officers who have returned from the battle at Châtillon. Everybody seems crazy with fear.

I have dinner with Pierre Gavarni, a staff officer in the National Guard, whom I have run into in the crowd. He tells me that he has been struck since the first defeats—he was at Metz and at Châlons as Ferri-Pisani's secretary—by the way everybody moves around in a void, by the lack of attention of the French mind at this moment for everything that concerns it. He has tried several times to find out what the rifle situation is at Mont Valérien without being able to get any information.

On the boulevards this evening there is a crowd, the immense crowd that gathers on bad days, an agitated, stormy crowd, looking for disorder and victims, from which continually rises the shout: "Arrest him!" At once on the scent of a man who is trying to get away, there is the brutal rush of a stream of men who dash through the promenaders after the man in flight at a pitch of violence which makes them ready to tear him to pieces.

Tuesday, September 20

I get off at Batignolles; among the shops full of produce and every kind of merchandise my eye lights on a store with closed shutters and open door, on which the word *Hospital* is written in big letters between two red crosses.

Inside the shop a man is laying out bandages on a little table; at the foot of the beds women are making lint. The man, the women, the empty beds waiting for amputation and death, this stiff rehearsal of the dreadful things that are going to take place tomorrow, all this is more impressive than if there were wounded men in the beds.

I stand before his tomb. He has been dead three months, three months ago today. Leaning on the grille, I push my mind back to a past shared by two, already so far away; as I cough, I think that the bronchitis from which I suffer and which causes me to have a fever might well reunite us fairly soon. The conversation of my thoughts with what is left of him under the stone is constantly interrupted and disturbed by the orders given to the Mobiles who are drilling outside the cemetery.

There aren't many of us at Brébant's this evening—just Saint-Victor, Nefftzer, Charles Blanc, and Charles Edmond. We talk about Renan's letter to Strauss. Saint-Victor tells us about the Emperor's correspondence, which is to be published; Mario Proth, the secretary of the committee, has given him some information about it. Among others there is a letter from the younger Guizot asking the Emperor to pay 100,000 francs worth of debts for him.

"Fine," I say, "if they publish everything, and acquaintances, relations, and friends are not exempt from the dishonor inflicted on the rest."

"You know, it's very hard! Kératry has already had the Bazaine dossier pulled out. He is the children's godfather; and then this is not the time . . ."

Saint-Victor adds a little later: "It would seem that there are some scarcely admirable letters from Uhrich, the famous defender of Strasbourg. . . . They say there are also letters from three or four editors of *Le Figaro* proving that they were bought; but they are not to be published because the government doesn't want to make an enemy of that paper at election time."

And I think to myself about the justice of History.

We come back to the defense of Paris, and everybody is very sceptical about the strength of the defense and the courage of the Mobile Guards, and very doubtful about the usefulness of the barricades.

Nefftzer interrupts: "But there are people who want to blow Paris up, I warn you! I know one, an editor of *Le Réveil*, who is all set to blow Paris up with sixty barrels of oil; he says that will be enough!" And in the midst of our rather sad seriousness everybody makes fun of such exaggerated resolution. Some one breaks in:

"Look, if they burn Paris, it ought to be rebuilt with chalets . . . yes, chalets, for Haussmann's Paris!"

"Yes," we reply in chorus, "we shall be forced to become a serious, well-behaved, reasonable people. It is urgent that we find another use for the Opéra: it is no longer in keeping with our means. We won't have enough money to pay the tenors; we will have an opera like that of a second-class city. . . . We are going to be condemned to become a virtuous people."

We realized how much to the point we had spoken when menacing shouts rose up to our windows with the cry: "Down with the lupanar! Put out the gas, put out the gas!" And we are obliged to have the chandeliers extinguished to the vociferations of a vulgar mob who, on the pretext that they have seen a call girl in a private room, take pleasure of an envious and violent sort in preventing the bourgeois from having dinner, though they keep their own whorehouses and cabarets wide open.

Wednesday, September 21

Today on the anniversary of the proclamation of the Republic a demonstration with torches by riffraff and street urchins who bear ahead of them a huge canvas on which the figure of Liberty is lighted up by the torches behind the canvas—a real transparency of the Ambigu Theatre, which makes you disgusted with liberty and this clownish people.

It is half past nine. I am going along the Rue de la Paix. All the shops closed. Not a passer-by. Three omnibuses are the only sign of life on the dead street, three omnibuses, each carrying the red-cross flag of ambulances above the driver's head.

Thursday, September 22

On the Trocadéro heights in the windy air resounding with the incessant drumming from the Champ de Mars are groups of curiosity-seekers, among them some correct Englishmen, binocular cases over their shoulders, holding enormous glasses in their kid-gloved hands. You see young girls with charming awkwardness raising a long telescope with one skinny hand while they cover one eye with the other hand in a childish gesture. At intervals the telescopes, which in peacetime are focused on the sun and moon, are directed at Vanves, Issy, Meudon; and among the curious people standing in line a Mobile, his rifle on his back, stands out on a little ladder like a pyramid as he puts his eye to the enlarging glass. The horizon is only fog and dust with a little white smoke which seems to have come from cannon shots.

Behind the opera glasses and the telescopes bursts out the noise of youngsters of fourteen, who are formed in companies and as banners carry boards attached to long poles bearing the words *Ambulance Aides, Engineer Aides, Firefighter Aides.* These battalions of ragamuffins, with cigarettes in the corners of their mouths, are improvising roles in the revolution, making a commotion which is something like an uprising of brats.

You see faces of all sorts, blouses of every color; included among them are pale barracks-raised soldiers' sons and rosy little baker boys with white caps.

This evening when I get off the train all the passengers for Auteuil and the belt-line take a serious look at a sort of armored cage in which the engineers will ride from now on.

Friday, September 23

Pélagie was telling me yesterday evening that she was not at all afraid, that this seemed to her a joke of a war. In fact, this morning's terrible cannonade, as she said, is hardly more than the noise you make when you shake a rug. But wait!

Near the gateway in the fortifications the road to Sèvres is covered with little tables surrounded by stools and laden with loaves of bread, bottles of wine, bowls of café au lait—a series of open-air restaurants with tricolor flags tied to the trees, with little stoves and steaming cooking pots, with canteen women who protect themselves from the sun by means of paper Pierrot hats.

At the Palace of Industry a group of men and women, silent and grave, are clustered around the little door at the left, waiting with anxious hearts for the ambulances to bring in the wounded.

On the pavement of the Place Vendôme in front of the staff headquarters there is always an expectant group disturbed by everything that comes in, is brought in, or goes out. I see a pale man in a white cap go out under the escort of two Mobiles. I am told that he is a looter and will be shot tomorrow. To the huzzas of the crowd an old priest comes in, gallantly mounted on a horse, which we recognize as a Prussian horse. With great boots on his legs and the red-cross insignia on his arm, covered with dust, he is bringing at full spur information about the battle which he has just left.

These ups and downs of hope are terribly upsetting to the system. It is terrible to see how the most sceptical contract illusions from the mob, from the false good news flying from mouth to mouth, from the contagion of group credulity, illusions suddenly destroyed by the dry reading of an official communiqué.

Constant pushing open of café doors. An incessant din of laughing conversation. The carefree life of the capital still going on in company with the horror of war on its doorstep.

September 24

In this capital of fresh food and early fruits and vegetables it is truly ironic to see Parisians pondering in front of the canned goods displayed by food merchants and cosmopolitan grocers. They finally decide to go in, and come out carrying under their arms *Boiled Mutton*, *Boiled Beef*, etc., all the possible and impossible canned meats and vegetables, things you would never have expected to become the food of the Paris rich.

Pasted everywhere on the walls are great bands of white canvas with red-cross hospital insignia on them, above which you sometimes see at a window a soldier's head in a blood-stained bandage.

Businesses are all transformed. Disderi bullet-proof vests are spread out among the exotic flowers at a florist's; National Guard jerseys and tunics fill the show windows of white-goods shops.

Through the basement air vents along the Rue de Rivoli you hear hammering on iron; through barred windows you see workmen forging breastplates.

Restaurant bills of fare are becoming limited. The last oysters were eaten yesterday; eels and gudgeons are all that is left in the way of fish.

After I leave the Pied de Mouton I cross through the Central Market, where the resounding noise of food being unloaded is mixed with the thin sound of pins falling in the National Guards' piston rifles. In front of Saint Eustache apprentice butchers hoist sides of beef on their shoulders and carry them along, with one hand on their hips, among the fat, happy rats which dart out from the iron trellis surrounding one tree and disappear at once behind another.

On the boulevard I run into Charles Blanc and Chenavard, who remind me of Rome and our walks among the ruins. Charles Blanc, who, along with his brother, has gone to the municipal office to sign up, is very indignant at the mayor who, showing no respect for the illustrious enrollees, stupidly asked them if they were armed.

Sunday, September 25

The two banks of the Seine full of cavalry horses and barelegged Mobiles, who are washing themselves in the waves made by the incessant plowing along of river boats. The usual placid anglers, but today they all wear the National Guard kepi. The Louvre gallery windows are protected by sandbags. In the Rue Saint Jacques women in groups of two or three talking, with anxious voices, about the rise in the price of food.

The Collège de France covered with white posters superimposed one on another, advertisements of *Pagliari Paper* for wounds, advertisements of *Phenol Boboeuf*, advertisements announcing publication of *The Emperor's Papers and Correspondence*. A newly posted notice on violet paper announces the formation of the Commune and calls for suppression of the Prefecture of Police and for mass mobilization. A wounded or dead man is carried by on a stretcher under escort of a band of Mobiles.

At the back of a second-hand store courtyard there are heaps of wine merchants' counters up for sale, all the counters from the suburbs outside the walls.

In the Luxembourg the thousands of sheep crowded together and shifting about in their narrow enclosure make you think of the swarming of maggots in a box. In the Place du Panthéon, in the areas where paving stones have been removed, little girls barely able to walk do acrobatic exercises with uncertain steps. In the courtyard of the Sainte Geneviève Library a mountain of sand. Posters on the columns of the Law School announce the formation of a Women's Committee, with Louise Colet's name at the head of the list.

On the Boulevard de Port Royal, near the Capucins, I think, camp followers in Sunday dress singing patriotic songs; farther on, seated on the ground among his sheep in a big enclosure, a shepherd reading *Le Petit Journal*. At a wine shop with the sign: *Au Grand Arago*, some women catch your eye with blood-red bands stuck in their black hair.

On another street over the door to a business house a name in gilt which seems to radiate the well-being of established fortune—Colmant, the name of the fancy-man in *Germinie Lacerteux*.

All along the boulevards and on both sides of them uneasy, menacing cattle pushing against the horse-chestnut trees and the urinals; in their inclosures they crowd back into a corner, then rush forward in a confused and agitated mass that is dominated by a big bull mounting a cow, which carries him along almost standing up. Another, lowering his horns, lets out a bellow that goes echoing down the endless avenue.

The sun sets in a great gold-yellow burst, which turns the outline of the church at the head of the Rue Saint Jacques to violet, and makes dark and vague the silhouettes of armed men returning home in the blinding glare of the dusty street.

Monday, September 26

Today a deep silence has followed the cannonade of recent days. The whole road from the Point du Jour to the ramparts seems to have been fortified by the barricade engineers. There are classic barricades made of paving stones and others made of sacks of earth. There are picturesque ones made of tree trunks—regular fringes of forest growing out of a ruined wall. It is like an immense Clos Saint Lazare, erected again by the descendants of the men of '48 against the Prussians. All the walls are crenelated and pierced with gun-slits. The ground, full of round holes close together, looks rather like the tin platters on which they cook snails in Burgundy.

In Gavarni's garden workmen are getting ready to cut down the quincunx of horse chestnuts.

The arches of the viaduct bridge, barricaded and closed by great cross-pieces, are filled with a crowd of men and women who are looking through the openings at the gleaming river and the green hills, where their glasses are trying to spy out the Prussians. Men in blouses seated on the parapet wait for the first cannon shots, just as though they were waiting for the first burst of fireworks shot off on the Trocadéro. As they work, the masons chat about the carbine shot they just sent into the target; you still hear it echoing against the plaque next to which some women of a certain elegance are bravely eating fried potatoes in a restaurant improvised under a tent.

Nature seems to be obliging with one of those contrasts of which novelists are so fond for their intimate catastrophes.

Never was September so gaily clad; never was the sky of so pure a blue; never was fine weather so perfect.

Tuesday, September 27

Yesterday a big demonstration by people on the Boulevard des Italiens against the butchers. They demand that the government sell its cattle without the intermediary of these speculators in human misery. In front of the municipal offices on the Rue Drouot a woman makes a harangue on the scarcity and dearness of the chief necessities of life. She accuses the grocers of concealing half their supplies in order to double the price a week from now. She finishes by saying in an angry voice that the people have no money to lay in supplies, that they must buy from day to day, and that always, always things are so ordered that the poor suffer and the rich are spared.

At the foot of the Point du Jour bridge on the Quai de Javel above a palisade with gun-slits, on the other side of the barricade, a whole landscape under a sky and over a river both luminous and grey. To the left a tall poplar black as a cypress. Straight ahead and to the right factory chimneys and hillsides looking as though they were covered with the white wash of a gouache. Shadows in bluish, violet, lead-colored tones, flashes of silver. A bit of nature standing out in contrast with the harsh colors of the tricolor flag floating above the wooden barricade, like a landscape drawn in molten metal, recalling to my mind what I have seen at the bottom of the shovel when I melted a piece of lead.

Turning my back on the landscape, I see black smoke bringing darkness into the sunshine, darkness like that of an eclipse. The people around me say it is the fire in the Bois de Vincennes; others, that it is a fire on the Buttes.

I return to Paris on the top deck of the American omnibus, which is held up for a long time in front of the Quartermaster's Depot, so encumbered is the quay with wagons full of cases of biscuits, omnibuses crammed to the very roof with loaves of bread which you can see through the glass of the closed windows, drays of every kind sagging under barrels of flour, all pressing and pushing for entrance or exit at this gigantic depot of our soldiers' food.

A pretty detail on the Rue de Rivoli: to the deafening noise of an artillery battery going by, an artilleryman caressing the brass of a cannon with amorous hand as though he were stroking beloved flesh.

Paris is disturbed, Paris is anxious about its daily pittance. Little groups of women gesticulate vigorously; at the corner of the Rue Jean-Jacques Rousseau and the Rue Saint Honoré I come upon an angry group beating against the closed shutters of a grocer's shop. A woman says that the grocer sold a dried herring to a Mobile Guard for fifty centimes; the latter hung it on the end of a stick with a sign reading: *Sold by an officer of the National Guard to a poor Mobile for fifty centimes.* A little farther on I hear two women behind me sigh in unison as they say: "Already there's nothing left to eat!" And in fact I see the meagre display in the pork butchers' windows, where there are only a few sausages in their silver wrappings and some jars of truffles. I return from the market by the Rue Montmartre. The white marble counters of the Lambert establishment, at this season normally laden with venison, pheasant, game, are empty; the fish tanks are empty. In this little temple of gastronomy a thin man walks back and forth with a melancholy air. In contrast, a few steps away a big jolly girl is selling beef extract, under the bright gaslight which makes a wall of tin cans sparkle.

A serious look comes over the faces of promenaders as they approach the white notices shining in the gaslight. I see them read slowly, then go off hesitantly, thoughtful and withdrawn. These are notices of the regulations of the courtsmartial established at Vincennes and Saint Denis. You are stopped short by this statement: "Sentence will be carried out on the spot by the squad ordered to guard the meeting place." You realize with a little shiver that the dramatic and summary events of a siege have begun.

Wednesday, September 28

What lively and colorful pictures the siege has composed in every nook of Paris, pictures that painters will neglect to paint or that will be sentimentalized by some Millevoye of the brush like Protais! What a feast of color is provided under the trees along the Champs Elysées by the red kepis, the red trousers, the grey-brown shirts, the horses' shining croups, the sabers hung in the branches, the brass helmets with horsehair manes; in the middle of all this an officer dressed in royal purple, lost in a big red-flannel robe, sitting on his chair in a pose at once bold and indolent.

At the Tuileries for the whole length of the Orangerie terrace a moving up and down on strings of canteens which are being filled down on the quay by winesellers' helpers harnessed to little carts. In the dusty, parched trees shirts drying on the highest branches look like scarecrows.

On every street the butcher shops are without a scrap of meat, their grilles closed and inside curtains drawn, a sinister sign of famine.

The whole length of the endless Rue de Vaugirard, which is both rural and commercial, nothing like the deadness of other neighborhoods, nothing of the warlike stamp of the other completely militarized districts. Hens peck away in the middle of the street; goats wander along the sidewalks; you would think you were in the Paris of yesterday if it weren't for a future winner of the Prix de Rome who, in a round blind window, is making a huge head of the Republic capped with a Phrygian bonnet, and if from time to time a rapidly passing tilbury driven by a butcherboy did not carry a Mobile on his way back to his post.

This evening as I am going toward my raiload carriage I bump into a gentleman taking the air along the platform in his big apron; he is an orderly in the railway ambulance service.

Thursday, September 29

During the day I look for a shop to rent where I can store my collections.

On my way to Burty's this evening my eye is caught in the shadows by the letters of fire outlined by the gas in the zinc openings of the columns: *Spectacles.* Flamboyant advertisements beneath which the rotten, dusty notices of the last performances that took place flutter in the night like the wings of grey bats.

Burty is a member of the *Commission on the Papers and Correspondence of the Emperor.* He is as happy as a fisherman with permission to fish in the pool at Fontainebleau. He tells of baskets of papers, enough to fill an audit office. But I do not see anything very strange or very new in all that he says or announces or has discovered. Receipts for money paid to men whom everybody suspected of receiving it; proof of thefts which are a secret from nobody; dispatches as brief as the telegrams they are, tag ends of accounts. Not an intimate document, not a letter that might cast light on the history of the human soul. I hope the memoirs will have more to tell us.

I make the observation that this government, which began with Morny's phrase: "Gentlemen, you know we are risking our skins," and ended with Filon's dispatch: "We must flee to Belgium," has the quality of an epic by Robert Macaire.

Burty has seen an album with photographs of all the Empress's masked-ball costumes; among them is one of her in the Greek style, with almost nothing on. He is seriously urging the government to have it reproduced, and he repeats: "I am sure it would have a very great effect on the people." I can't help feeling a bit of scorn for the means used by the government to stir up the masses to revolution, and that upsets him a little.

Friday, September 30

Awakened by cannon. A red dawn rising in a milky fog and bathing the trees, which are grey with dust. In the distance the dull growl of the *brute*, shattering bursts of shells, the continual crackling of rifle fire.

In the afternoon I seek out information on the spot. A gentleman with a decoration, who is copying handwritten dispatches in front of the municipal offices on the Place Saint Sulpice, tells me that the news is not good. I go up the Boulevard Saint Michel in a crowd that becomes larger and more compact as we approach the barrier. I reach the end of the Rue d'Enfer and the newly built church at the angle of that street and the Rue du Faubourg Saint Jacques. The way is barred.

There, a large crowd of waiting people next to empty carriages drawn up on either side of the street, a silent crowd of men and women. The women wear madras kerchiefs or little cotton bonnets on their heads. They are sitting on the ground at the edge of the street; near them are their small daughters, who put their handkerchiefs over their heads to keep off the sun and watch their mothers' faces without attempting to play. Men, with hands in the pockets of their blue blouses or with arms crossed, look ahead into the distance, their dead pipes in their mouths. Dispatch-riders go by at a gallop, among them youngsters with their shirt tails billowing out behind. People are not drinking in the cabarets; they are not even talking. A solitary workman in the middle of a group is telling what he has seen, emphasizing each of his statements with a gesture that repeatedly brings a big finger in front of his nose. You would say the population was transfixed; there is so stern a gravity in these men and women that in spite of the eternal sun and the eternal blue of the sky the setting seems to take on something of the sadness of this silent waiting!

Every eye, every look is turned toward the Rue de Châtillon. From time to time a red cross on a white flag emerges from the dust of the road. Then a swelling murmur which says quietly to every ear: "Some wounded!" At once the crowd, eager to see, makes a brutal rush to either side of the vehicle. Next to me an infantryman gets down from a hired carriage, his face dirty, his expression one of astonishment; two National Guards help him to the dressing station in the church, on which you read in freshly painted Gothic letters: *Liberty Equality Fraternity.* I see another go by, his poor handkerchief knotted around his head, a green quilt over his legs. All sorts of carriages, coupés, carts, breaks, moving vans carry pale faces past our eyes or let us see bits of red trouser on which blood has made great black stains.

Saturday, October 1

Horsemeat is slipping quietly into the Parisian diet. Day before yesterday Pélagie brought home a piece of steak which, seeing her doubtful expression, I did not eat. At Peters' yesterday they brought me roast beef; I examined the meat, which was watery, without fat, and striped with white nerves; my painter's eye discerned the blackish red color, so different from the rose red of beef. The waiter assured me, though not very firmly, that this horse was beef.

Sunday, October 2

At breakfast this morning a thin, hollow-flanked cat, a real siege-cat, slips into the dining room with famished meow.

Today nothing of the painful emotion and sadness of the last two days, no memory of the wounded going by. The Sunday sun has swept it all away. Gay and joyous, Paris streams out to all her gates for a promenade, as giddy as though she were going to Longchamp for the races. Women in summer costumes, wearing the big bows on their behinds and the tiny hats which are still in style, trot along on the circular paths or slip between the big vans by the openings on the belt-line.

You see young girls who have climbed up the sandy banks like goats, their eyes at the rifle-slits. Under the escort of a National Guard with silver braid, American-type coaches carry elegant women who steal the show, and who with their pince-nez in their hands speak of *bastions, ramparts, gabions, horsemen.* Commercial vehicles are full of members of the family in their Sunday best, some of them bouncing on the added seats. And the roads are full of little boys who cut up and play to the encouraging smiles of their parents.

What is most popular at the moment is to make the tour of Paris by the belt railway, a journey on which you see women not afraid to show their legs as they clamber awkwardly with brave little movements up to the top deck, from which they can look over the line of fortifications. I do the same and see new interior fortifications begun only a few days ago, barricades of paving stones, crenelations on truck-garden walls, moats being dug, all the work for a second line of defense. From a distance the ramparts under incessant construction take on the sharpness, the almost artistic finish of a little model of fortifications made of cork, of a finely constructed toy made for a young prince, to teach him to play siege.

I come back on foot along the quays in the gathering dusk at six o'clock. In the warm haze retained from the scorching day, in the dust stirred up all day long by the feet of men, women, horses, and carriage wheels, Paris is bathed in an African grey, the grey which Fromentin painted so well, into which the houses introduce a white accent and the trees a few violet blobs.

I keep on walking in this greyness, which deepens as night comes on, and out of which the red lantern of a river boat suddenly shines. I am still walking, lost in the silly dreams which the imagination makes out of the vague words that come to it from the passers-by, when I hear a man leaning against the quay say to another: "Well, they're going to jump on us now!" That statement wakens me and immediately convinces me that Strasbourg has fallen, a presentiment which is confirmed when I buy a newspaper on the boulevard.

This evening I do not observe in Paris the reaction I had expected from this sad piece of news. I think I see much more indifference than irritation.

Monday, October 3

Through the grillework at the bottom of my garden this morning I see the Breton Mobiles encamped in one of the villa paths reading their prayers from the little *Semaines Saintes* which they pull out of their pockets.

I don't know why, but for the last two days memories of my brother have again occupied my mind, which has been somewhat distracted from thoughts of him because of the horror of the present, the menace of the future. This memory is suddenly as vivid and cruel as it was in the first days after his death.

Why is it that I, who hold so little to life, I, who could take as my motto: *No longer does anything matter to me; nothing is left me*, do not seek death? Is it out of cowardice that I have avoided service in the National Guard? No, it is not cowardice. It is a feeling of proud, individual personality, which would lead me, if I could, to give my life all by myself, to do something great, to direct, to give orders, in short to be an individual in this war, but which prevents me from resigning myself to being a cipher, an anonymous piece of cannon fodder. Such a death, glorious as it might be, I consider beneath my place in literature. This is true, for nothing forces me to say it. . . . However, this sentiment might easily be silenced by the warm "Are you coming?" of a friend, who would by his company save me from the dirty and repulsive unknowns of the National Guard.

Two drunks sleeping off a spree on a bench at my entryway emit now and then in their drunken military dreams the hoarse cry "To Arms!"

The special beauty of this fine autumn, the russet trees, the soft blue sky, the great soft dripping shadows, the milky fog spread out and floating in the distance, the reflected vapors of the sun, the shimmering neutral-toned air, the very light itself, almost violet and not unlike the color of water in a cabaret glass, all this soft natural setting makes the shining implements of war and the multicolored swarming crowd stand out in harmonious color.

As I go out from dinner, I am accosted by a very well-dressed man who says to me, bowing like a man of the world, "Sir, would you give me enough for a meal? I have not eaten since yesterday." I refuse. Then I give him something. In times like these he may well have been telling the truth.

The men who govern us are mediocre, and on that account reasonable. They do not have enough *audacity* and have no idea at all of the *possibility of the impossible* in times like these. After all who are our saviors? A fine-talking general, a commonplace man of letters, an unctuous lawyer, and a middle-class replica of Danton.

Paris has never had such an October. The night, clear and full of stars, is like a night in the Midi. God loves the Prussians.

Tuesday, October 4

Opening the paper this morning, I read that Callou, the director at Vichy, has had a mental breakdown. He is only forty-two. This year there have been so many minds of forty worn out and done for by pressure of business, politics, literature: Callou, Langlé, Paradol, my brother. . . .

As you get off the train the first thing you notice is the wounded at the hospital, who are seated or lying on the grass wearing their hospital nightcaps and overcoats.

Bombardment is imminent. Yesterday they came to check whether I had water on every floor. Today I find barrels of water in all the alleyways; in front of the church on the Rue de la Chaussée d'Antin a great iron cylinder standing on legs is apparently a municipal cistern.

Standing next to the sidewalk, her feet in the gutter, immo–

bile, seeing nothing, hearing nothing, heedless of vehicles which graze her, an old countrywoman in a tile-shaped bonnet is, in her petrified rigidity, enveloped in pleats like those of the stone figures on the tombs at Bruges. She shows such great stunned sorrow that I go up to her and speak. Then, slowly awakening, she says to me in a voice which is like a lament: "I thank you for your kindheartedness. I do not need anything. I am only grieving."

These soft, sad words make me speculate for a long time about the unknown tragedy that this old exile from the fields bears silently within herself.

There are only five of us at Brébant's. We talk of the Aristophanic quality of the National Defense Government. Arago, whom Saint-Victor calls a regular Pantaloon from Italian comedy; Mahias, whose activity consists in getting drunk one day and recovering the next; Gagneur, that louse from *Le Siècle*, until now known only through his wife's visits to editorial offices in attempts to place his copy, Gagneur, now responsible for publication of *The Correspondence of the Emperor*. We are shocked by the lack of seriousness, decorum, correctness evidenced in this work, to which the editors give witty headings, as if they were writing copy for *Le Figaro*.

Nefftzer always brings the same darkly ironic view of things, the same scepticism about what can be done to save us. At times, hearing the diabolical laugh with which he habitually announces the most terrible disasters, I wonder whether this Alsatian is a Frenchman, so striking is the sceptical, even mocking, indifference of a foreigner in his talk about all this.

Wednesday, October 5

In the neighborhood of Boulevard Exelmans, in the little bouquets of greenery which suddenly came into view with the removal of the fences burned by the Mobiles, the open-air restaurants under the hazelnut trees are charming in the bright sun. The details have a picturesqueness that would enchant a Knaus: tables and benches in roughed-out wood, little kegs heaped up on an upside-down stool, the baroque coffee pots boiling on little terra cotta stoves, a disorder of bottles and glazed pots with blue designs on them, above them floating the heads of peach-colored women with flaxen hair.

For a moment this evening the setting sun completely fills the opening of the drawbridge, and the people and things passing through this square of fire stand out in almost supernatural fashion, as if on the gold of an enamel.

Thursday, October 6

This morning for the first time the sun rises in autumn fog. There is a touch of winter in the air today. You feel penetrated by the cold dew that wets the leaves of the trees.

The awakening of the Mobiles takes place without songs. They make their toilets without gaiety, without noise. Little drapers' wagons, such as you see in the most rude and out-of-the-way villages of France, pass among them, offering for sale knitted vests and cotton nightcaps, in which some of the men cover up their ears.

They are camped all along Boulevard Exelmans, some under the railroad arches, others in the cleared area where the new railroad line is being constructed. Little by little they shake off their lethargy and, seated on railroad ties which they have converted into benches, they plunge their spoons into the mess tin placed on a table improvised out of a door torn from its hinges.

With soup and a warm belly gaiety returns and the insouciant laughter of youth spreads from table to table. Some match pennies. Some shine their rifles. Some whiten their leggings. Under an arcade over which *General Staff* is written on a piece of board, some officers write letters on the corner of a table, while in their midst a tall thin priest in his round hat smokes a short briar pipe.

This grey winter weather makes you sad; and it seems that now, when there is no sun, the little irritations of life these days are unbearable and your mind takes a sly pleasure in coming back to them over and over. First, there is the difficulty in getting meat. Then yesterday it was announced that no trains will run after nine-thirty. All first-class seats have been taken over for the military, and you have to ride with dirty, smelly, jostling workmen. And then all the nearby houses have been occupied by soldiers, ready to spill over into yours, who make you fear their drunkenness, their thefts at any hour of the day or night.

Friday, October 7

Just as I am crossing the Seine on the viaduct the gunboat is covered with a white cloud and the terrible detonation of a cannon resounds, repeated by echoes from the Sèvres and Meudon hills.

I am in the Avenue de Vincennes. Behind the ramparts it is closed by a formidable barricade made of cyclopean stone blocks. In front of the ramparts there is a palisaded breastworks made of whole trees which thrust out the menacing spikes of their sharpened branches. The defense here is on a gigantic scale and is worthy of this suburb of uprisings, this Faubourg Saint Antoine, which seems to have mixed a genius for war with a genius for street-fighting.

Beyond the rampart, beyond the palisaded breastworks,

you walk between tree trunks, cut off even with the ground, which once were the handsome trees shading the avenue; to left and right extends a great empty space where the demolished houses have left a white area surmounted by a few heaps of plaster in the dirty green grass.

Then houses start again, closed houses. Only one is open, the house of a blacksmith, the sound of whose hammer is the only sign of life on this silent street. Now and then the corner of an elegant little garden, no longer watered by its owner, shows its poor leaves covered with all the dust that has been raised by the wheels of vehicles moving people out night and day for a whole month.

Suddenly in the distance a black mass and a dull rolling sound. Borne on the shoulders of eight National Guards, a coffin advances, on it the kepi of a National Guard; a drummer precedes it and at intervals beats out a funeral march on the black-palled drum. The route goes on between houses looking even more abandoned, even more shut up. A red horseman, a Spahi, goes by like the wind, perched on his high saddle.

You see big trees trimmed of their branches advancing from the woods, carried by teams of men marching in cadence. Poor Bois de Vincennes, with its trees cut down, with its chalets from which the doors and windows have been removed, with here and there ashes indicating a bivouac! Poverty-stricken women are everywhere in the woods, armed with hatchets and gathering firewood, which they carry along on wheelbarrows and children's wagons. You meet streetwalkers sweeping the empty paths with sagging skirts which, as their hands continually try to pull them up, you notice are pulled in by red belts. In contrast to these denizens of the main streets, in a corner you see two charming women sitting on the ground beside an elegant officer, who is playing with the parasol of one of them.

As I get on the omnibus for Paris a young girl sits down beside me. On her shoulder she has a spray of argentea, and between two spittoons tied together with string she carries, so she tells us, the last strawberries from her little garden at Nogent.

This evening a voice hails me out of the darkness. It is Pouthier, the model for Anatole in *Manette Salomon*, whom I have not seen for many months. We go to a café to talk about *him*, whose death he heard of in the provinces. The poor devil is as badly off as ever and is trying to get into the National Guard so as to earn thirty sous a day.

Saturday, October 8

In the streets you run onto old streetwalkers with red crosses on their left breasts, fat fancy women too old for their trade, who rejoice at the prospect of caressing the wounded with sensual hands and picking up a little love among the amputations.

This evening for the first time I meet Louis Blanc, whom his brother brings to eat at my table at Peters'. His head, set on a ridiculously small body, is a cross between that of a bad actor and a meridional seminarian. There is something horrible about this beardless man; it is the juxtaposition of childishness and senility in his face. He has the rosy cheeks of a baby with a sexagenarian's darkness inside the nostrils and around the mouth.

October 9

Science with its calculations is truly amusing. It will tell you it is as true as two and two make four that so much meat, so much salt meat, so much bread containing so much albumin-fibrin content, will provide nourishment to everyone in the same degree, as if the apparatus where this cooking takes place were always the same and blood, humors, bile were the same in every individual. I don't believe that for a minute. I am sure that there are people so constituted inside that they rebuild themselves only with meat and wine, and nothing else, however great the quantity, gives them nourishment, whereas other people, women especially, need only to eat *vegetables.*

For my part, a meatless diet, however good, however copious, leaves a void in my stomach; I recall that in my youth I used to die of hunger when at the château of my Villedeuil cousin, a great gourmand, they made me fast on Friday and Saturday. On the other hand, I have never seen my old cousin Labille eat anything but some lettuce leaves and fruit; yet she was always plump and in good health. In that green stuff she clearly found albumin-fibrin elements and carbon and everything.

Monday, October 10

This morning I go for my ration card. I feel as though I am beholding one of those long lines of the time of the Revolution, such as poor old Cousin Cornélie used to describe to me: a mixed group of people waiting, old women in rags, guardsmen in kepis, and lower-middle-class men all standing about in improvised premises with whitewashed rooms where you recognize your none-too-honest local tradesmen seated around a table, all-powerful in their National Guard officers' uniforms and supreme disposers of what you get to eat.

I bring home a piece of blue paper, a typographical curiosity for future times and the Goncourts to come, which gives me the right to buy every day for me and my servant two rations of raw meat or four portions of food prepared in the municipal canteens. There are coupons for the period up to November 14; no doubt a good deal will happen between now and then. . . .

All around La Muette ditch-diggers are making an entrenchment linked to a barricade at the entrance to Passy. I stroll as far as the Avenue de l'Impératrice, where I see some women leading cows to pasture on what is left of the grass, great clods of which are being carried off in carts to cover the slopes or protect the powder magazines. Lawn, bridle paths, main walks, all are full of close-set holes such as you see on the road to Billancourt; and two broad moats are cut across the whole width of the immense avenue, one in front of the railroad station, the other level with the Avenue Malakoff. Out of this avenue rush artillery horses, led in groups of three by horsemen, among whom you see the heads of children who are completely happy at having received permission to climb on a saddle horse.

Everywhere horses, gun carriages, soldiers, and field kitchens, where the fire that boils the pot at the same time dries a freshly washed blue-checked handkerchief—a spectacle that a big-bellied Bank employe in his tricorne hat considers at leisure.

On the horizon, dominating all this spectacle of war, against a sky of sun and rain, the white mass of Mont Valérien is silent.

Tuesday, October 11

At the doors of the new buildings where the municipal offices of the invaded suburbs are installed some pale women are talking together in plaintive voices about the impossibility of finding work. On the streets nuns, walking in pairs, look into the palms of their plump hands at the rice which they have taken from sacks by the doors of the grocery shops. Some bric-a-brac merchants, leaning on Gothic credenzas which are set out on the sidewalk, personify the melancholy state of business in hard times.

In front of the Gare du Nord I start out for Saint Denis in the typical open omnibus of the Paris suburbs, a bus upholstered in shreds of something green, driven by a youngster whose face has been burned in a fire. When there are ten of us, we set off. My companions are portly merchants with rings on their hands, old men with red ties and unbuttoned trousers, a white-haired old model from the Ecole des Beaux Arts with a short pipe in his mouth, and an officer's lively mistress, carrying in her suitcase the soft fixings for a night of love.

Still the usual barricades, still the usual destruction in the military zone, where occasionally in the middle of a field of rubble fragments of wall exhibit samples of wallpaper. On this road the houses which have not been demolished have an air of even more complete abandonment than elsewhere; on the shutters and porte-cochères of factories and livestock markets which are no longer open, posters on which the rain has washed the ink and curled the corners are now only white spots on mud-colored wood.

We come to the little bridge over the canal. But we are only permitted to see the Basilica from afar. Zouaves and Mobile Guards bar the entrance to the city and keep mothers, sisters, relatives, friends, and mistresses on the far side of the bridge. There is a rumor that a Prussian spy has slipped in and that, in order to catch him, all communication with the outside has been cut off. After an hour all these disappointed people decide to go back to Paris, having had a siesta on the hillside, from which you can see before you as far as eye can reach fields dotted with every color: men and women gathering up the leavings of the harvest.

Coming back on foot, I notice from time to time along the road that there are squared-out holes in which menacing pieces of barbed wire twist along.

This evening someone next to me says that all afternoon they fired from the Vanves fortress at a target they could not see, one which was visible only from the observation post on the towers of Saint Sulpice. Saint Sulpice transmitted the co-ordinates to the Opéra, and from there they were sent to Vanves with corrections of "To the right," "To the left," "Higher," "Lower," conveyed by signal flags.

Wednesday, October 12

A sad day, as sad as one I passed at this time last year at Trouville with my poor Jules. The cannons on Mont Valé-rien or the heavy voices of the naval guns from the Morte-mart battery continually make the windows rattle and send your blood in a rush to your temples.

These days you are glad to forget yourself, to strip yourself of your nothingness, to bury your waking life in a dream, with your imagination intoxicated by the cannon fire making you fancy yourself a partisan leader ambushing a convoy, killing off Prussians, lifting the siege of Paris—in this way living for long moments in a patriotic hallucination. You invent a means of flying which enables you to see and discover the enemy positions; you invent a murderous machine which kills by battalions and puts whole segments of an army to death. And you go around in a state of absorption like that of a child reading his first book; you range through the open spaces and the grand adventures of the impossible, the hero of a fiction which has being for an hour.

How many turns I made around this garden while my imagination, having nothing to do with the little promenade my body made on the winding paths, was completely absorbed in a daydream about taking the oxygen or hydrogen out of the air and making it mortal for the Prussian lungs of a whole army!

Thursday, October 13

It is a strange feeling, one of humiliation and pain rather than of fear, to know that those hills so near at hand are no longer French; those woods are no longer thronged by promenaders such as Gavarni drew; those houses, so pretty in the sun, no longer shelter your friends and acquaintances. How strange it is with a pair of glasses to try to pick out on that Parisian landscape men in Prussian helmets with a black and white flag, to detect the vanquished men of Jena hidden on the green horizon 4,000 meters away.

I find that the ruins and torn-down walls on the slope from Passy to the Trocadéro have been scaled by men and youngsters who follow the cannonade with their eyes from their perches on the crumbling stone. Beneath them are women in madras kerchiefs looking stupidly around. At every moment against the violet and russet landscape you see projected little bursts of smoke, which leave in the sky little round clouds that look like balls of cotton wool.

Around me opera glasses and good eyes follow the trajectory of the shells, leaving in turn from the Issy and Vanves fortresses and passing each other above the hill and woods at Clamart. The crowd is huge and the grand stairway of the Trocadéro is covered with curious people.

On the Pont de la Concorde, from the top of the omnibus, among a squad of Mobiles preceded by a troop of shouting, singing, dancing children, I see seven dirty red heads in bluish uniforms: they are Bavarian prisoners.

From the Panthéon I go to the Place d'Italie by way of the Rue Mouffetard. Among the mean shops which are like those in a village, among the butcher shops where posters announce that horsemeat will be sold for the duration of the siege, among the bakeries before which there are huge drays full of sacks of flour, and through handcarts carrying little red onions there is a tumultuous movement of bare-armed women who wear handkerchiefs knotted on their heads and blue calico aprons, of sickly old men wearing St. Helena medals, of fat vagabonds with Véron collars—a swarming crowd continually made larger by National Guards in slippers who are on their way to drill.

Everywhere, from the Place d'Italie to the Jardin des Plantes, they are covering the cattle sheds with oilcloth; everywhere they are building barracks, the beams of which are being used as trapezes by children; everywhere military formations of blouse-clad men, imitated by swarms of little ragged girls with frizzy hair and bright gypsy eyes, armed with sticks. Carts as high as the second floor continuously go by, carts loaded with cheap wood tables, benches, canteens, and all the utensils necessary for the thousands of guardsmen from this population at arms.

Night has come. Little bats zigzag in the pale sky above the dark violet towers of Notre Dame; outlined down below are the bayonets of the armed multitude parading like black pins over the bridges.

This evening Burty tells me of his little revenges carried out somewhat slyly against the people at the Louvre, against timid

Reiset, against Chesneau, who, in his eyes, has committed the crime of making Nieuwerkerke pay a bit too dearly for his copy. I am truly surprised at the petty jealousy and ignoble rancor of this man, who is not bad or without intelligence.

Friday, October 14

It is surprising how accustomed you become to this life measured by cannon shots, to the fine distant rumble, the startling burst, the powerful vibration of the air; and when these vigorous, sounding waves cease, you turn your ear toward the distant horizon.

I go to pick up Burty at the Tuileries. While waiting for him I look about. National Guards are playing *galline* in the courtyard. Near the heaped up camp beds under the peristyle a horrible canteen woman has set up her little table. A horseblanket is lying on the ramp of the staircase; a piece of paper bearing the words *Death to Thieves* is pinned to it.

As Burty shows me around the palace, his step seems happy, almost exalted, over treading those floors. You feel his heels beat out the victory of a cheap-jack merchant's son who has taken up residence in the seat of royalty. I don't know what kind of low satisfaction of envy I perceive in the bourgeois triumph of my friend, who can rest his ass on a chair where the imperial rump used to sit.

Under the old ceilings, blackened by the fetes and suppers of the Empire; under the beautiful tarnished gold, reminiscent of the gold in Venetian ceilings; among the bronzes and marbles which emerge from the mess of incompletely packed furnishings; in the depths of the splendid mirrors, you see the surly faces of bureaucrats, the long-haired heads of republicans, heads with a fringe of reddish grey and the humorless features of the *pure* and virtuous.

Unpainted wooden filing cases are ranged against the walls clear to the ceiling, and overflow with papers in bundles and cartons. Tables on sawhorses sag under the disorderly mountain of letters, papers, receipts, bills of sale. Held by a tack stuck into the gold frame of a mirror is the *Instructions for Inventory of the Correspondence.* I feel as though I have entered the black chamber of the Revolutionary inquisition, and this detestable opening up of history is somehow repugnant to me.

The members of the Commission hold their meetings in the Louis XIV room. The great sorting out takes place there. I pick up one of the papers at random; it is a bill to that great spender Napoleon III for darning his socks at twenty-five centimes apiece.

Saturday, October 15

To live on yourself, to have no exchange of ideas except those few and unvaried ones of your own which always revolve around a fixed idea; to read only the news that you expect about the miserable war, to find in the papers nothing but rehashes of defeats glossed over with the name of *offensive reconnaissances;* to be chased off the boulevard by the necessity of economizing on gas; to be unable to enjoy modern life in this *early-to-bed* city; to be unable to read; to be unable any more to rise to the realm of pure ideas and thought because you always plummet back to earth thinking of food; to be deprived of everything that was the intellectual recreation of the Parisian man of letters; to lack everything that *is new* or *renews;* in short, to vegetate in this brutal and monotonous condition of war means for the Parisian to suffer in Paris boredom like that of a provincial city.

This evening a man was walking down the street ahead of

me, hands in pockets, humming almost gaily. All of a sudden he stopped and cried out as if he were waking up: "Things are bad, God damn it!" This vague passer-by expressed everybody's basic feeling.

On the Boulevard de Clichy the Mobile barracks, where the men are going to bed, is full of the murmur of patois; through the canvas, where it is not backed by boards, there looms up, fantastic and enormous, the Chinese shadow of a Mobile in his nightcap. At every corner of nearby streets cut-rate prostitutes, driven by misery, grab hold of the belated Breton.

At the end of a narrow little passageway, lighted by a sort of gas globe, the door of the Reine Blanche opens to the crowd who slip inside. A dance hall decorated like all the dance halls on this boulevard; a hall with ceiling pictures which end abruptly at the red-paper lambrequins, with little narrow mirrors paralleling the columns, with zinc and glass lusters overhead in which there are only three lights because of the situation.

Where in calm times the filthy rabble dance, they rule in times of revolution. The orchestra platform is the tribune occupied by the black-clad, austere members of the bureau and the official speakers; the parliamentary jug of water is in front of them on the balustrade, where the necks of the basses rested yesterday. In the bluish haze of pipe smoke, on benches or facing each other at the little refreshment tables are National Guards, Mobiles, suburban philosophers, russet-colored from the bottom of their hats to the tops of their shoes, workmen in blue blouse and kepi. There are women of the people, tarts, young girls in red hoods, and even some lower-middle-class women who don't know where to pass the evening in times like these.

Finally a bell rings, a bell like the one with which the common people take a childish pleasure in playing at the Chamber of Deputies. Tony Révillon gets up and announces the formation of the *Montmartre Club* for the purpose of establishing liberty and, logically, as he asserts, of destroying the monarchy, the nobility, and the clergy. Then he proposes to read to the audience the issue of *Le Journal de Rouen* which was reprinted in this evening's *La Vérité*. It is painful to see the degree to which this herd of men are dupes of the printed word, the degree to which they lack critical judgment. Sacrosanct democracy can make up a catechism even richer in lies than the old one, and these people are ready to swallow it devoutly.

And yet, basically, underneath this nonsense, this crude swallowing of impossibilities, you perceive at any given moment a generous impulse, a warm devotion, a warm brotherhood. Thus when at this meeting the news is given out that we have 12,300 prisoners in Germany, a shout from all throats breaks into a murmur of grief, while the whole roomful of people give each other an indescribable look.

After Tony Révillon sits down, Citizen Quentin speaks and demonstrates with tear-jerking words and emotional bluster that all our misfortunes since Sedan would not have happened if we had had a Commune. And the *providential character* of a Commune having been duly established, everybody goes out to the anteroom to sign a petition for the immediate establishment of such a Commune.

Sunday, October 16

I am full of disdain and anger over the fabrication of *sensational news*, lies, or lying exaggeration of the truth, for the sake of a few sous. Journalists of this day and hour rob the public in exactly the same way as the merchants who behind the counter substitute an inferior object for the one listed on the door.

Today civilians can get as far as the Saint Cloud bridge. When you go into the Bois de Boulogne among the somber cuttings that have opened up a view clear to the town of Boulogne in one direction and to the lakes in the other, your eyes are amazed. They no longer recognize the place; they have an entirely different conception of distance. Remote places seem to be close by, the white church at Saint Cloud seems to rise over Boulogne.

The sky is leaden with rain. The hills, painted in harsh reds and greens and blotted out in places by fog, look like gouaches by Houël after they have been rubbed together in their boxes on the quays and exposed to the open air. The grey mass of the still burning château at Saint Cloud looms through the white veil of wispy smoke.

As I walk along, I pause before the marvelous genre pictures brought into being by the felling of the trees. Imagine an immense field or rusty-colored underbrush, in the middle of which trunks and branches are the color of green bronze, with behind them as a boundary a curtain of great trees which have kept their summer color and a little line of poplars with golden foliage. Underneath, all the disorder and architectural picturesqueness of cabins of mossy earth, huts of still green fir branches, shelters made of dried branches the color of dried currants, grey canvas tents with azure smoke over them, rags of all colors drying on lines, and the red trousers of the soldiers standing out in this harmony of color like vermilion pistol shots.

All sorts of vehicles pass along the road, artillery trains with men boldly standing on their noisy carriages, and private carriages, in one of which you see a gentleman carrying a stuffed owl in his hand.

I reach Boulogne. The street is full of infantrymen who, standing or seated on boxes of hardtack, bar the way. It is raining. Some of the soldiers have made Arab burnouses for themselves out of the canvas of their tents. There are sacks of rice on the ground and the men are taking their portions in handkerchiefs and the corners of bedcovers. Pieces of fatback, hanging on long poles, make the men carrying them dance to avoid their swaying. Soldiers burdened with sacks, from which pot herbs stick out and garland them in greenery, go over to the tin soup pots. The civilian population of Boulogne seems to be reduced to two or three old women hobbling along the sidewalk, and Rabatjoie's pork-butcher shop is practically the only place open.

As I go out of Boulogne between the closed-up houses where there is nothing living, nothing moving, I proceed to the intermittent sound of rifle shots, which seem quite close. I arrive in this fashion at the circular drive and take my place at the end of a line of National Guards, infantrymen, and Mobile Guards, who are sheltered somewhat by the angle of a shop which shows the newly made scar of a Prussian bullet. It is amusing to stick one's head out a bit and with the aid of glasses pick out the Prussians in Saint Cloud who, under the fire of the snipers hidden along the banks of the Seine, rapidly and self-effacingly cross a little street up above a little green reservoir. Mice disappear no more quickly; they are gone almost before you see them. And since, in these parts, every spectacle must have its Parisian side, there is a small boy at the very end of the line who shouts: "Umbrellas down!"

As I go home, vespers is ringing in Boulogne, but the sound of the bells is drowned out constantly by the thundering voice from Mont Valérien. I go into the church and in a chapel see a gathering of men in grey overcoats, some of whom are holding poor little prayer books in the paper binding of the Delalain classics. Among them a young infantryman is playing the melodion-organ while a comrade in red trousers rests his elbow on the organ case as he bends over the music. From this vulgar group of soldiers, whose similarity to Lemud's lithograph *Maître Wolframb* transfigures them, there rises soft and penetrating music, which in this time of nerves shattered by the cannons and the nearness of death brings an indescribably strong emotion, at once sweet and sad. When I leave, the voices of these *morituri* singing in the choir follow me, to the accompaniment of the "Jesus Christ!" of their companions on the square.

I am somewhat curious to see once more those places where we took our sad walks all last winter and spring. The pool at Auteuil has its little mound rutted by carts and its pretty shade trees lie fallen into the dirty water. I hoped they might have spared the three centenary oaks; where they once stood are gigantic stumps even with the ground; around them is piled a heap of firewood which a burgrave's fireplace would not be able to consume in a whole winter.

Monday, October 17

All day long the thundering noise from Mont Valérien, the rumbling of the gunboat echoing across the Sèvres and Meudon hills, and the nervewracking crackling of the Mortemart battery.

Tuesday, October 18

What a thing life is, good fortune for some, disaster for me and mine! Reading the paper in bed this morning, pell-mell with the news about the war I come upon the name of Marie de Villedeuil. My thoughts go back to the time when I saw my very young cousin with her modest curtsey and gentle brown eyes enter the virtuous drawing room of her Aunt Villedeuil, who, with her costumes and brusque tone, seemed like a second Duchess of Angoulême. I can see her seated in a little armchair, almost hidden behind the jardiniere bought at the sale of the Duchesse de Berry's effects, not daring to breathe a word, gracefully hunched up with her little arms crossed, showing the pure beauty of her head. Since then I have heard a good many things. But what do I read today: She, the granddaughter of the minister Laurent de Villedeuil; she, who grew up in that devout establishment; she, now the Countess Marguerittes, fallen to the lowest level of adultery! At Asnières she keeps a miller, a workman, and provides the inhabitants of the area with the shameful spectacle of her drunkenness and her quarrels with her lover. I pity them, the poor dead, who were so proud of their nobility, so justly proud of the honor of their family, whose last male descendant was to be poor Charles de Villedeuil and whose last female descendant was to end in a police court with a sentence of four months in jail.

The cannonade draws me to the Bois de Boulogne and the Mortemart battery. There is something solemn about the serious gravity and reflective slowness with which the men responsible for a gun execute the loading operations. At last the cannon is loaded. The artillerymen stand motionless on both sides, some of them leaning with fine sculptural movements on the tackle with which they have maneuvered the gun into place; one artilleryman in shirt sleeves standing on the right side holds the cord in his hand. A few seconds of immobility, of silence, I would almost say of emotion. Then with the pulling of the cord, thunder, flame, a cloud of smoke in which the cluster of trees masking the battery disappears. For a long time there is a white cloud, which dissipates slowly and sets off the yellow sand of the embrasure whipped up by the shot, the grey sandbags, two or three of which have been burst open by the sidewise recoil of the cannon, the red caps of the artillerymen, the white shirt of the man who pulled the cord.

This thing that kills at a distance is a regular show for Paris, and, as on fine days on the lake, there are barouches and landaus stationed around the butte while their women passengers mingle with the Mobiles and press as close to the awful noise as possible. Among the spectators are Pelletan, whose grey beard and head of an antique philosopher do not go well with a kepi; Jules Ferry; and Rochefort, who speaks, laughs, and jumps about like a man whose nervous system is played upon by the disturbances in the air.

The cannon fires six times; then the old officer takes from its tripod the little copper instrument that measures elevations and puts it carefully in a wooden box, which he shoves in his pocket; he goes away, while on the piece now being given a rest a young artilleryman sits. He is blond with a feminine face which has the imprint of that heroic something that Gros gives to his military figures. With police cap askew on his head, a vividly striped Algerian belt around his waist, his cartridge case over his belly, relaxed and charming in his picturesque disorder, he rests after the fatigue of this exercise of death. The performance is over; the spectators go away.

Some go toward Boulogne, toward a milky blue landscape like those you find in Switzerland and the Tyrol, recreated here today by the smoke from the cannons. Some turn back toward the Auteuil ramparts, where they have begun firing today for the first time; their shells pass over your head with a panting whish. Below the cannons some poor old women quietly gather up faggots, youngsters fish in the pool with horsemeat sausage as bait, and some young women, delighted to feel the vibrations from the cannon, are pulled back by their prudent husbands but are slow to go away.

At Brébant's this evening the conversation ranges from the political inconsistencies of Gambetta to the *blond men*, the race which in remote times came from the Baltic, spreading out into France, Spain, and Africa, whom neither changes of climate nor intermixture with the dark races has modified or darkened.

What we are eating makes each of us tell about the most extraordinary thing he has ever eaten, and Charles Edmond avers that he has eaten mammoth from Siberia, a piece of which Saint Petersburg was so gracious as to send to the Warsaw authorities. We all defer to him. A waiter brings the six of us a piece of Gruyère cheese the size and thinness of a twenty-five-franc note with as much ceremony as if he were carrying the Blessed Sacrament, and our dinner ends with a big dissertation on *sucking*, which was the vogue among the worn out and enfeebled of Napoleonic times.

Thursday, October 20

At Batignolles endless lines of people signing up for meat rations. At the doors of butcher shops, too, endless lines made up of broken-down old men, ruddy National Guards, old women with little stools under their arms so they can sit down, little girls strong enough to bring home the niggardly ration in the big market basket, and tarts with their noses in the air, their hair flying, and their eyes full of coquettish glances for the veterans who keep the line in order.

From Montmartre to the Rue Watteau, where I have dinner, you see nothing but billposters in white blouses covering the walls with notices about the manufacture of cannons.

All the stores have exercised their ingenuity to convert their merchandise into *rampart goods;* there is nothing but rampart bedding, rampart furs, rampart beds, rampart kerchiefs, rampart gloves. The show windows of merchants and provisioners have a somewhat sinister air by reason of their emptiness. The dirty napkins of the regulars is all you see at the cheap restaurants; two sickly laurels among empty earthen jars are all you see at the pork butchers'. In contrast, little handcarts being pushed along the streets are mobile pancake factories.

The big Central Market is very strange. Where they used to sell fresh fish all the stalls are selling horsemeat; instead of butter they have beef or horse fat in big squares like yellow soap. But the movement and animation are at the vegetable market, which is still in good supply, thanks to the foragers. There is a crowd around little tables laden with cabbages, celery, cauliflower, which the women vie for and middle-class women carry home in napkins. In the bedlam of bids, words, jokes, insults, you suddenly hear an *Oh! My God!* noisily breathed out by the market women as they see a sniper's body go by behind the open curtains of the litter in which he is being taken to his home.

The great news at Burty's this evening is that Rochefort, with all sorts of difficulty, is learning to ride horseback so that he can ride at Trochu's right when they make a triumphal return from an *offensive reconnaissance.*

Friday, October 21

From my window what I see is the color of a cannonade.

Above Meudon the upper sky half aureoled with big white

stripes, like the aurora borealis effect which Gudin loves to use to light his stormy seas. Lower down, the hill and its green thicket appearing through rents in the white mist which close almost at once, letting you see the countryside with the intermittent confusion and clarity of a pair of glasses which you are attempting to focus. Here and there the sparkling windows of distant villas looking like the sparkle of crystal chandeliers. Nearer at hand the houses at Parc aux Princes and Billancourt and all the built-up area clear to the Seine standing out violet against clumps of pale trees and seeming to be furrowed with little shining rivulets where the sun strikes the slate roofs. Beyond that a second area of azure fog, striped without a break from the Point du Jour to Auteuil by a perspective of cannon shots which spit out big clouds, thick clouds that look like spilled-out entrails.

Everywhere smoke filling the hollows of the earth and giving a kind of foggy base to solid things.

In the foreground on the Boulevard de Montmorency people stand watching from their carriages. In the cold transparency of a sunless corner and the grey reflection of the pavement carriages and people have no color; they are almost like the black spots in a photograph of *high life*.

A little to the right is the naval gun on our ramparts. Each time it is fired the gunners disappear in a whirlwind of burning smoke, which the wind carries off toward the Point du Jour in a big red cloud that rises against the white sky. Then they reappear, wrapped around with scarves of smoke, which are slow to detach themselves from their clothing; they reappear in a kind of halo, the red of autumn foliage mingled with the light of day.

On the hills opposite, almost substantial apparitions and fantastic constructions built by the caprice of the clouds are sketched out and given body at every burst of a shell.

For a long time I watch a white stalactite grotto stand out against the green of a little copse. And in the small patch of blue far up in the sky little bits of smoke remain for a long time unwilling to dissolve, so that you might take them for balloons.

It smells of powder in the open air as it used to in the old Franconi Circus. The distance fades out; over the slowly disappearing landscape there rises a white shroud like a gigantic cloud of flour, which is made rosy by little fires that have been started in the woods.

Saturday, October 22

This evening Chennevières was telling me of his unsuccessful efforts to have Simon make a radical change in the administration of art. Nieuwerkerke, Maurice Richard, and Jules Simon are absolutely identical in their conservatism.

Sunday, October 23

A Sunday of rain and wailing wind. Why this torpor which keeps me from doing anything, from going out, which leaves me stupidly trimming the shrubs in my garden, when everything outside is such an object of curiosity?

This evening I go to the Luxembourg. In the darkness of its black grandeur, with only one light illuminating the court of honor, I cannot describe the air of antiquity which invests Rouher's palace; it seems to be the domicile, not of things of yesterday, but of very old dead things. Everything, including the rows of tubs piled against the walls, gives it the picturesqueness of a ruined Roman *casino* drawn by Hubert Robert.

In the utter darkness of the Rue de Tournon a hole of light under an awning from which cauliflowers and strings of garlic are hanging. A group of people in front of it. It is a fruit store where half the display spills out over the sidewalk; in a pool of blood you see two large deer, their throats slit and their entrails cast aside as though to a pack of dogs. Enormous carp push their bluish noses to the surface of the rippling water in a child's bathtub. By the light of a candle guttering in an old copper candlestick you see the golden neck of a young bear pierced by a round hole, and his four paws folded in death. These were boarders at the Zoo whom ravenous Paris will fight over tomorrow.

In the brown-out under the somber sky the Seine rolls its dark waters, the waters of Phlegethon. The darkness of this city, whose location you could once discern from ten miles away by the reflections it made in that part of the sky that serves it as ceiling, of this city which once turned night almost into day with the brilliance of its shops, its cafés, and its thousands of street lights—this darkness, these new shadows change Paris, give to even its newest districts the imprint of age, pushing them back into the past, so to speak. You wander along the dark stones without recognizing them, astonished and a bit disturbed over your loss of direction.

As I am walking along in this fashion, a spot of light makes me stop in front of a pink poster on which the unquenchable *ego* of Legouvé promises the public to appear in a literary matinée. Empires may follow on constitutional governments, and republics on empires, but we shall always have M. Ernest Legouvé—who will talk on Sunday about *moral nourishment*.

Monday, October 24

I go out today by the Maillot gate, where the drawbridge and the section provided with gun-slits have been painted green in order to simulate a continuation of the grassy bank of the fortifications. This strikes me as rather Japanese.

The one thing standing among the rubble is the Duke of Orléans' chapel. Gillet's restaurant has become a staff headquarters; at the door two sentinel boxes have been improvised out of boards from the demolished buildings. A crowd is standing in line to get passes.

The whole Avenue de Neuilly shows the signs of a long encampment, and at the foot of almost every tree there is a little mound of blackened bricks, sardine cans, and old shoes. The civil population seems to have departed. Only Gamache, the fencing master with the triumphant sign, still has curtains at his ground-floor windows. Invasion by soldiers everywhere; the numerous boarding schools for young girls and establishments for *young ladies* have russet-colored Mobiles on guard at their doors. A constant stream of people passing in both directions, a continual coming and going as the three barricades are crossed by infantrymen, Mobiles, and scouts returning from reconnaissance bent under the load of green stuff and vegetables they have gathered on their way. A constantly renewed parade, where weariness is full of verve and gaiety!

There is a mine all prepared under the second arch of the Neuilly bridge; the house which curves off to the right has its terrace and upper windows protected by sandbags in which openings have been left for guns. On the pretty leafy islands in the Seine, now completely cleared, you see grey overcoats under yellow knapsacks maneuvering in the rain among the trunks of poplar trees.

Soon the rain becomes a downpour, through which the horsemen gallop away, shrouded with bedcovers which make them look like equestrian ghosts; picturesque carts with heavy blue canvas flapping over them rush away too; so do the artillery wagons, on one of which, braving the deluge, a svelte canteen woman in tricolor-bordered skirt and a little white apron with pockets and border outlined in red, and with rooster feathers on her head, bold and striking in her colorful attire, appears for a second against the landscape crisscrossed by rain, lighted by a shaft of sunlight as in a March shower.

The pavement at the Etoile barrier has been taken up, and the bas-reliefs of the arch have been enclosed in great wooden boxes. As I go down the Champs Elysées I look at La Païva's town house, which is closed, and wonder if it was not the Prussian espionage headquarters in Paris.

This evening above the whole length of the Rue Saint Lazare, above the white edifice of the railroad station, a blood-colored sky; a cerise light staining even the somber nighttime blue of the sky; a strange sight of the prophetic kind that used to disturb the people of remote antiquity. Someone near me says: "The Forest of Bondy is burning." Another says: "It's an experiment with light on Montmartre." Still another: "It's the aurora borealis."

Tuesday, October 25

Today the sky has kept something of the magic of yesterday evening's phenomenon. What an electric color in the clouds, what beauty for the eye! There was an autumn effect in the gold-brown tints of the trees and the pigeon-breast tints of the stones with something theatrical added, something that does not belong to this era: the infinite detail of distant structures which are set back, outlined, and given sharp contours as though under the clear light of the southern sky. The structuring and stratification of the clouds was equally surprising and full of strange mirages. It was as though Paris was bounded by a chain of mountains on the other side of Grenelle, with a real lake at their feet, both mountains and water made of a big violet cloud with silver crests.

Today Parisian eyes are interested only in displays of things that may be eaten, products with which to simulate the food of ordinary times. It is interesting to watch a passer-by's study of the advertisement for one of these products, his indecision, his inner struggle evidenced by his moving his umbrella from one arm to the other, his uncertainty, his going away and coming back. In the Passage Choiseul I watched the behavior of a siege-bound citizen in front of a completely new product; he was inhibited in his desire to use it in his kitchen by reason of its well-known purpose and perhaps by personal memories. For a moment prejudice got the upper hand, and he went away; he walked a few paces, then suddenly turned around and retraced his steps, feverishly entering the pastry shop to buy some *cocoa butter.*

Wednesday, October 26

I go to the offices of *L'Officiel* to see Théo, since I have heard that he is back from Switzerland:

"Why the devil did you come back to this sinister mess?"

"I'll explain it to you," Théo says, coming down the stairway. "Lack of money! You know how fast a twelve-hundred-franc note goes; that was all I had. Then too my sisters here in Paris were at the end of their resources. That's why I came back."

He begins to talk, from the depths of his heart, about the Princess, about her drawing room which for us was like a family gathering place, about Saint Gratien, which was the pleasant recreation in our lives of continuous work:

"As a matter of fact, I had a letter from the Princess while I was in Switzerland, a wonderful letter, I'll show it to you. Three pages, wonderful, I tell you! Not a word about her in it. . . .

"This revolution is the end for me; I'm through. Anyhow

I'm a victim of revolutions. No joking! At the time of the July Revolution my father was very much a legitimist; he gambled on a rise as a result of the July Ordinances: you know how that came out! We lost our whole fortune, 15,000 pounds a year. I had been destined to have an easy life, to be a man of leisure; instead I had to earn my living. Well, after several years I had things in pretty good shape. I had a little house, a little carriage, two little horses. February [1848] took care of that. I got back on my feet, was going to become a member of the Academy, of the Senate: with Sainte-Beuve dead and Mérimée dying, it was not unlikely that the Emperor would want to appoint a man of letters, was it? At last I was in a snug position. Everything went to pieces with the Republic. You can imagine that at my age I can't very well start my life over again. I have lost everything. Now I am a hired-hand again, at my age. All I want is a wall where I may smoke my pipe in the sun and eat some soup twice a week! What's most horrible is the kind of hypocrisy I have to put into everything I do: you know, my descriptions have to be red, white, and blue!

"This tinned stuff is certainly tragic," he resumes, as we go past Chevet's show window, which a short time ago was full of succulent dainties but now has only canned vegetables. After a short silence during which he leans heavily on my arm as he meditates, he says suddenly: "What a disaster! How complete and solid! First, capitulation; now, famine; tomorrow, bombardment. How artistically composed this disaster is!"

He continues: "It's a funny thing about French courage and valor, so French a product—everybody was convinced that we were heroic by birth—now it doesn't exist any more! Everybody is out to save himself. You've seen those clowns with their coats inside out at whose faces the crowd is told to spit? Now isn't that an official acknowledgment of the cowardice of the army!"

"My dear Théo," I say to him as I leave, "my opinion is that cynicism has killed off all heroic imbecility, and that nations which don't have that any more are condemned to death."

Thursday, October 27

At the Point du Jour viaduct piles of sand and lime, mountains of gravel, the ground rutted by wagons and your feet stubbing in the mud against the rails of the new railroad line which will add another track to the old one. Everywhere masons, scaffoldings, water buckets coming up from the Seine on a picturesque pulley, mortar being mixed, stones flying from hand to hand, supports being set up to buttress walls, walls rising to support a series of light arches, steam engines whistling. A scene of urgency, haste, and feverish work such as I have never seen before, in which people seem to pant with patriotism: the picture of a nation at work to the sound of cannons firing all along the line.

Through the holes and openings of this unfinished work, in the same direction as the trajectory of the French shells, a remarkable sunset. You might say that it is a light wash of violet shadows on gold-leaf paper, with in the middle a big streak of gold-green opening out like a fan and giving the pale light of dawn to the hills above Saint Cloud, which are already asleep and extinguished in the blackness of dusk.

Friday, October 28

The astonishing, the amazing, the incredible thing is the complete lack of communication with the outside world. Not an inhabitant who has had any news from his family for the last forty days! If by the greatest chance a copy of *Le Journal de Rouen* slips in, it is run off in facsimile as the most priceless rarity. Never before have two million people been shut up in so absolute a Mazas Prison. Not an invention, not a discovery, not a single happy, audacious act: there is no imagination left in France!

Bit by bit we begin to feel the ugly side of the war. In the main street of Auteuil, preceded by a soldier leading a horse by its bridle, two infantrymen with grey faces go by on a packsaddle. Their poor backs flinch at each bump and it is an effort for their weary feet to span the stirrups. That hurts. Wounded men you expect from war. But people killed by cold, rain, lack of food, that is even more horrible than the wounds of battle. "They're from my regiment, the 24th infantry," says a canteen woman next to me on the omnibus. "Every day they bring some away like that!" And the discouragement of those she serves is echoed in her own voice.

Against the grey stone and beneath the golden cross of the Panthéon there stands out an immense tribune trimmed in red and reached by wine merchants' ladders. A big white banner carries the words: *Citizens, your Country Is in Danger! Volunteer Here for the National Guard.* Up above, a coat of arms with the silver vessel of the City of Paris is surrounded by a cluster of flags, a black one at the top with the names of Strasbourg, Toul, Châteaudun inscribed on its funereal folds. The dates 1792–1870 are written at the two extremities on red, white, and blue oriflammes. Attached to the pillars are cardboard shields on which you read the two letters *R. F.*

The huge tribune is full of kepis trimmed with silver braid and the shining shoulders of wet rubber coats; through them the crowd mounting the stairs filters and pours, a crowd in tiers of backs in white blouses and blue blouses, all this to the rolling of the drums and the blare of bugles. A spectacle with something of the fair in it, yet moving by reason of the electricity that emanates from great generous actions and multitudes ready to sacrifice themselves.

People cover the square, dominated by pyramids of women and children who have climbed between the columns of the municipal offices of the Fifth Arrondissement and those of the Law School. Their faces are pale with the yellow tinge brought both by siege rations and by the emotion of this spectacle, which is punctuated by bursts of the *Marseillaise.*

At last to the rolling drums the interminable parade of the newly inscribed National Guards begins and passes in front of the desk in the middle of the tribune. With the late hour, the rainy sky in which a few flocks of starlings are scattered like dry leaves, the pale dusk which makes people's faces even paler, all these thousands of men, these thousands of bayonets crossing through the dark shadows of the tribune and emerging dark and as though veiled with crepe give something of the effect of a fantastic review, of a phantom army emerging from a lithograph of midnight by Raffet.

Indeed this is material for a painting; but, to tell the truth, it is too much a repetition of '92. It is humiliating to discover so flat a copy of the past, one so servile that they have even written on the façade of the Law School: *Unity and Indivisibility of the French Republic. Liberty, Equality, Fraternity, or Death.* Death, that's it!

Saturday, October 29

In the waiting room at the railway station, among the soldiers, on the benches, rows of nuns leaning on their umbrellas provide perspectives of sweet profiles coifed in white under the wavy motion of their black veils.

At Belleville I run into a group of school children singing the *Marseillaise* as they come out from school brandishing their boxes above their heads and dancing wildly, one leg in the air, like that little Japanese on my ivory box with the vari-colored lacquer.

At Romainville the cabarets and games of boule are closed; on this road beloved of Parisians there is scarcely anything but roving dogs of every kind, pathetically thin and circling each other in fright. It is raining; beyond the green band of the field that I am crossing I perceive what is in front of me with the dull colors and uncertain outlines of a landscape through a steamy window pane.

Soon, emerging through the distant mist and the streaking rain, you see the strange silhouettes of men and women who, though very close, look like a procession at a Court of Miracles. They are the returning foragers. You see every kind of ugly specimen clothed in a fantastic variety of rags. You see women in dresses shining with rain, their stockings spattered with mud up to their hips, walking weighed down, bent in two. You see other women who have made pockets all the way around out of the folds of their underskirts and who show large shameless expanses of flesh. You see men harnessed to carts and pulling their heavy burden of potatoes, and at their sides little children dragging something green in a cigar box at the end of a string. You see . . . but what don't you see there? You see foragers with wooden legs and even some middle-class people, strayed into this swarm of knaves, triumphantly bringing home a bunch of soup greens in their hands. You even see little girls who, straining to carry little sacks on their heads, show under tightly molded dresses the outlines of their tensed little bellies and thin thighs.

A tough, who might have posed for Gavarni in one of his Vireloque engravings, is at the end of the parade brandishing in his upraised arm a long, thin black cat, which has just been strangled.

A cab which I come upon by chance takes me through unknown streets to the rampart gate at La Chapelle. I pass between bits of field that have been turned over, fences that have been torn out, big trees that have been felled, heaps of stones, houses without windows or doors to which still cling the skeletons of half-uprooted shrubs, between walls on unlighted streets where there is no passer-by, no living thing. My way is always under the dissolving sky on a road that is melting away among ruined or abandoned things reflected with the dark night in pools of water, so that I finally have the feeling that I have been taken to the scene of a cataclysm.

This evening I have donkey steak for dinner.

Sunday, October 30

Ahead of my cab a line of little army ambulances with grey curtains topped by the red kepis of the drivers and the fluttering of the little red-cross flags.

I go into the Pasdeloup concert hall for a moment. The hall is jammed. At this time music has no power to make me forget, to send my thoughts off into daydreams; I do not feel myself carried away by Mozart's Pastorale and I go out to enjoy the spectacle of the streets.

The whole boulevard is like a fair. They are selling everything on the sidewalks: woolen tricots, chocolate at two sous a tablet, slices of coconut, *Sultan* pastilles, heaps of Hugo's *Les Châtiments,* weapons that look as though they had come from a theatre prop-room, surprise boxes in which you see *him or her you love*. On the bench opposite the Théatre des Variétés amateur fishermen are selling pickerel as big as gudgeons which they have just caught somewhere or other. The crowd, as carefree as on a Sunday in ordinary times, walks slowly along, musing over and stopping in front of every shopwindow to the yelling of frightful urchins shouting in voices already hoarse from alcohol: "Madame Badinguet or the Bonaparte woman, her lovers, her orgies."

Monday, October 31

. . . . .

On people's faces, in their attitudes, you feel the repercussion of the great and terrible things that are in the air. Behind the backs of people asking questions of a National Guard, I hear the words *revolver shots, rifle shots, wounded*. At the doorway of the Comédie Française, La Fontaine tells me the official news of Bazaine's surrender.

The Rue de Rivoli is in tumult and the umbrella-sheltered crowd grows as I approach the Hôtel de Ville.

There I find a mob, a disorder, a confusion of people of every kind through whom National Guards are constantly making their way, rifles in the air, and shouting "Long live the Commune!" The completely dark building, above which the clock goes nonchalantly on in its already lighted dial, has its windows wide open, with workmen's legs dangling out as they did on September 4. The square is a forest of upraised rifles, whose stocks shine in the rain.

On people's faces you see anguish over Bazaine's surrender, a kind of fury over yesterday's setback at Le Bourget, and at the same time an angry and heroically impulsive determination not to make peace. Some workmen in round hats are taking down in pencil on dirty portfolios a list which a man is dictating to them. Among the names I hear are those of Blanqui, Flourens, Ledru-Rollin, and Mottu. "It will be all right now!" a workman says in the midst of the eloquent silence of the people around me; and I find myself in a group of women who are already talking fearfully about a sharing of wealth.

It appears, as the workmen's legs at the Hôtel de Ville windows would indicate, that the government has fallen and the Commune been established. The list read out by the man in the square is to be confirmed by universal suffrage in twenty-four hours. This is the end. We may write down for this date: *Finis Franciae.*

Shouts of "Long live the Commune!" burst out all over the square, and more troops rush down the Rue de Rivoli followed by vociferating and gesticulating riffraff. Poor France, fallen into the power of these unintelligent bayonets! At this moment an old lady who sees me buying the evening newspaper asks me—what an irony!—if the quotations on government securities are in my paper.

After dinner I hear a man in a blouse say to the woman in a tobacco shop where I am getting a light: "Must we always be swept along like this! We are going to see another '93 and people will be hanging each other!"

The boulevard is completely dark, shops are all closed, there is no one on the streets. An occasional group of men, with strings around their fingers from which packages of something edible dangle, stand in the light from kiosks and cafés, where the proprietors come and go at the door, uncertain whether they should close up or not. A call to arms is sounded; an alarm is sounded. An apoplectic old National Guard goes by, kepi in hand, exclaiming: "The swine!" At the doorway of the Café Riche a National Guard officer summons the men of his battalion. A rumor circulates that General Tamisier is a prisoner of the Commune. The call to arms continues furiously. A young National Guard makes his way down the middle of the boulevard shouting at the top of his voice: "To arms, for God's sake!"

Civil war, along with famine and bombardment, is that to be our fate tomorrow?

Tuesday, November 1

Squads of National Guards advance slowly from the Place de la Concorde toward the Hôtel de Ville as the nightcaps of the wounded and the coifs of the nuns look out at them from the windows of the Tuileries. It is a counterdemonstration to yesterday's outbreak watched by a crowd such as holidays bring out in Paris streets.

There is an unusually large number of us at Brébant's this evening—Gautier, Bertrand, Saint-Victor, Berthelot, etc. Louis Blanc makes his first appearance there, with his priest's physique and his Levite's frock coat.

Naturally, yesterday's revolution is the subject of conversation. Hébrard, who was inside the Hôtel de Ville, says that we can have no idea of the vulgar imbecility he witnessed. He saw one group that wanted to elect Barbès: those good folk were unaware that he was dead! "For my part," Berthelot says, "very early on, wanting to know what the situation was, I went up to and asked a sentinel at the Hôtel de Ville: 'Who is in there? Whom are you guarding?' 'Hell,' he answered, 'I'm guarding the Flourens government!' He didn't know that the government he was guarding had changed. What can you expect if France has come to that point?"

Louis Blanc starts speaking words that are soft and slow to come out, holding each one in his mouth for a moment as though he were sucking a delicious bonbon: "All those fellows yesterday nominated themselves, and to give their names value they added some well-known name, some illustrious name, the way you put a feather on a hat." He says this in his half-wry, half-sugary way, secretly bitter that his name, so popular in '48, has so little weight with the masses, and it must be admitted that in general the illustrious and celebrated are of little importance to a population which seems to want to choose the masters of France from among its *relatives and friends,* from among its needy pals at the beerhall and the cheap restaurant. To support his remarks, little Louis Blanc takes out of the little pocket of his little trousers a printed list of twenty names submitted to the vote of the citizens of the Fifth Arrondissement for the formation of a Commune, a list of the most illustrious unknowns of which a government has ever been made up in any country in the world.

At this point Saint-Victor asserts that he has it from one of Trochu's friends that the general boasts that he will relieve the siege of Paris in two weeks. Everybody laughs, and those who know the Governor of Paris characterize him as possessing little intelligence, having the narrow mind of the military which is closed to any new invention, any new idea that might appear, bringing his veto to any serious suggestion as readily as to a fantastic one.

For the fantastic is not lacking, and there are people who suggest defending Paris with dogs, to be infected with hydrophobia and unleashed on the Prussians! Louis Blanc tells of one man, whose advocate he became, who wanted to deprive the Prussians of water at Versailles by destroying the Marly waterworks and drying up the reservoirs. Trochu cut off discussion of this by the one comment: "Absurd!" The next day Dorian was delighted with the idea.

Then a manufacturer of military equipment who is there, an artillery officer, and Berthelot give us a long list of inventions and products which have been turned down for one reason or another, usually for no reason at all, right off the bat, frivolously, without any understanding. There is the instance of the carbon rockets, of a balloon which would bring in 600,000 francs by setting up a *Correspondence-Journal* with the provinces, but which still awaits authorization.

"Imagine," Louis Blanc continues, "when I expressed my surprise at the lack of news to Trochu, he said to me: 'But the government is doing everything possible. Do you know that it is spending ten thousand francs a month?' That stupefied me, ten thousand francs for things of such prime importance, when they ought to spend a hundred thousand!"

From Trochu we pass on to General Guiod, whom Berthelot considers responsible for our disasters, a man who, not content with opposing the manufacture of Chassepot rifles, turned down Commandant Potier's cannon. "It's very simple!" he adds. "Since the beginning of the war it has been an artillery contest; the Prussian cannons have a range of six hundred to eight hundred meters more than ours! They are placed from one to two hundred meters out of our reach and destroy us at their leisure. The Potier cannons would have equalized things."

"You know," says the equipment manufacturer, "that during the week Commandant Potier was confined to quarters by General Guiod the two thousand men over whom he was in charge did not work, and in such times as these . . ."

He is interrupted by the artillery officer: "It's the same problem for the artillery. They say there isn't any: let's say rather that they don't want any! When an appeal was made for artillerymen, one of my friends presented a very capable former officer to General Guiod. Do you know how he was received by that old fool? 'Sir, I don't like untimely zeal!' "

Berthelot breaks in:

"Yes, everything is like that. Nefftzer does not understand my exasperation when I go to see him. He does not see things in detail as I do; he does not run into their stupid stubbornness all day long. And what about the decree recalling the old fellows from retirement when what we need is young men, ability that will develop, a general who will be discovered? We should have made little sorties, very frequent sorties, under the command of captains. The man who did best would have been made a colonel; if he distinguished himself several times, a general. In that way we would have rebuilt our cadres, we would have had a nursery for officers. But advancement is reserved for the army of Sedan. Yes, that's no joke: for the army of Sedan!"

And we talk about the end of France, her lack of men of valor, the convulsive state in which she is going gasping to her death.

Meanwhile Renan, exhausted, his hands crossed over his belly like a priest's, spouts verses from the Bible into the ears of Saint-Victor, who enjoys hearing Latin. In the midst of this hashing over the causes of our ruin, Nefftzer shouts:

"What has finished France is routine and rhetoric!"

"Yes, it is classicism," Gautier sighs, interrupting the analysis of the *Quatrains* of Omar Khayyam which he is making to good old Chennevières in his corner.

Wednesday, November 2

All day I have been haunted by an obstinate memory of another Day of the Dead. We were at Comerie. Edouard took us for a walk on the heights overlooking the Oise. We walked along in the north wind through a desolate landscape surrounded by the wheeling flight of crows. Jules was already having trouble with his liver, and we were sad, sad like the sad day.

Today at the cemetery people are lined up to enter and to leave as if they were at the door of an amusement park. I don't know why, but I am grateful to the crowd which presses in there. It makes me happy to see very few graves without a fresh wreath, and I lean over to look at the black forms and pious hands bent over the funerary stones. The dead, forgotten for the rest of the year, are surrounded by a murmur of prayers and of words.

Poor grave, it has only the wreaths which I have brought! When I am gone, nobody will bring even a sprig of immortelle. This grave will suffer the abandonment of the dead without family. The idea is painful, not on my account, but on his.

At the entrance to the cemetery there is one child's coffin after another. This makes the women say: "Still another little one!" It would appear that the siege is slaughtering the innocents.

Thursday, November 3

We live under a permanent call to arms.

Who is the unknown person destined to reach fame in these times? What unexpected event does the future have in store for us? The courageous reinforcement from the West of Mobiles and sailors, in contrast with the feebleness and cowardice of the rest of France, should this not have some weight in the formation of the next government on the side of restoring the monarchical and religious principle? On the other hand, Belleville's apparent desire to tyrannize over France, could it not bring a resurrection of the former provinces, already wounded by the centralization practiced under recent reigns, could it not bring about a dismembering of France, the seed of which is already evident this morning in the announcement from Brittany?

This evening as I walk along the viaduct, I amuse myself by looking at the fires in the Breton camps, those glowing coals in the dark of the cavelike areas between the arches, those glowing spots with a thousand flying sparks which light up the faces and hands of the men warming themselves in shadowy, vague groups.

Friday, November 4

The Hôtel de Ville square is calm, abandoned by the crowds of recent days. A few curiosity-seekers only.

All at once, legs are flying, everybody is running along the quay, where I see the Governor of Paris go by to the acclamation of the crowd and followed by an entourage of street urchins. A young, mild, agreeable face with the big beard of the African officer, a distinguished general as a novel or a play at the Gymnase would represent him.

During the evening I was in the Passage des Panoramas; in this passage which used to be blinding with light, I wondered if I were not in a tunnel underneath the Thames.

Saturday, November 5

At dinner Clément de Ris tells me that at *Les Débats* office they are worried about Renan's mental state because of his monomania over saving France with a plan of his own invention: the reestablishment of Henry V, with the Prince Imperial as his adopted son.

Sunday, November 6

The Prussians have refused an armistice. I believe that

never in diplomatic history has there been a more ferocious document than M. de Bismarck's memorandum. His pity for the hundreds of thousands of Frenchmen who are going to die of hunger resembles the Jesuitry of an Attila.

Monday, November 7

At lunch today at the Taverne de Lucas I find on my bill a charge of fifteen centimes for a napkin. Laundry service, it seems, is in confusion because of the withdrawal of the Boulogne, Neuilly, etc., laundryworkers into Paris, and also because of the government's requisition of potash and other materials for the manufacture of gunpowder.

I go to call on Hugo and thank the illustrious master for the sympathetic letter he so kindly wrote at the time of my brother's death.

He lives on the Avenue Frochot—at Meurice's, I think. I have to wait in the dining room among the remains of lunch and a mess of glass and porcelain bric-a-brac. Then I am ushered into a little drawing room, the walls and ceiling of which are covered with old brocade.

In the chimney corner are two black-clad women, whose features are vaguely visible against the light. Half-reclining on a divan around the poet is a group of friends, among whom I recognize Vacquerie. In a corner Hugo's fat son in National Guard uniform is playing checkers on a low table with a little blond-haired child in a cherry-red sash.

After shaking hands Hugo goes back to stand in front of the fireplace. In the penumbra of the antique furnishings, in the autumn light which is somewhat darkened by the faded colors of the walls and made blue by cigar smoke, against this background of another age where everything is a bit vague and uncertain, things as well as faces, Hugo's head in full light is properly framed and looks striking. He has some fine white disordered locks of hair like those of Michelangelo's prophets; on his face is a strange, almost ecstatic placidity. Yes, ecstasy, but now and then the dark eyes become lively again, it seems to me, and are infused with a sort of mean slyness.

When I ask him if he feels at home in Paris, he answers to this effect: "Yes, I like present-day Paris. I should not have liked to see the Bois de Boulogne thronged with carriages, barouches, and landaus. It pleases me now that it is a quagmire, a ruin. . . . It's fine, it's great! Don't think, though, that I condemn everything that has been done in Paris: the restoration of Notre Dame and La Sainte Chapelle is well done, and there are certainly some beautiful houses." When I say to him that the Parisian of the past finds himself lost, that Paris is Americanized: "Yes, that's true, an Anglicized Paris, but what keeps it from being completely so, thank God, is two things: the comparative excellence of its climate and the absence of coal. . . . As far as my personal taste goes, I like the old streets best." In answer to someone's remark about the great boulevards: "It's true, the former government did nothing for defense against foreigners; everything was done as defense against the population."

He comes over to sit beside me and talks of my books, which he is kind enough to say were among the distractions of his exile. He adds: "You have created types; that is a power that men of very great talent do not always have." Then, speaking of my loneliness on earth, which he compares to his own when he was over there in Guernsey, he preaches the value of work as an escape, lulls me into thinking of a kind of collaboration with him who is no more, ending with these words: "For my part, I believe in the presence of the dead; I call them the *Invisible Ones.*"

In the drawing room everyone is discouraged. Even those who are sending patriotic articles to *Le Rappel* admit aloud that they have little belief in any possibility of defense. Hugo says: "We shall get on our feet again some day; we cannot perish, for the world cannot endure this abominable Germanism; there will be revenge in four of five years."

At this visit Hugo shows himself to be friendly, simple, a good fellow, not in the least inclined to be enigmatically oracular or to lay down the law. His great personality reveals itself only in delicate nuances, as when he talks of the embellishment of Paris and mentions Notre Dame. You are grateful for his politeness, which is somewhat cold, somewhat that of a gentleman, but pleasant to encounter in these times of banal effusiveness when great celebrities receive you for the first time with a "Well, so it's you, old fellow!"

At every street corner there are people selling things to eat. In front of Thiers' house a man from the country with two rabbits. On the Place de la Bourse a woman who carries a live hen from group to group, pulling back its feathers to show how fat it is. The strange transformation that businesses are undergoing these days! Hatters tempt the collector of things military with the classic Prussian helmet surmounted by a spread-out eagle like a lightning rod or with the chocolate-colored helmet of a Bavarian *picked up at Châtillon*. Merchants of paintings and painters' supplies are selling oilcloth kepi-covers. The little delivery-service offices, now without clients, have become siege bazaars; in them you see revolvers, marine glasses, knives, bastion kits, sheepskin beds, ejectors for breechloading rifles, filter cups, etc. A butcher shop on the Rue Neuve des Petits Champs has changed its name to *Hippophagie* and displays under the bright gaslight an elegant skinned animal with the abdomen cut out in festoons and lace and garlanded with leaves and roses; the animal is a donkey.

Tuesday, November 8

The vegetable market which yesterday was on the Rue Tronchet, I find today all along the Avenue de Clichy from General Moncey's statue to the rampart gate, with a swarm of young peddlers, little ragamuffins with their shirt tails sticking out through the crates on which they are sitting and little girls in hoods, with three turnips in front of them. Other merchandise intrudes on this huge display of greenstuff: old trousers, pieces of stove pipe, lampshades, oil paintings of country houses made by their amateur proprietors, and models of the human jaw which open and close, bought from some bankrupt dentist.

I go across the drawbridge. Swallowed up in the fog, the sun makes the sky look like smoke from a big fire; behind me the great line of fortifications, standing out from all other constructions, looks like cliffs immersed in morning mist, where customs officers are in silhouette. As on all the avenues, the houses are abandoned, though they have *For Rent* signs in front of them, which is certainly ironical. Among the closed-up wine shops there is a shoe-repair shop the window of which is full of horsemeat, horse blood-sausage, etc. It has become a fry shop, a rotisserie, a homecooking shop, I think, and a horrible looking woman comes from the fire to hand an infantryman something nameless and stinking through the open window.

You see soldiers from every branch of the service, men and women of every sort, all of them carrying something in their hands, be it only a piece of board! Among them some frightful toughs, wearing hand-me-down infantry pants and gold-braided imperial police caps down over their eyes. There are miserable looking people who make you shiver; old women in rags with the rusty keys to their hovels hitting their legs with the sound of iron against wood. In one corner some soldiers in kepis are taking some whores off to a wine shop.

Every few feet you go through barricades, nearly all made of barrels full of sand with sandbags on top. As I am lighting my cigaret at one of the barricades, the sentinel comes up to me and says: "Don't throw away your match; those are my instructions."

Then I am past the Clichy church and into the market gardens which have no more palisades, among stakes still upright which once held up plank roofs, among lean-tos where all the laths have been pulled off as far as arm can reach. The wood everywhere has been used for the soldiers' fires. On the horizon of this devastation are the skeletons of big trees outlined against the sky—a rose cloud with a cerise sun—their branches resembling the leafy pattern of an agate. On the left a mixture of red and yellow buildings bathed in a cloudy rainbow light that would drive a watercolorist to despair.

The road goes on, to stop suddenly, as if the landscape were cut off sharp, between a gutted factory held up by some posts and a restaurant with boards painted brick-color on which you read the words: *Swimming school at the foot of the bridge*. At this point your view is cut off by a heavy yellow fog rising from the Seine, which is not visible; out of the fog looms a sentinel from the infantry who shouts: "You can't pass."

I take a road to the right which is black with coal and wander under the stunted trees of orchards where men are taking up squares of turf and loading them on carts. In vacant lots some National Guards, who look like homunculi, are practicing close-order drill. In every direction above the closed passages the kepis and bayonets of sentinels. On every side walls with openings for guns through which bits of sky can be seen. And far away along a path which goes between pieces of fallen wall an old woman drags herself along slowly under a staggering load of wood, like an ant under a piece of straw.

Still looking for the Seine, I take a street that goes around some factories which are silent and dark, the color of things always enveloped in smoke; in only one of them is there a rumbling noise and a burst of steam from the cellar air vent. I come to a starch factory, through the wide door of which I see some men cutting down big trees. Before me there is a redoubt which has openings for three cannons, and then the Seine, as Corot might have painted it.

Still a rosy sky, with houses crowded together on the farther shore like the dots of dominoes among the violet masses of the trees; the water is yellow, turned to salmon by the reflection from the sky; the island opposite, completely leveled, shows a bit of blue in the second-growth brush around its two rustic cottages. On one side the Asnières railway bridge, a black thread in the air. On the other side, the Clichy bridge, where the flooring over one arch has fallen into the water. The whole landscape has colors which are not those of day, but seem to be the coloring of opals and mother of pearl seen at dusk.

Under this fantastic sky and on this devastated road, prostitution is very evident. You see soldiers' women of every sort. I walk behind a creature on the arm of a young infantryman. She is bareheaded, with her hair heaped in a crown, or rather a pastry mold, on top of her head. She is wearing a black wool dress with a long train; the waist comes up to her breasts, and the ruching of her cape heightens her shoulders. She has a white scarf around her neck and a black straw basket in her hand. This is the distinguished get-up of the whore on service to the military in this year of grace 1870.

On the way back, lines of starving women and children besieging the municipal canteens repeatedly force me to get off the sidewalk.

Wednesday, November 9

We have had the Emperor's plan and Palikao's plan; now we are threatened with Trochu's plan. We know what the first two were like. God save us from the third!

This evening I run into Nefftzer, who takes me to drink a glass of half-and-half at Frontin's. We go down to the cellar frequented by the democrats. Nefftzer has already reached the condition of gaiety and expansiveness that comes from a few glasses of beer and his Swabian laughter is formidable.

In reply to something I say about Hugo, he gets started talking about the man, whom he saw a great deal of at the Conciergerie in 1852, where Hugo came to eat dinner every day with his sons and Vacquerie. He tells me of his complete unawareness of food. "Proudhon," he says, "and another of my friends had restricted themselves to dinners costing ten sous. We did as they did. Note that for the price of ten sous we had three courses, but what courses! Wine, but what wine! Now I can distinguish between good and bad and resign myself to the bad. But Hugo, no! I remember one day when he was late and we had given him up, we had thrown our scraps in a corner, a horrible mixture of things like veal liver and skate with black butter. Well, Hugo gobbled it up!

It was something to see. We watched him in amazement. And you know how he eats: he devours like Polyphemus.

"Hugo in those days was very amusing. It was at the time of the presidential election. I had the best room, one arranged for by Beauvallon, so they were all in my place. Hugo came to butter up Proudhon, making an effort to use him; but basically Proudhon despised him, as he would a musician."

"Hugo has said in my presence that Proudhon was an idiot," a man drinking at our table breaks in.

"I mentioned," Nefftzer continues, "that my room was used for everything. One day we had quite a dinner. Crémieux had brought some Constance wine which he had got from Rothschild, no doubt because he was a Jew. Madame Hugo, who at that time had a tendency, I won't say to get drunk, but to become pleasantly stimulated, had drunk a good deal of the wine. She talked too much. I shall never forget the look, one impossible to imitate, by which Hugo suddenly blistered her, reduced her to silence.

"In the old days when Hugo came to *La Presse* I never recognized him at first glance. My idea of the great poet never coincided, at the first moment, with the gentleman in front of me. Yes, he looked like a petty crook, like an eternal student. He was dirty, dirty. Then he had a mania too for wearing narrow trouser straps and pearl-grey trousers covered with stains, and always a black coat.

"When I saw him again in Belgium, he was a different man. He looked like an old cavalry captain. But I must do him this justice: whether it was the old or the new Hugo, he always received you warmly, with charming, gracious politeness. I remember when we used to go to his house with our wives how he wouldn't let any of them leave without helping them on with their coats or capes. In anybody else this would have been ridiculous; in him it was courtly manners."

Nefftzer's conversation becomes more elevated and turns to the dislocation of France. It is ten-thirty and in compliance with National Defense regulations a waiter puts out the gas and sets a candle on the table. The cellar begins to look like one of the cellars where I had supper in Berlin.

"Now I am a German, completely German," Nefftzer says; "I defend France only from a sense of duty. But I don't deceive myself. The day is probably not far off when you will see again a Phocean republic, a Grand Duchy of Aquitaine, a Grand Duchy of Brittany."

And in the dim light observations and thoughts full of profundity, ironies and paradoxes almost of genius come out of his gross Jordanesque face, reddish in the harsh light of the candle which makes the thick flesh and warts stand out, come out from his at times almost incomprehensible jargon, from his stubborn words which spurt out like belches. Beneath the Caliban appears the man I thought I had discerned—a fine intelligence in a gross material envelope. He says:

"It's the Saint Bartholomew's Day massacre which today is finishing France. If France had become Protestant, she would have been the leading country of Europe forever. You see, in Protestant countries there is a gradation between the philosophy of the upper classes and the free inquiry of the lower classes. In France there is a gap, an abyss, between the scepticism of the upper classes and the idolatry of the lower classes. Believe me, that is what is killing France!"

And he ends by saying: "M. de Bismarck, the first statesman of all time!" repeating several times: "He always lands his blow," but wondering whether he would have been as great if he had encountered circumstances as adverse as those which Pitt had to meet. He orders more beer and porter, saying that it is beer that puts him to sleep every night.

At the moment there is a general and immediate need on the part of everyone I see for tranquillity of spirit, for repose of mind, for escape from Paris. Everybody says: "As soon as it's over, I'm leaving." And they indicate the corner of France, the vague place in the country where, far from Paris and all that recalls it, they will be able for a while to stop thinking, reflecting, or remembering.

It could be that the great events of '89, which nobody, even its enemies and adversaries, writes about without all sorts of genuflections, were less providential for the future of France than has hitherto been thought. Perhaps it will be realized that since that date our existence has only been a series of ups and downs—up when by chance a man of genius was at hand—a series of adjustments of a social order forced to demand a new savior in every generation. The French Revolution destroyed the discipline of the nation, killed the self-abnegation in the individual which had been supported by religion and other feelings of idealism. Our first savior finished off whatever had survived of that idealism by the phrase of his prime minister: "Get rich!" and our second savior, by his example and that of his court, which said, in effect, "Take your pleasure!" And when all religion was quite dead, they conferred the true sovereignty of France on the destructive and disorganizing attitudes of the lowest level of the nation by means of universal suffrage.

'Eighty-nine might have provided the basis of government for some other people, a people who seriously loved liberty and equality, a people who were educated, discriminating, habituated to free inquiry. But for the sceptical, cynical, credulous French temperament, '89 seems to me destined to become a mortal illness.

Friday, November 11

The wounded man is in favor. As I go along the Boulevard Montmorency, I see a lady taking a wounded man in grey overcoat and police cap for a ride in her open carriage. She has eyes only for him; she continually adjusts the fur laprobe; the hands of mother and wife are constantly running over his body.

The wounded man has become fashionable. For others he is an object of utility, a lightning rod. He defends your dwelling from invasion by the suburban population; he will save you later on from fire, pillage, and Prussian requisition. Someone was telling me that one of his acquaintances had set up a hospital in his house. Eight beds, two nursing sisters, lint, bandages, nothing was lacking. But no wounded man in sight. The householder was full of anxiety about his house. What did he do? He went to a hospital where there were lots of wounded men and paid three thousand francs, yes, three thousand francs, to have one of them turned over to him.

I deeply wish for peace; I very selfishly hope that no shells will fall on my house and my treasures. However, I was walking sad as death the full length of the fortifications. I was looking at all those works which will not protect us against German victory. I felt from the attitude of the workmen, the National Guards, and the soldiers, from what people around me were admitting to each other, that peace was signed in advance and on M. de Bismarck's terms. And I suffered stupidly as from a disappointment, a disillusionment about one I loved. Someone was saying to me this evening: "The National

Guards! Let's not talk about them. The infantry will raise their rifles in the air; the Mobiles will hold out for a little while; the sailors will fire without conviction. That's how they will fight, if they do fight."

Saturday, November 12

Let posterity beware of telling future generations about the heroism of the Parisians in 1870. Their heroism will have consisted solely in eating strong butter on their beans and serving horsemeat instead of beef—without being too much aware of it, since the Parisian has little discrimination about what he eats.

Sunday, November 13

In the midst of everything that straitens and menaces life at this moment, there is one thing that sustains it and stirs it up, almost makes you love it: emotion. To go beneath the cannon fire, to risk your life at the foot of the Bois de Boulogne, to see flames leaping out of the houses at Saint Cloud as they are today, to live under the constant emotion of a war which surrounds you and almost touches you, to rub elbows with danger, always to have your heart beating fast: that has its sweetness, and I feel that, when this is all over, hectic enjoyment will be followed by dull boredom, very dull, very dull.

This evening in the resonance of a frosty night you can hear constantly repeated all along the ramparts in a striking chant: "Sentinels, on guard," accompanied by the continuous sound of distant cannons, which are like bursts and cracklings of lightning in the mountains.

Monday, November 14

Walking in the ruins of the Bois de Boulogne, I am curious

to see the houses at Parc aux Princes. All of them have been abandoned by their owners. All the pretty gardens are strewn with infantrymen; in the green trees the red cloth is in sharp contrast with the white marble of la Tourbey's house, which I almost bought.

I push ahead and walk at random along paths where I find a degree of abandonment I have not yet encountered in the Paris suburbs. The houses which begin in these undefined areas, in the true country—modest houses, poor little middle-class houses, miserable rustic chalets—have their iron gates or doors left wide open by some sharpshooter; and from the broken panes of their windows shreds of curtains flutter out, all puckered by the rain. Branches of broken climbing plants hang desolate over the vanished doors. Deserted doghouses guard deserted barns.

Among all these buildings there is one that moves me particularly for some reason. A building made from scraps of all times and places, a building which you feel some strange, bizarre Parisian, after having been architect and mason, erected for his retirement. I enter the little courtyard, which is encumbered with all sorts of things, among which I make out a child's bathtub. Hanging on a dead tree, the only tree, is the rustic philosopher's straw hat, a real Vireloque hat. I go into the ground-floor room through an old Louis XV doorway. The furniture is all smashed up; an empty buffet has only shreds of wood hanging where the doors were. A touching thing—in the midst of the raging devastation of this poor dwelling, a chair in one corner has remained intact. On this chair rests an old red-edged book with a marker, indicating where the owner stopped reading.

The sky is grey with big clouds which look like whirlwinds of ashes. The Saint Cloud hills are blue black, and the ruined château looks as though it were already a hundred years old. I look at it, through the smoke of four of five fires near the church, over the white tombs in a cemetery, where the decapitated wall has been converted into a barricade and reinforced with sandbags. Gusts of wind make the blinds clatter on the open windows of deserted houses. I have a sharp, almost cruel pleasure in walking through this desolation, this scene of death, in a raw wind which brings tears to my eyes.

There is something comforting about beating the pavement to the shouts which make the boulevard ring, shouts of "Orléans recaptured by the Army of the Loire," and thus to walk along in the resurrection of Paris.

Wednesday, November 16

Among thin women sexual pleasure is manifested by a nervous spasm; among fat women by a sort of convulsion. With the former it is rather a lengthening, a stretching out; with the latter, a drawing together, a contraction. The *little death* brings ecstasy to the faces of the first, apoplexy to those of the others.

Thursday, November 17

You overhear women on the Rue Richelieu exclaiming fearfully at eight o'clock in the evening: "Oh, but it's dark!"

Friday, November 18

. . . . .

Each cannon has its sound, its timbre, its resonance, its snoring, or strident, or dull, or shattering *boom.* I am now able to recognize with certainty the cannons at Mont Valérien, Issy, the Point du Jour emplacement, and Mortemart. I don't mention the naval gun on my own rampart, which is easy to recognize among all the others because in the daytime it shakes all the doors as if a gust of wind were enveloping the house, and at night shakes me in my bed like a light earthquake.

Saturday, November 19

They are inflating a captive balloon here. Naturally redheaded Nadar is on hand, with his naval officer's cap and his raglan coat of military cut, moving around, throwing himself about, making himself visible to everybody, with his whole body saying to the world: "Look at me carefully, me, the real, the only, the unique Nadar!"

Sunday, November 20

At the top of the Butte Mortemart I heard a little girl say to her little friends as she pointed to Saint Cloud: "Our house is still there, the last one, near those trees. Do you see it?"

That is the consolation of the moment. People big and small come here from time to time to take a look at their beloved homes. The other day a gentleman whom I did not know asked permission to look at the entrance to his workshop in Sèvres from one of my windows.

Nowadays in the restaurants you start your dinner in gaslight and end with candles as a result of the regulations shutting off gas at seven-thirty.

This evening I run into young Masson, who is enveloped in a Mobile Guard overcoat. I find that he, who used to date his letters with the *pluviôses* and *messidors* of the republican calendar, is greatly disillusioned by the republic of the republicans and soldier-democrats. He complains that when he marched forward with Goubie, his brothers did not follow him at all. A little of his bad humor toward the present recoils on '89 and brings a considerable diminution of his admiration for the First Republic. He is a symptom. I am convinced that many young people who, like him, felt a degree of exaltation are now becoming ardent reactionaries after contact with the despicable ruling riffraff of the present moment.

Monday, November 21

Several days of inactivity passed almost entirely at home, during which the sad memories of this house crept over me.

November 22

I go for a walk in the Bois de Boulogne, where autumnal sadness is today mingled with the sadness of war. Rain, which in its hurried fall hides and effaces the lines of hills in the distance; a dull sky, where from time to time a cannon shot fired from a fort makes a little white cloud appear; a wailing wind, in which you hear the repercussions of rifle shots on the right bank of the Seine. I have still in memory and before my eyes the paleness and exhaustion of numerous sick soldiers whom I have just seen going by on packsaddles.

No one walking or wandering idly in the main woods; not even the living cry of a little bird. I am alone. I go through the desolate felled area, among trees where I have sat with *him,* under which I saw him look so sad. They are dead too, those trees. Felled birches stretch out in front of me and their white stumps look like the corner of a cemetery. On the abandoned road dried branches and the soles of old shoes are mingled in the mud.

At last near La Cascade I pass an encampment under the trees, an agglomeration of huts, cabins, and shanties picturesquely put together from fragments of plank, pieces of zinc, fir branches, pressed clay, and random pieces of glass used as window panes. The Café de la Cascade, so popular with Parisian brides, is a hospital. The upper lake is dry and my step sends up a cloud of birds that are looking for worms in the ooze. No more cascading water; in a sort of mud that remains in the pool, infantrymen framed by the heaped up rocks are washing their dirty shirts.

The rain has stopped. Sharp, clear, crystalline daylight, cleared of all mist, outlines almost harshly the little villas in tiers on the hills and the rectilinear mass of Mont Valérien, behind which there is a spectacular sunset. The sky, palely blue and palely yellow, looks like the bed of a great dried-up river, the blue streaks being water, the yellow ones sand, with big heavy white clouds crested by molten gold being the banks.

Just in time, I return only a few minutes before the closing of the Auteuil gate. The closing is a military spectacle: blowing of bugles, belated people puffing, heavy soldier shoes pressing in the mud, drivers leading horses by the bridle, the people who are entering and those going out pressing against each other, all of this already indistinct in the falling night. The darkness of the two closed gates is set against the piece of red sky striped with violet clouds which was visible a while ago, and four long arms rise up into the nocturnal blue of dusk.

Wednesday, November 23

During the siege you feel boredom as you do at a tragedy that will not come to an end.

Veuillot has what few writers possess: he conveys a sort of alacrity to his readers. Moreover, his talent for irony has never expressed a more grandiose, a more disdainful scorn.

Thursday, November 24

Madame Burty was telling me today that her laundress says it costs her thirteen francs a day to feed her horse.

The ragman on our boulevard, who nowadays is standing in line at the public market for a cookshop proprietor, was telling Pélagie that he has bought cats at six francs apiece, rats at one franc apiece, and dogmeat at one franc a pound for his principal.

Friday, November 25

It seems to me that autumnal effects have never been so beautiful as this year. Perhaps that is because I have been looking at them more than ever before and have had my eyes continually turned toward the Prussian horizon.

This evening I could not get enough of looking at the dead heaps of brush, which as far as I could see were tinged by the sun to the pink color of heather; the hills were a harsh violet, and the houses at Saint Cloud an indescribable bluish-white caused by the smoke of the eternal conflagration which has been smoldering for a month.

This colorist's landscape has a sky of cherry flame containing in its embrace two or three odd spots of pale blue, that blue which Lessore puts on his pottery plates.

Saturday, November 26

This is the last day the gates will be open; tomorrow Paris ends at the ramparts, and the Bois de Boulogne will no longer be part of Paris. I want to walk there the whole day, before it disappears perhaps.

And here I am this morning in the circular path; above me the man with the telescope is shouting: "Who wants to see the Prussians? You can see them very clearly. Gentlemen, come take a look!" I walk through the fallen trees, stopping at piles of sand, at little smokestacks—coal ovens; stopping at huts abandoned by the soldiers which are marvels of labor and ingenuity, with doors made of branches turning on hinges of vines.

I constantly have to jump over big ditches, over mounds topped by fascines, over barricades which are part of the defense line; I reach the top of this winding road where the barouches used to go out on the racetrack, and in front of me I see Saint Cloud as though it were at the foot of the road, Saint Cloud with its burned houses and its streets that have been licked by flames.

The gate of Le Pré Catalan is open. Cannons are drawn up on the lawn, and artillerymen signal to make a wide detour as you pass. From Le Pré Catalan I go to Le Jardin d'Acclimatation by the pretty path along the brook under the green trees. There a band of men, women, and children are breaking up the poor trees which, after they have passed, are left with white scars, branches hanging to the ground, and heaps of twisted wood—a revolting act of pillage which reveals the Parisian population's love of destruction. An old man from the country passing by, who loves trees as he does all things old, raises his eyes to heaven in a sorrowing way.

On my way back I am somewhat calmed by the sight of the large island, which, protected by the water around it, has kept its green trees, its bushes, and its English neatness intact and is without wounds in the midst of the general devastation. On the edge of the lake near the once-frequented bank a tall thin priest walks all by himself as he reads his breviary.

I hurry to get back by five o'clock. The lawn which goes from the Butte Mortemart to the Boulogne gate is covered with Mobiles, who are going to camp there for the night. It is charming to see the bluish multitude, the little white tents, soldiers and tents diminishing down to little men in little microscopic squares of canvas among the smoke from their cooking fires, which makes a regular cloud on the horizon, against which the big trees on the hills stand out like a stage set. Far in the background you get just a glimpse of the Saint Cloud church sunk and submerged as in a scene of apotheosis at the moment the curtain falls.

Five o'clock strikes. People hurry and push. There is a pile-up of artillery caissons which makes it difficult to get through. A poor old man next to me on the drawbridge becomes frightened and falls. I see him carried away on the shoulders of four men, inert, his head dangling. He has broken his spine.

Monday, November 28

During the night I am awakened by cannon fire. I go to an upstairs room.

In the starless sky crisscrossed by the branches of big trees, from the Bicêtre fortress to the Issy fortress, for the whole extent of this wide semicircle, there is a succession of little points of fire, which flare up like gaslights and are followed by loud explosions. These great voices of death in the silence of the night are very moving. After a while the barking of dogs is added to the thundering of the cannons; the fearful voices of people who have been awakened begin to whisper; roosters send forth their clear notes. Then cannons, dogs, roosters, and people all return to silence, and my ear cocked out the window perceives nothing but in the distance, far off, a fusillade like the dull sound of an oar touching the wood of a boat.

What a strange collection of people you find in an omnibus! How many kinds and sorts of military men! I am next to a chaplain from the South with lively, gentle eyes, who tells me that since the gates were closed the morale of the Mobile Guards and of the army has completely changed, that discouragement and demoralization were constantly produced by foragers, by the prostitutes who went back and forth between the French and the Prussians, and indeed by members of the men's families. He adds that the soldiers felt that they were surrounded by treason, but now they are of a mind to fight and have confidence.

I go through the Luxembourg Garden. Near the pool there is a cart laden with barrels, and on the stone wall a collection of children and of men in shirt sleeves leaning over the water. I go nearer. Kneeling men are pulling a huge net, the corks of which graze the swans, which rise from the water with frightened wings, half-flying in anger. They are fishing the pool to get food for Paris; soon carp and monstrous cyprines appear on the bottom of the net as it comes to the surface of the moving water. The catch is put in the barrels in the harnessed cart.

It takes a certain amount of skill to get out of the garden without being hit by the pirouetting National Guards as they practice bayonet thrusts.

Opposite the Bullier dance hall and concealing its eastern door, on which is written *Hospital, Val de Grâce Branch*, stands an immense cart from which a man is tossing out mattresses as you would toss out forkfuls of straw.

The Boulevard Montparnasse is furrowed by the cannons and caissons returning to Paris, and sickly women with the look of the provinces are seated on the benches, shivering in their hooded capes. Among them an old toothless woman, whose chin sticks out further than her nose, looks just like the wooden carving on a fool's sceptre such as I have seen at sales. She seems to be in a wild state of agitation.

On the Boulevard d'Enfer horses and donkeys are tied to spindly trees which are without bark to the height of five or six feet. Standing by the croups of these nags is a wily, ruddy group of men with whips curled around their necks: a collection of aged and juvenile horsetraders among whom you see every type of seller and dealer in horses. An old Norman with his blue-striped cotton bonnet and his white beard that looks like a stock; a shepherd with a round hat, a bare neck, and a big rope slung over his blouse; here the well-to-do with their caps which have curly black-wool ear-flaps, their square-cut sideburns, their red scarves knotted around their necks; there, the unemployed jockeys with their long-sleeved vests and their wool mufflers; then, wearing flat caps which cover the back of the head, a whole group of sly, shifty young hooligans, with the faces of diplomats. A bold-eyed little girl with the kerchief of the Paris region on her pretty curly hair offers to sell me a donkey for 350 francs; it looks for all the world like a donkey from the Boulevard Montmorency.

This is the street of the horse market—the Poissy of today's Paris. I go on into the market proper, where the tethered horses are so hungry that they eat the wood of the railing to which they are tied and pick up from the ground the little pieces that they have gnawed off. They are led to the scales before which an infantryman who is weighing them kneels on a sack. You see hands pass over their flanks; you hear words whose meaning you don't catch spoken with diabolic smiles and winks—a sort of mysterious transaction lasting only a moment between these men made ruddy by outdoor life. The deal is made. Then the horse is led away to a corner where a thin little man lowers the iron handle of a bellows, by which coals are being kept red; at one side a man who looks as distinguished as an auctioneer stands smoking his pipe. He takes an iron from the fire and presses it against the horse's rump, which smokes. Another man in a wool bonnet and great casklike boots, who wears a coat over his blouse, uses scissors very artistically to make two or three cuts in the hair of the chest: symbolic marks. Now the horse is butcher's meat and has received his passport to the slaughterhouse.

Tuesday, November 29

The salt meat delivered by the government cannot be desalted or eaten. I have been reduced to killing one of my little hens with a Japanese sword. It was frightful, for the lively creature got away from me and flopped about headless in the garden.

Today everybody is withdrawn into himself. In the public vehicles nobody speaks; everybody is closed up, and the women of the common people seem to look blindly at what is going on around them.

The Seine is covered with river boats, which have their steam up and, draped with hospital flags, are ready to go to pick up the wounded.

In the Champ de Mars little army ambulances preceded by an interminable line of mules laden with campaign materiel. On the bridge artillerymen standing near their caisson in the damp cold draw around them their white greatcoats over which their carbines are slung.

The emotion of waiting is evident in the streets. There are groups standing in the squares. Any man who speaks, any man from whom you may hope for information, is surrounded. As night falls the groups become enormous, overflowing the sidewalks and spilling into the streets. Ambulances come slowly down from the barrier at the Porte d'Italie surrounded by a cortege of women, one of whom will sometimes risk opening the door at the rear to look at the wounded.

I have dinner at Brébant's. We talk of our black misery. Charles Edmond recounts this incident. While at the butcher's his wife saw a well-dressed woman, one dressed like a society lady, come in and ask for a sou's worth of *horse trimmings*. My friend's wife put a franc in her hand, and as an expression of thanks the other woman burst into tears.

We speak of the nervous overstimulation of women, of the fright caused by the events of these days, of the fear on the part of the authorities that they may have to put down an uprising of women.

Then the dangers of the future lead us to talk of exile. Some say that exile is a condemnation to death, which is the way the Romans understood it. Others, such as the cosmopolitan Nefftzer, say that there is no such thing as exile.

It is really strange how some men have no feeling of country. I notice this lack particularly among thinkers like Renan, who says that a feeling of patriotism was quite natural in antiquity but that Catholicism displaced it; and since the idealists are the heirs of Catholicism, they ought not to have such close attachments to the soil or such miserably ethnographic bonds tying them to the nation. "The native land of idealists," he bursts out, "is the one where they are allowed to think." And each word he speaks shows how little French he is, in the bourgeois sense of the word. A few minutes later, alluding to the capture and occupation of Paris by the Prussians, to Berthelot's nervous interruptions and strangled indignation, he asserts that this occupation will be no harder on him than were the first days after the Second of December. The fact of foreign domination does not arouse in him anything of what disturbs, affronts, and enrages patriotic hearts. William or Napoleon, it is all one to him.

This evening I find my friends decidedly too superior to humanity, and I am almost angry when I hear Nefftzer declare that Bazaine's behavior, his overt treason, was perfectly human, when I hear him take pleasure in it with his big, mocking laugh.

Wednesday, November 30

From one in the morning until eleven an uninterrupted cannonade, so rapid that separate cannon shots are not perceptible and you have the impression of the interminable rumbling of a storm which does not quite break. Or perhaps a celestial housemoving, in which the Titans move the heavenly chests of drawers about over your head.

I am in Gavarni's garden, which has become a sort of observatory for the passers-by, who enter by a break in the wall. With my neighbors, some National Guards, and some workmen I enjoy this shaking in the heavens which at times seems to be communicated to the soil beneath my feet.

The cannonade lasts all day. All day these rumblings and grumblings of death, not a second without a succession of their blasts which, at the distance at which they are, seem like the piling up of waves from a heavy sea on the horizon.

I am somewhat ill. I was unable to go to Paris this afternoon. I have no news. I turn my ear to the noise in the streets, which tells the good or the bad in public events by the steps of the passers-by and by the timbre of their voices. Nothing! The street tells me nothing this evening!

Thursday, December 1

This evening on the Rue Tournon, where candles light up a

porte-cochère and with their flickering gleams illuminate a livid face under a checked handkerchief, I see a man stiff with the immobility of a corpse brought down from an open carriage; his voice protests at each touch of the hands which help him down and carry him into the hospital. He is a Mobile whose thigh was broken yesterday at eleven in the morning and who has just now been brought in from the battlefield under the cover of night.

In the Auteuil omnibus there is a Parisian rifleman next to me holding a Prussian helmet of the Royal Guard on his knees. He tells of the enthusiasm of the troops, of the Zouaves, who during the attack on Villiers were admirable, of one company in which only four men got off without injury.

Tuesday, December 2

All of Paris is in the Avenue du Trône today. You witness the great emotion of the capital, its population staying close to the city gates, shortening the distance, getting closer to the news.

On either side of the street, kept open by the National Guard, all the way to the barrier with its columns bluish in the winter sun, two crowds rise up in tiers, standing here and there on heaps of stones, forming little mounds of men and women. The street is completely full of the coming and going of ambulances, of shell carriages, of vans carrying ammunition, of caissons, of vehicles of every kind which every fifteen minutes the closing of the bars across the railroad tracks causes to back up and bump into each other in a strident grating of metal. And the eyes of the crowd are all turned toward the culminating point of the avenue where you see the returning ambulances emerge; all eyes seeking out a priest's hat on the seat, the white coif of a nun on the bench, trying to pierce the dark shadows near the driver for the collapsed figure of a wounded man. In everyone you witness a painful shudder mixed with avid curiosity over the paleness, the lividness, the bloodstains, the ragged uniforms, the stiff-lipped control of the suffering wounded men, who know that people are looking at them and try to be equal to the occasion.

Next there pass by some wounded men sitting at the tail end of a cart, their legs hanging limp, their faces pale though vaguely smiling at the people they pass—smiles that make you want to weep. Wounded men go by, showing on their faces their terrible anxiety about their wounds, their uncertainty whether there must be an amputation, uncertainty whether they will live or die. Wounded men go by, posing in studied and theatrical attitudes, sitting on a heap of straw, perched on top of the carriage, saying to their public: "Go on, there's Prussian meat over there!" A big Saxon with a cheerful face and a good-hearted smile is smoking a cigar among the French wounded. A fierce-looking wounded man holds his rifle tight against himself; his broken bayonet is no more than an iron thumb. In the backs of little coupés you see wounded officers, whose gold-braided sleeves and slack hands rest on the pommels of their swords; and through the steamy windows of the omnibus files of bent backs and wounded soldiers constantly pass before your eyes.

The cold is sharp, but the crowd cannot pull itself away from this bloody sight. You hear women's little heels beating down, clicking on the frozen earth. You want to see, you want to know—and you don't know anything and the most contradictory rumors run about and spread every minute. Faces light up or become sad at a word from this person, at a word from that. Someone notices that you cannot hear the cannons at the fortresses any more; that is a good sign that the army is advancing. In one group I hear: "Things were going badly this morning, it seems, but they're going all right now. The Mobiles had given ground."

Eyes and glances continue to turn toward the wounded, the dispatch-riders, the aides-de-camp, toward anyone who comes from over there at a gallop. "Look, there's Ricord!" someone says as he sees the surgeon pass by in his carriage. A National Guard shouts to the crowd from his seat on horseback: "A half-league in front of Chennevières and hand-to-hand fighting now." And always you wait, you ask questions, you get everybody to say to you, "Everything's fine," a statement which every horseman is forced to repeat before he is allowed to go on. There is no positive news; but something tells the crowd that things are going well. Then a sort of feverish joy rises to all the faces made pale by the cold; men and women, caught up in a kind of playfulness, run ahead of the galloping horses and attempt to extract from the riders with laughs, jokes, coquetry, and gentle violence news that they do not have.

Saturday, December 3

At the gates of the city in the melted snow and through a fog like the fogs of London, always ambulances and soldiers returning in rags as if from a six-months campaign. Many of them have heroically put on cotton bonnets; among these men in cotton bonnets a very gay infantryman is teaching advanced horsemanship to his little donkey, which he has *appro-. priated* somewhere in the suburbs.

I go into a café, where I have to remove a drum from my table. Around me are sleeping Mobiles, lying against their knapsacks on which their exhausted bodies have fallen. The laughter, the diapason of words, the tap-tap of dominoes bespeak with their gay tumult a resurgence of hope.

Sunday, December 4

In spite of the cold, the piercing frost, the whipping wind, I can't refrain from going to see the spectacle at the Avenue du Trône barrier. On the interior road which goes from La Rapée to the Avenue de Vincennes well-muffled bourgeois men, women with red noses under their veils who are accompanied by sniffly children, all interrogate the horizon. On top of the fortifications in the sharp light you see the ridiculous silhouette of a National Guard wrapped in his wife's tartan in default of an overcoat.

In tiers on wooden beams at the Vincennes gate is a swarm of youngsters who tap the soles of their wooden shoes and give advance notice to the crowd of what they can see through the gun-slits. They know everything, they are informed about everything, these little kids; one of them, who makes me think of the street Arab in Monnier's *L'Exécution*, says to another: "That's usually an ambulance flag! It's the white flag for removing the dead!"

I come back by train with two infantrymen. They complain that they have not slept for five days:

"They have taken away our bedding, and we have to sleep as we are on the ground. No tents! No straw! Nothing! You know, it can't be done. You light a fire. You keep yourself warm. You tap your feet."

"My eyes hurt," adds the other; "they hurt like everything today. It's because of the green wood we burn; the wind sends the smoke in our eyes. If this goes on for a month, I think I'll be completely blind."

Monday, December 5

In his article yesterday Saint-Victor asserted in brilliant fashion that France must give up the idea of Germany which she has held up to now, a conception of that country which, on the word of the poets, she has been accustomed to consider the land of good-fellowship and innocence, the sentimental setting of platonic love. He reminded his readers that the ideal fictional world of Werther and Charlotte, of Hermann and Dorothea, has produced the toughest soldiers, the most perfidious diplomats, the most cunning bankers. He might have added the most rapacious courtesans. We must be on guard against that race, which deceives us with an image of childlike innocence; their blondness, on the contrary, signifies the hypocrisy and the cunning implacability of the Slavic races.

Ups and downs of hope which undo you. You think France is saved. Then you think she is lost. A few days ago we had broken through the enemy lines and the Army of Paris had joined hands with the Army of the Loire. Today Ducrot's retreat across the Marne brings a gloomy sense of failure and despair.

At street corners you see horrible sights: ambulances from which they take out men whose heads are covered with bloody towels.

At the market there is a scarcity of salad greens and vegetables. The little tables in front of the market women are bare of all verdure. Here and there a woman parsimoniously pulls two or three leaves of sorrel or cabbage out of a basket and shares them among women who fight over them, and you see the broad hands of soldiers close over two or three little onions which a woman has handed them.

In the Rue Montmartre in front of a wine merchant's window, where a fry merchant has set up shop, some men, women, and children are dining, to the warmth of a little flame, each devouring his pancake hot from its newspaper wrapping.

Paris under Siege

On today's bill of fare in the restaurants we have authentic buffalo, antelope, and kangaroo.

In the open air this evening under any light, under any improvised street light, consternation-struck faces bend over squares of newspaper. It is the news of the defeat of the Army of the Loire and the recapture of Orléans.

Thursday, December 8

If the Republic saves France—I don't yet want to give up hope for my country—we must understand that France will have been saved not by the Republic, but in spite of it. The Republic will have only supplied the inadequacy of its men, the noisy proclamations of Gambetta, the cowardice of the battalions from Belleville. It will have disorganized the army by its commissions à la Garibaldi, will have undermined Parisian morale by the eternal Prussian propaganda of *brothers and friends*, will have killed national resistance in the provinces by the fright evoked by its very name. That is its whole contribution to the National Defense. It will have given nothing but pillagers to the army and not one of its popular names will have fallen on a field of battle at the side of a Baroche or a Dampierre for the deliverance of our country.

'Ninety-three is indeed dead, there are no more republicans. Now the men at the top are whining lawyers; the men at the bottom, riffraff carrying on political wreckage, breaking everything in the State as in the houses which they enter as National Guards. Behind the words *Republic* and *republican* there is no longer any religion—a false sentiment, if you wish, but still an ideal, an elevated feeling which raises humanity above itself and renders it capable of greatness and devotion.

You talk only about what is eaten, can be eaten, or can be found to eat. Conversation does not go beyond that.

"You know, a fresh egg costs twenty-five sous!"

"I hear there is an individual who is buying up all the candles in Paris, and out of them, by adding a little color, he makes that grease which is so expensive."

"Oh, keep away from cocoa butter; it stinks up the house for at least three days."

"I saw some dog cutlets; they're really very appetizing: they look just like mutton chops."

"Now tell me, who has eaten kangaroo?"

"Let me tell you about something good! You cook some macaroni and put it in a salad with plenty of greens. What more can you ask for in these times!"

"Don't forget. There are still some canned tomatoes at Corcelet's."

Hunger is beginning and famine is on the horizon. Elegant Parisian women are beginning to turn their dressing rooms into henhouses. You figure, you count, and you wonder whether even by using all the waste, all the scrapings, all the parings, there will be anything left to eat in two weeks.

We shall lack not only food, but also light. Oil for lamps is becoming scarce, candles are at an end. Worse than that, with the cold weather we are having we are getting close to the time when we will be without coal, or coke, or wood. Then we shall endure famine, cold, and darkness; the future seems to hold sufferings and horrors such as have not been experienced in any other siege.

Friday, December 9

What weather for a war in this frost and snow! You think

of the suffering of men condemned to lie down in this frozen dampness. You think of the wounded finished off by the cold.

Today the rampart, with the white lines of its fortifications where the stiff and freezing National Guards walk back and forth, with the dark background powdered with white, with the slippery slopes of the forts, with a low sky the color of an unpolished glass where a captive balloon floats—the rampart looks like a corner of the Russian countryside.

As I come home at sunset, the rosy trees around me rise out of the whiteness of the earth into a pigeon-breast-colored sky. I feel as though I were walking through one of those Japanese pictures of snowy earth and pinkish trees which that country of naturist art uses to represent winter.

Saturday, December 10

Nothing more unnerving than this state in which hope stupidly tries to believe for a moment all the untruths, the lies, the nonverities of journalism, then falls back immediately into doubt and unbelief about everything. Nothing more painful than this state in which you don't know whether the provincial armies are at Corbeil or at Bordeaux, or whether those armies even exist any more. Nothing more cruel than to live in darkness, in night, in ignorance of the tragic fate which threatens, surrounds, and stifles you. It really seems as though M. de Bismarck has shut up all Paris incommunicado in a prison cell.

For the first time I see people in line at the dry-grocers'— disturbing lines of people pouncing indiscriminately on all the canned goods that are left in these shops.

In the streets, collections on behalf of the wounded cross convoys of the dead; and big calico alms bags, looking like those you see in Italy at carnival time, are carried even to the second floor to solicit charity from the people at the windows.

These days there is nothing more provincial than one of the big Paris cafés. How is that? Perhaps because of the scarcity of waiters, because of the endless reading of the same newspaper, because of the crowds that form in the middle of the café to talk about the things they know, as people talk about local things in a small city, or indeed because of a stupefied habituation to the place, where in former days, distracted only by light thoughts and eager for the pleasures and thousand distractions of Paris, people paused only for a moment, with the lightness of birds of passage.

Everybody is losing weight; everybody is getting thin. You are always hearing of men who have to have their trousers taken in: Théo laments that he has to wear suspenders for the first time, since his belly won't hold up his pants.

The two of us go together to see Hugo at the Pavillon de Rohan. We find him in a nondescript hotel room with a dining-room buffet of yellow wood and a mantelpiece decorated by two Chinese porcelain lamps with a bottle of brandy in the middle. The god is surrounded by female creatures. There is a whole sofa full of them; the honors of the salon are done by an old silver-haired woman in a dress the color of dead leaves, with a low-cut neck revealing a considerable expanse of old skin—a woman who has at the same time the air of a marquise of other days and that of a strolling player of today.

As for the god, he seems old to me this evening. His eyelids are red; his complexion is the brick-color I saw at Roqueplan; his beard and hair are tangled. A red jersey sticks out beyond the sleeves of his coat; a white scarf is wound around his neck.

After all sorts of activity, doors opening and closing, people entering and leaving, actresses coming for permission to recite something from *Les Châtiments* in the theatre, after mysterious goings-on in an anteroom, Hugo drops down on a low chair and in his slow speech which seems to come out after laborious reflection, he begins, apropos of microscopic photography, to talk about the moon, the great desire he has always had to know about its details, a night he once passed with Arago at the Observatory. He says that the telescope of that day brought the moon within ninety leagues of the eye, with the result, he says, that if there were a monument—and he always mentions Notre Dame when he talks of a monument—you would see it as a dot. "Now," he adds, "with improvements, with lenses of one meter, you ought to be able to see it much closer. It is true that excessive enlargement produces chromatic accident, diffusion, and an irised contour. But that is unimportant; photography ought to be able to give us more than maps full of mountains."

Then somehow the conversation turns from the moon to the elder Dumas: "You know," he says to Gautier, "they say I have been to the Academy. . . . I went there to help get Dumas elected. I would have succeeded, for when you get down to it, I have authority with my colleagues. But at this time there are only thirteen of them there and you need twenty-one members for an election."

Tonight I come home from Passy to Auteuil on foot. The road is covered with snow. The sky merges with a watery fog pierced by the diffuse light of the moon. Every branch has a coat of snow, as though it were *candied*. Each twig seems covered with mother-of-pearl vegetation. You seem to be walking in the troubled, vitreous, electric light of an aquarium among great white madrepores. It is the fantasy of melancholy, and in this landscape of moon and snow the idea of death becomes almost sweet. You could fall asleep without regret in its poetic coldness.

Sunday, December 11

For lunch I am almost reduced to shooting the sparrows in my garden.

Monday, December 12

Last night it froze, thawed, and froze again, and for the first time I notice a minor phenomenon of nature which smacks of fairyland. Each leaf on the trees is covered with another leaf of ice, so that when you try to raise up a bush that is crushed under the weight of this crystal, it tinkles like a chandelier and at your feet all this flora of ice makes a sound like broken glass. As long as this perishable melting matter lasts, it is amusing to watch the holly leaves with their swellings and spiny knobs apparently enclosed in diamonds.

Someone tells me that the other evening he heard a woman come up behind him and say in a bold voice: "Monsieur, come up to my room." The invitation was repeated twice in different tones. The third time it was a supplicating: "Monsieur, please come up to my room!" which sounded like the voice of hunger trembling on the verge of tears.

Today Pélagie was visited by her nephew, a Paris Mobile encamped at the moment on the Avron plateau. In the most naive way he told her of his pillagings in houses and châteaux, saying that the officers turned a blind eye on condition that they be given the best part of the loot.

She was almost frightened by his bandit manner and told me this curious detail, that the soldiers had probes to sound the false walls and hiding places made for concealment from the Prussians. Our soldiers have probes in order better to rob the houses which they are supposed to defend and protect! That aroused the indignation of this daughter of the Vosges, who reacted with horror after his visit and could not understand such unconcern for our country and its invaded mountains on the part of this man who finds the trade of soldier fine, except for his very considerable fear of being killed.

Nights of insomnia produced by the continuous cannonade from Mont Valérien, which abruptly bursts into rapid fire resembling the six revolver shots of a man suddenly ambushed.

Tuesday, December 13

At Brébant's we talk of the devastating suburban population now camping in the houses of Paris. Du Mesnil tells us that one of these refugees has made a ragpicker's dump out of the house he is living in. Another has turned his dwelling into a house of prostitution, not clandestine but as ignobly public as a big Number 8 on the Avenue de Vincennes.

Then with his complete lack of patriotic feeling, Renan starts predicting the impossible, prophesying the chimerical.

Thursday, December 15

I had dinner at Voisin's this evening. While eating, I hear a gentleman say to the man seated next to me: "I certainly wish I had news of my poor wife! Imagine, since last September . . ." Then the man with the poor wife, having finished his dinner, goes away. After a few moments another customer comes in and sits down next to my neighbor, whom he knows. They chat: "Imagine," my neighbor says to the new arrival, "X . . . has just this minute been complaining to me about not having any news of his wife; I didn't know what to say to him!"

"Yes," the other replies between two mouthfuls, "she died . . . at Arcachon."

"Exactly, but he doesn't know a thing!"

Isn't it frightful how in these times we are in ignorance of the life and death of those we love?

Friday, December 16

Today the official news of the fall of Rouen. I am happy in my confidence that Flaubert's threat to blow out his brains was nothing but hyperbole.

To be overcome by a stupid love for my shrubbery, passing hours trimming the old ivy of its dead stalks, cultivating my violet plants, mixing up earth and fertilizer for them—all this while the Krupp cannons threaten to make a ruin of my house and garden; it's too stupid! Grief has turned me into an animal, has given me the manias of an old shopkeeper in retirement. I am afraid that under my man-of-letters skin there's nothing left but a gardener.

Sunday, December 18

Today there is a concert at the Opéra. I notice that all the men handling pass-out checks are dressed in National Guard uniforms.

Prices listed on the Brébant menu this 18th day of December: *Chicken wing, 9 francs. Thigh, 6 francs.*

Tuesday, December 20

I don't know whether it is the lack of red meat, the lack of nutritive elements in this boiled mess of canned meat, or the lack of nitrogen, but the bad, the adulterated, the ersatz food which the restaurants have provided for the last six months leaves you in a permanent state of unsatisfied appetite. You always feel a dull hunger, whatever you eat. Last night I had to get up and nibble some chocolate.

On the way to the cemetery, around General Moncey's statue in the Place Clichy I see National Guards under mobilization getting ready to leave. They are in grey overcoats, and the knapsacks on their backs have tent stakes on top. Women and children surround them, keeping them company until the last minute. A little girl who has a little knapsack on her back, with a sea biscuit simulating ration bread, clings to her father's legs. Young girls, at once embarrassed and a little frightened, hold the rifle of a brother or lover who has gone into the wine shop. And a canteen woman in a coat with fluttering red lapels passes rapidly by as she pours out drinks here and there.

Some bags arrive; they are packages of cartridges that are spilled out on the pavement, which is soon covered with the debris of their greasy wrappings. Some kneeling on the pavement, others seated on the edge of the pedestal of the Marshal's statue, put the hundred cartridges they have just received into their unbuckled knapsacks, while hearses file by between National Guards whose rifles are lowered to the ground.

Across from me at the restaurant is that stupid creature named Mario Uchard, explaining his plan of campaign to the firstcomer unfortunate enough to sit beside him.

Since the siege began the Parisian's walk seems entirely changed. It was a fine way of walking, always a little hurried, but you felt it was leisurely, pleasurable, and aimless. Now everybody walks like a man in a hurry to get home.

Wednesday, December 21
Going to watch the cannonade from the rampart, I pass by

the Mobile camps where, under the cedars of Lebanon stripped of branches with only a tuft of green at the top, like the bouquet masons put on the chimney of a new house, you see the debris of crockery, fragments of tarpaper, and cat skins stiffened by the frost.

Thursday, December 22

All Paris is a fair, and there is everything for sale on the sidewalks. They sell vegetables, they sell muffs, they sell packages of lavender, they sell horse fat.

The siege stimulates the imagination of crooks. Today Magny was waiting for an officer who had ordered a dinner for twelve comrades. He had insisted on fish, fowl, and truffles. The whole order was given merely in order to cheat the coachman who took the officer to Magny's out of five francs.

Saturday, December 24

As I get off the train, I see a peasant lovingly holding a rabbit in his arms; he is asking forty-five francs for it from the passers-by.

In spite of the Prussians Paris is beginning to put up its booths for New Year's Day. Opposite the Passage de l'Opéra some are almost finished already, poor little booths made out of the leftovers from lumber for the Mobile barracks and meagerly furnished with pitiful toys.

I go into a shoemaker's on the Place de la Bourse. His wife is speaking in a voice in which there are traces of tears and little nervous laughs about a Mobile garrisoned in the East fortress; he is her son. Suddenly addressing me, the mother reveals herself with these words: "When there's a cannonade, you probably won't believe it, sir, but from the sound—it's strange, isn't it, but that's the way it is—I can immediately tell the cannon from the East fortress."

In that dirty, dark Rue du Croissant in front of shops with the sign *Newspapers Sold Wholesale*, the strange spectacle of a mass of croaking urchins, the stentorian little Paris newspayer boys who, even as they cut up, keep a record of the papers sold on a wine merchant's barrel. Their headquarters is in front of the Vallée Press, the leprous establishment of *Le Siècle*. There they warm themselves in the steam of a stream of hot water running down the tumultuous street. There they get their meals from the trays carried around by Jews, who are selling pieces of bread, tablets of chocolate, big pickles, and barley-sugar candy in every color.

Charles Edmond told me this. His son-in-law's aunt, a poor old woman who was once rich and isn't any longer, has her whole life and soul centered on a son who gave up his job at the Bank and became a soldier. Every day the poor woman stands in line for her meager ration of horsemeat, prepares her little meal, sets two places, divides the meat between her son's plate and her own, and cuts the bread into two pieces. When the meal is quickly over, the old woman hurries off to give her son's portion to some poor person.

Next to me at the restaurant is the empty, noisy cackle of a woman in velvet sitting with what looks like a Polytechnic student transformed into an artilleryman. This cackling which I could not have stood a little while ago is pleasant; it takes me back to other days.

Sunday, December 25

It is Christmas. I hear a soldier say: "By way of celebration we had five men frozen in our tent."

What a remarkable transformation of business and what a

bizarre transformation of shops! A jeweler on the Rue de Clichy now shows eggs wrapped in cotton wool in his jewel boxes. In the part of the window usually given over to silver, you see chickens, ducks, jellied meat; and a big sign announces: *Roast Goose by the Piece.*

Right now the mortality is very high in Paris. It is not absolutely the result of hunger, and the deaths are not confined to the sick and sickly who are finished off by the restricted diet and present hardships. Much of this mortality comes from grief, displacement, homesickness for the sunny corners in the Paris region from which these refugees came. Of the tiny migration from Croissy-Beaubourg—twenty-five people at most—five are already dead.

Monday, December 26

A new foodstuff has been discovered for the unsatisfied Parisian appetite; it is arsenic. The newspapers talk complaisantly of the vigor this poison gives to chamois hunters in Styria and suggests for your lunch an arsenic pill to be procured from any doctor.

In the streets near the Avenue de l'Impératrice I fall in with a threatening mob, frightful women's heads coifed in madras kerchiefs and looking like the Furies of the common people. They threaten to *skin alive* the National Guards who are closing off the Rue des Belles Feuilles and standing guard over it.

It is a question of a supply of wood for making charcoal which people have begun to pillage. The cold, the frost, the lack of fuel with which to heat the little meat that people get has put the feminine part of the population in a fury and they are falling on trellises and wooden fences, tearing away everything on which they can get their angry hands. These women are aided in their work of destruction by horrible children who jump on each other's shoulders to get at the bushes along the Avenue de l'Impératrice, breaking off what they can reach and dragging their little bit of firewood along with them at the end of a string held by a hand pushed into a pocket.

If this terrible winter weather goes on, all the trees in Paris will go down to satisfy people's urgent need of fuel.

Tuesday, December 27

As I go up the Rue d'Amsterdam there is a hearse in front of me; the black pall is covered by a gold-embroidered vest instead of epaulettes. The body is followed by a National Guard and a member of the hospital committee. Around me people say it is the coffin of a Saxon officer.

At the doors of wood merchants there are threatening lines.

In spite of the deadening effect of the snow which falls in dispersed, fluffy, crystalline flakes you can hear everywhere a distant and continuous cannonade from the direction of Saint Denis and Vincennes.

In front of the Montmartre cemetery the hearses are lined up, their horses breathing noisily, the coachmen in black silhouette against the white snow as they stamp their feet.

I stop for a moment at La Chapelle gate and amuse myself as the lanterns are being lit by watching the incessant going in and coming out of soldiers, vehicles, wagons—the traffic of war in what looks like a bivouac in Russia.

The first paper that I buy informs me that the bombardment has begun.

At Brébant's we have nothing in the way of news except what is in the evening communiqué. We talk of the bombardment, which for the moment we believe intended to irritate rather than terrify the Parisian population—this in opposition to the statement of a German paper that the psychological moment for bombardment has arrived. *Psychological moment for bombardment,* now isn't that ferociously German?

We talk of the government's inertia, the discontent among the population caused by General Trochu's inactivity, his endless tergiversations, his do-nothing attitude. Renan says the general has no military ability, only the qualities of a politician and orator; and Nefftzer interrupts Renan to say that this is also the judgment of Rochefort, who has had a good deal to do with the general and admires him somewhat. The general's eloquence, in the beginning sounding like that of M. Prudhomme, seems to warm up and quicken after a few minutes into compelling and persuasive speech.

From Trochu the conversation leaps to Jules Simon, whom somebody, I don't remember who, calls an honest man; Nefftzer denies this and tells how he broke his word. Another speaks of the gross charlatanism of his lectures and the clown's tricks he uses in them. As for me, I simply suspect that he is a rotter, because of all the moral books he has written, *L'Ouvrière, Le Devoir,* etc. It is too obvious an exploitation of the sentimental rectitude of the public, and the idea of carrying out such an exploitation would never occur to an honest man. I might add that among the men of letters with whom I have had to do in my life I have known only one completely pure man, in the highest meaning of the word, and that is Flaubert—who, as we know, customarily writes books that are supposed to be immoral.

Finally someone compares Jules Simon to Cousin. This causes Renan to eulogize the minister—all right! The philosopher, I have nothing against that. But also the man of letters, calling him the first writer of the age! That we cannot take, Saint-Victor and I, which provokes a discussion and the trotting out of Renan's favorite thesis, that people can't write any more, that the language ought to be confined to the vocabulary of the seventeenth century, that since we are so fortunate as to have a classical language, we ought to hold to it, that right now in particular we must reattach ourselves to the language which conquered Europe, that we must seek in it the model for our style, and only there. We shout at him: "But what seventeenth-century language are you talking about? Is it Massillon's, or Saint-Simon's, or Bossuet's, or La Bruyère's? The languages of that time are so varied and different!"

I interject: "Any great writer of any time is to be recognized only by the fact that he has his own personal language, a language which to the informed reader is like a signature on each page, in every line, and by your theory you condemn the nineteenth century and all the centuries to come to have no more great writers."

In the face of argument Renan shifts his ground a bit, Jesuitically, as he is accustomed to do in discussions; and his remarks turn to a defense of the university, which has remade style, which, he says, has *purified* the language, after it was corrupted by the Restoration. At this point he interrupts himself to proclaim that Chateaubriand wrote badly.

Shouts and vociferations greet this odd critic's bourgeois assertion that old Maimbourg is a good writer and the prose of *Les Mémoires d'Outretombe* is detestable. He returns to his fixed idea that the vocabulary of the seventeenth century contains all the expressions we need today, even of a political nature; and he proposes writing a political article for *La Revue des Deux Mondes*, every word of which will come from the

Mémoires of Cardinal de Retz, boring us for a long time with the idea of this miserable little tour de force.

During this discussion I couldn't help laughing to myself as I thought of that seventeenth-century word, the word *gentleman,* which Renan used to characterize the super sacred *chic* of Jesus Christ.

Recently Bertrand the mathematician was lunching on the Avron plateau with Stoffel, the former military attaché to Prussia. Stoffel told him that he had just ordered the destruction of the crenelated wall of the Maison Blanche, which would no doubt cost a dozen men. "But," Bertrand said, "that's a place to use dynamite; you will save men." "Do you have some in your pocket?" "No, but if you will give me a horse, I'll bring you some within two hours." Needless to say, dynamite was not used.

The last train leaves at half past eight, the last omnibus at half past nine. Tonight I was forced to come home on foot, walking on the frozen snow with a starless sky overhead and the dark Seine at my side. Only two sounds broke Paris's sleep of death, the distant noise from the Quartermaster's Depot at Chaillot and the aeolian hum of telegraph wires carrying the stupid orders of National Defense.

Wednesday, December 28

Life is sad in this scene of removal, when the eyes no longer have the pleasure of the things they love, when everything that was hung on the walls has been taken down because of the cannon shocks, when unframed drawings are in cartons, and frames with their delightful carving and radiant gilt are wrapped in old newspapers, when books lie on the floor tied in bundles, when the room you live in looks like the back premises of a grocery store.

In these times many lower-middle-class people go to bed at seven and get up at nine. They are less hungry in bed, and they are not cold.

Potatoes are now twenty francs a bushel.

An expression and an image born of the siege: I hear one soldier say to another: "What I'll have waiting for me is a *fricassee of dry bread!*"

Thursday, December 29

Much has been written about the demoralization of the upper classes caused by the last regime. But I am especially struck by the demoralization of the working class by the luxury and well-being given them by the Emperor. I see this class completely flabby and spineless. Once virile, martial, daring, it has become talkative and extremely careful of its own hide. That blind love of battle which made it possible in any uprising to count on five hundred Parisians ready to fight for the joy of fighting, for the heroic feeling of being under fire, that love of battle has disappeared, as the government discovered in a few hours on October 31; and National Defense has found nothing but cowards in the battalions from La Villette.

The swinishness of the National Guard exceeds anything that a well-bred man's imagination might invent. I am on the train among three National Guards, whose every tipsy gesture is practically a blow for their neighbors, and who can't make a statement unless it is accompanied by the word *shit*. One is a stupid drunk; another, a teasing sly drunk; the third, a brutal drunk. During the journey the sly drunk tells the brutal drunk that the stationmaster has ordered his arrest when he gets off on account of the disturbance he made when he got on. I see the man pull out his knife, open it, and put it back in his pocket. I get off at the next station, not at all eager to be present when my neighbors leave the train.

Today there is a crowd above Belleville, trying to see something of the cannonade, which is unceasing. On the mounds, the little hills of the Montagnes d'Amérique, which are white with snow, small crowds of people stand out black against the sky. I take a path skirting the wooden brickworks which their owners are tearing down in order to forestall marauders. I make my way, not without the aid of my hands on the frozen ground, by a goat's path between excavations and little precipices, along green clay banks where some hooligans have made slides; I reach one of the little eroded peaks which in all this snow give the tormented landscape the appearance of a small reproduction of a volcanic region. A bird of prey wheels above my head, perhaps one of Bismarck's falcons sent to attack our pigeons. I can see nothing of the shelled area. My disappointed curiosity turns to Le Bourget, lighted by a pale ray of sunshine, to fires on the Prussian side, to a German helmet which I think I see shine out.

Contradicted by the indignation of some, by the incredulity of most, a rumor about evacuation of the Avron plateau begins to circulate. Then there arises, visible to all eyes, a sense of discouragement such as defeat of the Army of the Loire and the Army of the North did not bring, a state which it seemed nothing could produce.

Burty tells me today that a general, whose name I have forgotten, had exclaimed: "This is the first act of our agony!"

Late at night when you walk along the walls of Paris you are surprised to hear the crowing of roosters shut up as though behind a village wall; and you see no lights except at the windows of houses with the word *Hospital* over their doors.

Friday, December 30

Only today is the abandonment of the Avron plateau made official; and the inept military report which accompanied the announcement has killed the energetic resolution to resist. The idea of capitulation before the last mouthful of bread has been eaten—unthinkable yesterday—has entered the minds of the people, giving advance notice that the Prussians will be entering the city one of these days. The things that are happening betoken such incapacity in high places that the people may well make a mistake and take this incapacity for treason! If that happens, what a responsibility before history for this government and for Trochu, who with such ample means of resistance, with an armed mob of 500,000 men, have without a battle, without winning anything, without one noteworthy action, without even one noteworthy defeat, indeed without doing anything intelligent, audacious, or foolishly heroic, made the most shameful defense in recorded history, one that gives ringing testimony to the military nothingness of France today!

Truly, France is accursed! Everything goes against us. If the cold and bombardment continue, there will be no water with which to put out fires. All the water in the house is frozen, practically up to the chimney corner.

Saturday, December 31

Horsemeat, a meat that brings bad dreams and nightmares. Since I began living on it, I have had a series of sleepless nights.

Last night at the approach of 1871, the year which I am going to begin alone, my sad thoughts brought my beloved brother before me in the discomfort of my dreams. I saw him as he was during the last months of his life, as he was a year ago; and all the time that the deception of sleep lasted I felt again the cruel inner suffering that I experienced during his illness. I don't know how or why we were calling on Janin. During the whole long visit, which I would not and could not shorten, my pride suffered from his lack of attention, his absences of mind, his awkwardness, his entrance into death ahead of time, and I watched people's faces to see whether they were aware of what was bringing me to despair. And in my dream I had all those painful perceptions in an acute state, absolutely as though I were reliving them.

At last when I had managed to cut the visit short and was relieved to be able to take him away before people could realize what had happened to him, as we were going through the door and saying good-by, the poor child began to stammer. The sorrow I felt woke me up.

In the Paris streets death meets death: the undertaker's hearse crosses the path of the military bier. At the grille of the Madeleine I see three biers covered with Mobile overcoats and with wreaths of immortelles on top.

I am curious enough to go into the shop of Roos, the English butcher on the Boulevard Haussmann. I see all sorts of bizarre spoils. Hanging on the wall in the place of honor is the trunk of young Pollux, the elephant in the Zoo; and among nameless meats and exotic horns an employe offers camel kidneys for sale.

The proprietor is exhorting a circle of women: "It's forty francs a pound for filet and trunk. . . . Yes, forty francs. . . . You think that's high? But you know, I'm not sure that I'll manage to break even. I counted on 3,000 pounds, and it has only come to 2,300. . . . The feet, you want to know the price of the feet? . . . Twenty francs. . . . Other cuts run from eight to forty francs. . . . Oh, let me recommend the blood sausage. Don't forget that elephant blood is the most generous blood of all. His heart, did you know, weighed twenty-five pounds. . . . And there is onion, ladies, in my blood sausage."

I settle for two larks which I carry off for tomorrow's lunch.

As I leave I meet a bearded man who is haggling over a single duck at a fruit seller's on the Rue du Faubourg St. Honoré! It is Arsène Houssaye. He complains over the little knowledge members of the government have about people and quotes this pretty remark by Morny when he was annoyed by the pretensions of newspapermen to be able to run things: "Your journalists? But they haven't been ministers!" And the poet, who is a bit of a speculator, laments France's financial ruin, repeating a statement by Rouland, hot from the latter's mouth this morning: "If we may estimate the wealth of France at 1,500 billion, we must consider that today it has fallen to 900 billion."

New Year's Day in Paris this year is confined to a dozen miserable little stalls scattered here and there on the boulevards, where shivering merchants offer the frozen passers-by puppet caricatures of Bismarck.

At Voisin's this evening I see the famous elephant blood sausage again; indeed I dine on it.

1871

Sunday, January 1

What a sad day this is for me, the first day of the years that I am condemned to live alone.

The food we are getting and the perpetual interruption of sleep by the cannonade give me a migraine headache today that forces me to stay in bed.

Cold, bombardment, famine: these are the New Year's gifts of 1871. Never since there was a Paris has Paris had such a New Year's Day; in spite of that, drunkenness explodes its bestial joy on the frozen streets tonight.

This day makes me think that from the point of view of human history it is very interesting, very amusing, for one who is sceptical about progress to observe that in this year of 1871, in spite of so many years of civilization, so much preaching about the brotherhood of man, and so many treaties to establish a balance of power in Europe, brute force can still assert itself and prevail with as little hindrance as in the time of Attila.

Monday, January 2

Every day poor women become ill from cold or fatigue or starvation during the hours they have to stand in line for the distribution of meat.

An interesting subject for meditation. All Europe would have opposed us if we had been the stronger and had wished to establish our frontier on the Rhine, which is after all our ethnographic boundary! The victorious Germans are getting ready to take Alsace and Lorraine, to annihilate France by this amputation, and all Europe applauds! Why? Can it be that nations are like individuals? That they don't like aristocrats?

Wednesday, January 4

Still ill today, I spend the whole day in bed in a vague half-sleep. In my head float formless ideas, ready in an instant to become dreams but stopped on the threshhold of sleep by a detonation from Mont Valérien or by the triumphant cackle of three hens which I have in a cage near my little fire of green wood. These three lively creatures are my last line of defense against today's *nag* meat and tomorrow's hunger.

When you stand in line at the Paris butcher shops, one time they'll offer you a package of candles in place of meat, another time, hot spiced wine.

Thursday, January 5

Today the bombardment has begun on our side. You can see nothing; your view is stopped on the other side of the ramparts by a thick fog, but in the white opaqueness you can hear formidable detonations. I was listening to this noise and watching in Gavarni's garden with several people when we heard a shell whine overhead. Someone came at once to tell us that a shell had just fallen in M. Hardy's courtyard.

In the afternoon I come back again to wander around in the Auteuil cemetery. An occasional whistle of shells; then suddenly two men, who are thirty feet ahead of me, hastily fall back toward me, one of them carrying in his hand a piece of lead weighing more than two pounds which has just missed them. There is talk of people wounded at Billancourt and Javel. However, everybody there, men and women, refuses to go away and gives proof of fearless curiosity. The cannonade of the last two months has habituated the Parisian population to the cannons; and far from frightening them, the bombardment seems to push them, albeit nervously, to a disdain for danger.

Friday, January 6

Walking in the garden, where in the warmth of the thaw a tender green is beginning to push through the white snow and ice, I constantly hear the whistling of shells, sounding like the howl of a heavy autumn wind. Since yesterday this has come to seem so natural to the population that nobody pays any attention to it; for example, in the garden next door two little children stop their play at each explosion and say in their still half-stammering voices: "There went one," then quietly continue their game.

Shells begin to fall on the Rue Boileau and the Rue La Fontaine. Tomorrow they will no doubt fall on my house; if they don't kill me, they will destroy all that I still love, my house, my bibelots, my books.

Standing at the door of every house, half terrified, half curious, women and children watch the medical corpsmen go by in their white blouses with red crosses on the arms, carrying stretchers, mattresses, and pillows.

Saturday, January 7

The suffering of Paris under siege? A joke for two months. But in the third month the joke turned to privation. Today the joke is at an end and we are moving rapidly to famine, or at least for the moment to universal gastritis. The ration of horsemeat weighing 330 grams, bones included, allotted for the nourishment of two people over a three-day period equals the lunch of one ordinary appetite. Prices of chickens, of edible meat-pies are out of reach. It is impossible to get hold of vegetables to make up for the lack of meat; a little turnip costs eight sous and you have to pay seven francs for a liter of onions. Nobody mentions butter any more; and fat, except for what is made of candles or axle grease, has disappeared. As for the two foods on which underprivileged populations maintain themselves—potatoes and cheese—cheese is only a memory, and you have to fight to get potatoes at twenty francs a bushel. Coffee, wine, and bread make up the diet of most of Paris. [See Illustration 3.]

This evening at the station I ask for a ticket to Auteuil; I am told that beginning today trains will not go beyond Passy. Auteuil is no longer part of Paris.

Sunday, January 8

Last night behind my curtains I wondered if there were a hurricane. I got up and opened my window. The hurricane was the unceasing and continuous whine of shells passing over my house.

I go out for a moment to look at the face of Auteuil. In front of the station street urchins in military caps are selling to National Guards the shell fragments which they continually go out and gather up near the cemetery.

Curiosity-seekers, but not very many and not inclined to venture beyond the station. In the streets patrols of National Guards, customs officers, and forestry officers who melt away into the wine shops. Many gentlemen who are moving away with traveling cases in their hands. I see a very old lady with white curls painfully trying to get away on the arm of a workman who is carrying her overnight case. People are standing in front of the house of Mongelard, the pastrymaker; his house had its chimney carried away by a shell yesterday, but he is heroically making pastry again today. Everybody is on his doorstep alert for a shell, women having forgotten to finish dressing, some of them still in nightcaps.

In the little Italian-looking square small girls, shielded by the entrance to the church, are watching the shells fall at the end of the boulevard. At the huge barrack-like Sainte Périne building, with all the windows closed and no sign of life behind the panes, it would seem that the aged inmates have been evacuated or taken down to the cellar.

I am worn and weary: I eat so badly and I sleep so little. The closest thing to an ordinary night since the bombardment began would be a night spent on board ship during a naval battle.

Monday, January 9

Nobody on our boulevard; just National Guards going to their posts and stretcher-bearers on their way to the Point du Jour.

The omnibus is about to shorten its run, ending its trip at the Pont de Grenelle, and I watch them move out from the depot, where a shell last night killed eight horses and wounded eight others, five of which had to be shot.

At the Passy railroad station groups of men talking about shell bursts, groups of women exchanging recipes for making something out of nothing; a young infantryman showing where a bullet is supposed to have ricocheted off his arm. At the shop of the woman newspaper dealer, who is not there, a

National Guard artilleryman leafs through the pictures in *Omnibus*, as he leans on two loaves of ration bread, which are strapped together. On a bench a divisional chaplain, with a white cross on his chest attached by a broad, red-bordered ribbon, polishes his glasses and flirts with a woman; he has the evasive looks and silly smiles of Got in *Il ne faut jurer de rien*.

Tuesday, January 10

The gunfire this morning is so rapid that it seems as regular as a steam-engine piston.

As I ride into Paris with a sailor from the Point du Jour battery, he tells me that yesterday there was such a hail of shells that they had to endure seventeen salvos lying on the ground without being able to return the fire. After that they fired a whole battery and blew up an ammunition dump. In spite of the terrible fire they so far have had only three wounded: one with his thigh severed who died, another seriously wounded, and a seaman who had his eyes and beard burned when a shell burst in front of his face.

There are a good many of us at Brébant's this evening. Everybody who has been under bombardment wants to hear what has happened to other people. Charles Edmond gives a fantastic description of the bombs that rained on the Luxembourg. Because a shell fell in the Place Saint Sulpice, Saint-Victor deserts his lodgings on the Rue Furstenberg at night. Renan has emigrated to the Right Bank.

The conversation concentrates on the despair of the high brass in the army, their lack of energetic determination, the discouragement which they spread to the soldiers. Somebody tells of a meeting at which poor Trochu threatened to blow out his brains because of the cowardly or undisciplined attitude of the old generals. Louis Blanc sums things up when he says: "The army has lost France; it doesn't want her to be saved by the civilians."

Tessié du Motay tells of two pieces of stupidity on the part of our generals which he claims to have witnessed. At the time of the December 21 affair he saw General Vinoy, who had been ordered to take Chelles at eleven o'clock, arrive on the scene at two; he saw him arrive at two, accompanied by a fantastic and tipsy staff, and ask where Chelles was. Du Motay was also present—the same day, I think—when General Le Flô arrived on the Avron plateau; he also asked whether that really was the Avron plateau.

This same Du Motay asserts that, after our complete success on December 2, the army had received the order to advance when someone came to tell Trochu that we were completely out of munitions.

This makes Saint-Victor proclaim rather verbosely that we need a Saint-Just. Someone tells of a threat to burn Paris if it does not surrender, which is supposed to have been received by the Ministry today.

In a corner Berthelot levels charges, comic in their exaggeration, against Alphand, who, he says, is responsible for everything that has gone wrong—this in a fairly original way by refusing nothing that was suggested to Ferry, but doing it himself as badly as possible. He mentions the salting down of meat, which went bad; the setting up of hospitals in the Luxembourg, where the wounded froze; the digging of trenches at Avron, and many other sorry items which, he says in his fiercely unjust antipathy, will get Alphand a job as William of Prussia's Haussmann.

These sad remarks are punctuated by the mournful snorts of Renan, who predicts that we shall witness scenes of the Apocalypse.

Wednesday, January 11

Fleeing the bombardment, frightened hordes of women and children burdened with packages go through Auteuil and Passy, their shadows running along the walls, on which posters announce the taking up of temporary cemetery concessions.

From my window this evening I see a huge fire, which seems to be devouring the Issy fortress.

Thursday, January 12

I make a tour of the bombarded areas of Paris. No terror or fright. Everybody appears to be living normally; café proprietors, with admirable sang-froid, are replacing windows broken by exploding shells. However, among the people coming and going you do now and then meet a man who is carrying his clock in his arms; and the streets are full of handcarts dragging sorry-looking furniture toward the center of the city. On them occasionally you see a poor old crippled man who can't walk.

The vents of the cellars are stopped up with sacks. One shop has an ingenious protection made of layers of planks reinforced with sandbags to the level of the first floor. On the steps of Saint Sulpice furious voices are accusing the generals of treason. They are taking up the paving stones in the Place du Panthéon. A shell has carried away the capital of one of the Ionic columns of the Law School. In the Rue Saint Jacques perforated walls and scarred spots from which little pieces of plaster are constantly falling. Enormous blocks of cut stone, part of the entablature of the Sorbonne, providing a barricade in front of that ancient building. But where the bombardment really hits the eye is on the Boulevard Saint Michel, where all the houses at an angle to the streets parallel with the Thermes de Julien have been scarred by shell bursts. At the corner of the Rue Soufflot the entire balcony of the first-floor apartment has been torn away from the stone and dangles menacingly.

From Passy to Auteuil the snowy road is rose-colored as it reflects the fires at Saint Cloud.

Friday, January 13

You have to do justice to the Parisian population—and admire them! It is astonishing that they do not break the windows and rough up the merchants and their merchandise in those establishments where insolent show windows tactlessly recall to the *starving* people that the rich, having money, can always procure game, fowl, and other delicacies. That is reason for astonishment. But no! At most a pleasantry or a cynical remark in which there is no anger.

I have only seen a bit of indignation in front of Hédé's bakery on the Rue Montmartre; he is the only baker who still makes white bread and croissants. The common people, accustomed to white bread but now condemned to bread fit only for dogs, seemed to suffer from this exhibition of privilege, which is purchased after all by hours of standing in line.

When I once read in Marat's journal the furious denunciations of the *People's Orator* against grocers, I thought them a maniacal exaggeration. Today I realize that Marat was right. This business, completely *National-Guardized,* is a business of hoarders and crooks. Personally I don't think there would be anything wrong in hanging up two or three of these slick chiselers in their own show windows, for I am sure if that were done the cost of a pound of sugar would no longer go up at the rate of two sous an hour. Perhaps in time of revolution a few discriminating executions are the only practical means of holding the rise of food prices within reasonable limits.

At Peters' this evening I saw the maître d'hôtel's carving knife make two hundred slices out of a leg of veal. Two hundred slices at six francs a slice, that's 1,200 francs. Let's not dissolve in pity over the sorry lot of the restaurant keeper.

A remark overheard next to me: "Our wives have abandoned us this evening." "So much the better; we can go to look at the Panthéon and the bombardment." Visits to the bombarded areas have taken the place of the theatre.

Tonight I passed part of the night at my window, kept awake by the cannonade and rifle fire around Issy. In the silence of the night it seemed close, very close, and with the heightened imagination of fearful, troubled hours, it seemed to me for a moment that the Prussians had taken the fortress, which was not firing, and were attacking the ramparts.

Saturday, January 14

M. Dumas, the industrialist, was telling me today some sorry details about the behavior of the Breton Mobile officers. His brother-in-law has a very fine estate at Neuilly. Some soldiers and officers, among them M. Legonidec, were quartered on the estate. These gentlemen did not content themselves with building fires in the middle of the bedrooms; when they left they took away twenty-five pairs of sheets which had been lent them, and M. Legonidec had fifteen potted palms taken from the greenhouse and sent as a New Year's gift to a tart. M. Dumas made a complaint and got an order from the General Staff for return of the sheets and the palms.

Universal suffrage in the election of Mobile officers has been a great mistake. They have elected *good fellows*, that is, officers who, when they are not encouraging everything, prevent nothing.

Not having the courage to go to Paris and having nothing to eat, I kill a blackbird in my garden for dinner. When I have thrown the bird, its wings stiff, on my table—now I don't believe in metempsychosis—I come somehow or other to make an association between the memory of my brother and the dead bird. I recall its arrival every evening at dusk, the sharp whistle by which it seemed to announce itself, the two or three forays across the garden it made with its pretty, quick flight. I recall its pause of a few seconds on a branch, always the same one, of a sycamore next to the house from which it looked out motionless and enigmatic. Then its sudden disappearance into the shadows and darkness. There came to me, then, like a superstitious belief, the feeling that something of my brother had passed into this little winged creature, this airy creature of mourning. I felt a vague fright over having destroyed with my rifle something friendly from beyond this world which was watching over the safety of my house and me. It's stupid, it's crazy, it's absurd, but that was my obsession all evening!

Sunday, January 15

The most frightful cannonade that the southeast [*sic*] rampart has yet heard. "It's a real pounding!" a man of the people says as he runs by. The house, shaken to its foundations, pours out all the accumulated dust of its ledges and ceilings.

In spite of the frost and the biting wind there is always a crowd of the curious at the Trocadéro. In the Champs Elysées heaps of felled trees onto which, before they are hoisted on wagons, a swarm of children precipitate themselves, armed with hatchets, knives, anything that will cut, and hack off pieces of bark with which they fill their pockets, aprons, hands, while in the hole left by the tree you see the heads of old women who are busy unearthing what remains of the roots with picks.

In the midst of this devastation a few men and women promenaders who give the impression of nonchalantly taking their before-dinner constitutional as in former days.

In a boulevard café seven or eight young Mobile officers parading and coquetting before a whore whose hair is dyed in the Venetian style, as they draw up an imaginary witty menu for the evening meal.

As property-owner my situation is a strange one. Every evening as I come home on foot my eyes try to see from as far away as they can whether my house is still standing. Then when I am sure, as I approach to the accompaniment of whistling shells, I examine it in detail and am astonished to find neither hole nor scar on my building—of which, by the way, the door is left half open so that I won't have to wait to get in.

Monday, January 16

King William's birthday. The cannons kept me from sleeping all night and I was still in bed at eleven, drugged with fatigue. In the midst of thunderous sounds from the Mortemart battery I noticed a noise overhead and supposed that Pélagie had just moved a piece of furniture. A few minutes later Pélagie came into my bedroom and told me jauntily that a shell had just fallen next door, in the room right on the other side of my wall. The shell, or rather two shell fragments, went through the roof and fell into a bedroom where a little boy, whose chilblains kept him from walking, was in bed.

The child received no hurt except for fright over the fallen plaster.

Today there begins distribution of bread, a piece of which will be a true curiosity for future collectors: bread in which you find pieces of straw.

Tuesday, January 17

They say that a Prussian battery has been set up at the Porte Jaune, near Saint Cloud, which will make Auteuil untenable in a few days.

Wednesday, January 18

Today the ration is 400 grams per person. Imagine that there are people condemned to live on so little! Women were weeping in the line at the Auteuil bakery.

Now it is not just a few stray shells as on previous days but a hail of lead, which bit by bit surrounds and hems us in. All around me explosions which burst fifty, twenty-five feet away: at the railroad station, on the Rue Poussin, where a woman's foot was blown off, in the house next door which had already had its first experience day before yesterday. And while I am at the window picking out the Meudon batteries with my glasses, a shell fragment almost hits me and spatters mud against the door of my house.

At three o'clock I am passing the Etoile barrier and, seeing troops filing by, I stop. The monument to our victories, illuminated by a shaft of sunlight; the distant cannon fire; the immense parade, the last bayonets of which send sparkling light under the obelisk, all this was something theatrical, lyrical, epic. A great and proud spectacle, this army going to the cannons which we hear; among the men are white-bearded civilian soldiers, the fathers of families; beardless faces, who are their sons; and in the open ranks women carrying the rifles of their husbands and lovers slung over their shoulders. You cannot express the picturesqueness the war took on with this civilian multitude convoyed by hacks, unpainted omnibuses, moving vans for Erard pianos, all transformed into military supply vehicles.

There were of course some drunks, some merry songs clashing with the national anthem, and always a bit of that cutting up of which French heroism cannot rid itself, but all in all the spectacle was moving and grandiose.

Thursday, January 19

All Paris has gone out of doors and walks about waiting for news.

Rows of people at the straw-strewn doors of hospitals. Before the municipal building on the Rue Drouot a crowd so packed that, as a man of the people said, "you couldn't toss in a hazelnut." In National Guard uniform Marchal, the big painter, whom the siege has not slimmed down, stops vehicles from passing. Good news circulates. The first newspapers arrive, announcing the capture of Montretout. People are joyous. Those with newspapers read them to the groups that form around them. Everybody goes joyfully off to dinner; all around you is the murmured account of the happy details of today's battle.

I go to see Burty, whom the shells have chased from the Rue Watteau and who is now provisionally lodged on the boulevard above the Lacroix bookstore. He saw Rochefort around four o'clock and got the good news from him along with a rather nice story. During the fog Trochu complained about not being able to see his divisions. "Thank God,"

Rochefort exclaimed, "if he saw them, he would call them back!"

D'Hervilly, who is there, still has his pretty railing wit of other days. He gives us a droll and whimsical picture of the Asnières bridge crossed under a green autumn sky by Hyacinthe, whose nose only was visible but who had the necks of two bottles of liquor sticking out of his pockets as he brought them back from his country house. Then he tells us of his visit to the good old fellow in *mammalogy* at the Zoo; he was in his office with his mounted stuffed birds and from time to time passed his hand lovingly over a stuffed deer—a pretty little Hoffmanesque anecdote.

Burty showed me a Japanese painting of great interest. It is a study, on several panels, of the decomposition of a body after death. It has a German macabre quality which I did not expect to find in the art of the Far East.

I am back on the boulevard at ten o'clock. The same crowd as before dinner. Deep dark groups in the unlit night. Everybody standing watch before the kiosks and, in a hope that has become a little anxious, waiting for the third edition of *Le Soir*, which is late in appearing.

Madame Masson was telling me of the visit she made to young Philippe Chevalier at the Ministry of Foreign Affairs hospital before his death. The rooms still had the mirrors, the chandeliers, the gilt decoration of Legislative Corps parties; and the dying man, who remembered those affairs, said to Madame Masson: "Right here where I am they had the buffet."

Friday, January 20

Trochu's dispatch last night seems to me to be the beginning of the end; it poisons my stomach.

Paris under Siege

I hear National Guards running past my gate uttering these words: "Since I'm going to die anyhow . . ."

I send part of my bread over to a neighbor, a poor National Guard who is recovering from illness and whom Pélagie found lunching on two sous worth of pickles.

At the Maillot gate a crowd, less numerous, however, than the one that waited at the Trône barrier after the Champigny incident. Everybody with a look of sad foreboding, though still unaware of the sorry *fiasco*. Pell-mell with the ambulances and the mule litters men of the National Guard infantry companies march in, a bit stragglingly, without music, morose, all-in, harassed, covered with mud. From one of these companies issues the stridently ironic voice of a returning soldier who tosses out to the stupefied crowd: "Well, aren't you going to sing a song of victory?"

Someone hails me from the top of a returning vehicle. It is Hirsch, that Jewish harbinger of misfortune who told me of the Le Bourget disaster at La Chapelle gate. He shouts to me in a gay tone: "It's all over; the army is coming back!" And in a bantering tone he tells me what he has seen and heard, things that seem to go beyond the limits of human ineptitude.

The crowd becomes silent, withdraws into sadness. Wives of National Guards wait on benches in poses of despair. Into this crowd, who are glued to the sad spectacle, who will not go away, who keep waiting, there hop two men, each with a leg amputated, displaying their brand-new crosses as they go along on crutches. People look after them for a long time with emotion.

I pass by the Princess's house, where the grille is open as on the days when we used to come there by cab for intelligent pleasure. From there I go to the cemetery. He died seven months ago today.

In Paris, on the boulevard, I encounter anew the despairing discouragement of a great nation which has done much to save itself by its own efforts, its resignation, its morale, and feels that it has been lost by military stupidity.

I have dinner at Peters' next to three of Franchetti's scouts. Theirs is absolute despair under the mask of irony, the special form that French despair takes: "We've had it, we've had it!" They speak of the Army of Paris which is unwilling to fight any longer, of the heroic core which kept it together killed at Champigny and at Montretout, and always, always, they speak of their leaders' incapacity.

It is odd that in the situation I am in, in the grief that devours me, I still have a cowardly desire to live, and on the way home I seek to avoid the shell whistling by me which might bring me deliverance!

Saturday, January 21

I am struck more than ever by the silence, the silence of death, which disaster brings in a great city. Today you can no longer hear Paris live.

Every face is that of a sick man or a convalescent. You see only thin, drawn, pale faces; you see only yellowy pallor like horse fat.

In front of me on the omnibus are two women in full mourning: mother and daughter. The black-gloved hands of the mother are constantly twisting and moving mechanically to her red eyes, which are unable to weep any more, while a tear, slow to fall, dries from time to time at the edge of the daughter's eyes, which are raised to heaven.

On the Place de la Concorde near the tattered flags and withered immortelles on the Strasbourg statue a company is encamped, blackening the walls of the Tuileries garden with their fires, their heavy knapsacks making a sort of shield for the balustrade. As you go among them you hear words like these: "Yes, our poor little adjutant is being buried tomorrow."

I go up to the Luxembourg Palace, to Julie's house; she reads me a letter from her son-in-law saying that in the Montretout battle he had to drive the fleeing National Guards and Mobiles back with a stick.

We have seen the pork-butcher shops become empty places one by one, decorated only by yellow pottery and aucuba plants with leaves veined like white marble; the butcher shops have drawn curtains behind padlocked grilles. Today it is the bakery shops' turn, and they have become dark holes with hermetically sealed show windows.

Burty had it from Rocheforte that when Chanzy saw his troops flee, he charged them sword in hand; then, seeing that blows and abuse were of no use, he ordered the artillery to fire on them.

A curious and very symptomatic phrase. A girl whose heels clip-clop behind me on the Rue Saint Nicholas says to me: "Sir, will you come up to my room in return for a piece of bread?"

Sunday, January 22

This morning as shells fall all around me, I move my most precious possessions, fearful lest a shell kill the single horse of the moving van, fearful lest a shell kill or wound one of those poor devils who are helping me move.

I am at Burty's; he has put at my disposition a part of the apartment he is occupying on the boulevard at the corner of the Rue Vivienne. He helps me move with a charming friendliness which makes me repent certain unjust ideas I have had about him.

Suddenly a frenzied call to arms. We go out. We are told that there is fighting at the Hôtel de Ville. In the street there is effervescence, agitation; in the midst of it, however, I see policemen tranquilly looking at pictures in the stereopticons. On the Rue de Rivoli we learn that it is all over. We see General Vinoy pass by rapidly under escort of some dragoons and riflemen. And while the infantrymen from Puteaux, all garlanded with bits of garden trellis, go back up the Rue de Rivoli, cannons deploy on the quay and move toward the Hôtel de Ville.

In the evening the boulevard takes on the menacing look of revolutionary times: Discussions ready to come to blows. Parisian Mobiles accusing Trochu's men of having fired on them without provocation. Women shouting that the common people are being murdered. These are the last convulsions of our agony.

Monday, January 23

A strange sight! In the restaurants that are still open the customers bring their own bread under their arms, as a result of a notice posted yesterday stating that restaurant keepers can no longer furnish bread to their customers.

Here and there an old, decomposing notice mentioning Le Bourget or the Avron plateau; on our walls we have a consecutive history of our reverses.

Well, so much the worse! When I think of the death of Regnault, that promising young painter, I find a crying injustice in the equal obligation for defense which exposes to bullet fire the best-endowed equally with the most accomplished imbeciles.

I go to see Duplessis at the Bibliothèque Royale; and in the darkness of the Print Room, where my brother and I passed so many hours, an employe has to tell me to watch out for a basin of water or a pile of boxes. Today it is a cellar where all these precious objects which are the envy of Europe are piled up as if for removal—and I am afraid that is what may happen.

Tuesday, January 24

Vinoy's replacing Trochu is like changing doctors for a man on the point of death.

Today a frightening calm. No more cannon fire. Why? This silence seems to me to be a bad sign.

The bread we now get is of such quality that my last surviving hen—a funny, speckly hen—complains, cries, and scolds when I give her some and only decides to eat it when night falls.

On the boulevard opposite the Opéra Comique I come upon a crowd which fills the street and bars the way to the omnibuses. I wonder if there is another riot. No, all those heads in the air, all those arms pointing at something, all those women's umbrellas being shaken, all this anxious and hopeful waiting is on account of a pigeon lying on the pipe of one of the theatre chimneys.

In the crowd I run into Christophe the sculptor, who tells me that overtures for surrender are being made.

I call on Burty to take him to dinner at Brébant's. While I wait for him, his wife tells me of the horrible material suffering of the artists at this moment, the suffering of Bracquemond, who has such an appetite that he could eat a leg of lamb all by himself and who is dying of weakness in order to prevent death by starvation of his pretty little wife, who has as big an appetite as he has. She tells me of a cab trip with Madame Meurice, during which the two of them in an access of good-heartedness saw and overcame Charles Blanc, extracted an order for an important commission almost by force from Rousseau the porcelain merchant, captivated dry Madame Simon with the open black gloves, and finally won for the engraver the position of curator at Sèvres. When I asked how much Rousseau had paid Bracquemond for his dinner service, she told me that Rousseau had made 55,000 francs from it but had only paid 600 francs for it—600 francs which Bracquemond had used to bury his mother.

At Brébant's in the little antechamber before you come to the large dining room everybody has collapsed in exhaustion on the easy chairs and sofa, talking in low tones about the sad events of the day and about the morrow which awaits us.

People wonder if Trochu is not crazy. In this connection Berthelot says he has heard of a notice destined for the Mobiles that was printed but not posted in which Trochu speaks of God and the Virgin in terms a mystic would use.

Over in a corner someone remarks that what is especially criminal about men like Trochu and Favre is that from the beginning they despaired to their intimates and yet in their speeches and proclamations gave to the multitude a belief in, a certainty of, deliverance, which they allowed to continue to the very end. "There's danger in that," Du Mesnil continues; "you don't know whether when surrender is signed it won't be rejected by the virile part of Paris." Renan and Nefftzer make signs of disagreement. "Take care, I'm not talking about revolutionary elements but about the energetic, middle-class elements, about the infantry who have fought and want to fight some more and cannot accept giving up their rifles and cannons right off the bat."

Dinner has been announced but nobody has heard. Berthelot tells of an interview with Ferry, that monstrous fool, who had the insolent stupidity to answer his complaint about breadlines set up in places where shells were falling and the unfortunate women were in danger by saying: "Well, they don't have to go there!"

We sit down at table. Everybody pulls out his piece of bread. Someone says: "Do you know what Bauër has called Trochu? An Ollivier on horseback!"

We eat our soup. Berthelot gives the real reason for our defeat: "No, it wasn't superior artillery, as has been said; it was just the one thing I'm going to tell you about. This is it. When a Prussian staff officer is ordered to move an army corps to such and such a position at such and such a time, he takes out his maps and studies the country, the terrain; he estimates the time it will take each corps to cover its route. If he sees a slope, he takes out his—an instrument the name of which I can't remember—and takes the delay into account. So before he goes to bed he has found the ten routes by which the troops will come out at the time set. Our staff officer doesn't do anything like that; in the evening he has his pleasure and next day when he arrives in the field, he asks if his troops have arrived and where the attack is to begin. Since the beginning of the war—and that was the reason for our defeat —from Wissembourg to Montretout we were never able to mass troops at a given point at a given time."

They bring in a saddle of mutton.

"Oh," Hébrard says, "they'll be serving us the shepherd at our next meal! This saddle of mutton is a fine saddle of dog."

"Dog, you say it's dog?" Saint-Victor bursts out with the whimpering voice of an angry child. "Now, waiter, this isn't dog, is it?"

"But this is the third time you've had dog here!"

"No, that's not true. Monsieur Brébant is an honest man;

he would tell us . . . and dog is impure meat," he says with comic horror. "Horse, yes, but not dog!"

"But I have never eaten such good mutton," Nefftzer says with his mouth full. "Now if Brébant gave you rat. . . . I have eaten that, it's very good. Its taste is a cross between pork and partridge."

Meanwhile Renan, who has appeared preoccupied and anxious, becomes pale and green, throws down his money on the table, and disappears.

"You know Vinoy," someone says to Du Mesnil. "What kind of man is he and what is he going to do?"

"Vinoy is a sly one: I think he won't do anything but play the policeman!"

Then Nefftzer breaks out against journalism and journalists. He has become absolutely apoplectic and his Germanic speech, strangling at times in anger, growls at the ineptitude, stupidity, and ignorance of his colleagues, whom he accuses of having brought on the war and of having made it such a disaster.

Hébrard has pulled a piece of paper from his pocket: "Listen, gentlemen, here is a letter from M. Dudevant, George Sand's husband, asking for a decoration and citing his cuckoldry as a reason. Yes, gentlemen, his cuckoldry: *domestic misfortunes which belong to history.*" An Homeric laugh greets this piece of Prudhommesque buffoonery.

Then the seriousness of the situation leads the diners to a discussion of how the Prussians will treat us. There are some who think they will empty the museums. Berthelot says they will carry off our industrial materiel. Then somehow the conversation veers off to a big discussion of coloring matter and *turkish pink,* after which it gets back on the track. Nefftzer, in opposition to everybody else, takes the stand that the Prussians will seek to astonish us by their generosity and magnanimity. Amen!

After we leave Brébant's, on the boulevard the word *capitulation*, which it would have been dangerous to utter a few days ago, is on everybody's tongue.

Wednesday, January 25

Nothing of the vigor and feverish agitation characteristic of the passers-by a few days ago. A population, inert and beaten like a bird, dragging along under a grey sky where heavy flakes of snow continually fall.

There is no longer room for the absurdities of hope. People are lined up before the only shops that have anything left to eat—the chocolate shops. And you see soldiers who are triumphant at having conquered a pound of chocolate.

Thursday, January 26

The shells are getting closer. New batteries seem to be revealed. Shells fall every minute on the railroad line, and people cross our boulevard crawling on hands and knees.

In everyone you witness the painful adjustment of mind by which people are coming to accept the idea, the shame, of surrender. However, there are some energetic men and women who still resist. I heard some poor women this morning who were still shouting in the breadlines: "Let them cut our rations down even more; we are ready to suffer anything rather than surrender!"

Uneasy and agitated crowds on the boulevard.

Friday, January 27

This morning I go to Regnault's funeral. There is an enormous crowd. In weeping over the corpse of this talented young man, people are weeping for the burial of France. What a horrible thing this equality in the face of brutal death by cannonade or rifle fire, which strikes down genius and imbecile alike, the precious existence and the useless one!

I had thought of having him do a portrait of my brother like the one he did for Countess Nils Barck. My brother will not live again through his young talent, for which I heard the muted *De Profundis* played to the sound of bugles and the roll of drums. I saw a young girl in widow's habit pass behind the coffin like a shadow. I am told she was his fiancée.

After I leave there I go into Goupil's shop, where there is exhibited unframed a watercolor by the dead man in which Morocco looks like something out of *The Thousand and One Nights*.

The firing has stopped. I go for a turn in the Auteuil area. A woman shouts to a neighbor: "We are still here in the cellar but we're going to come up."

Holes in roofs, scars on the fronts of buildings, but really remarkably little material damage from all that hurricane of iron that passed over our heads. Most striking is a tongue of land between the viaduct and the Auteuil cemetery. It is full of big craters three meters across where shells fell so close together that they duplicated on a large scale the regular arrangement of holes which the barricade commission built at the Point du Jour.

Near the Michel Ange gate I climb up on the viaduct. A hundred houses are burning in Saint Cloud: it is the bonfire by which the Prussians celebrate their triumph. A sick soldier leaning on the parapet bursts out: "It's a shame to see that!" At the Point du Jour gate they are loading trucks with shining new copper-pointed shells, shells which will not be used.

As I come home I have to be wary of leaping, drunken Mobiles who are celebrating our defeat by dancing as the night comes down.

Saturday, January 28

The journalists are happy, and they seem almost proud of what the Republic has done to defend the nation. They proudly cite the homage paid our heroism by the Prussians and even hope that Trochu will be recognized by them as a great warrior.

In contrast to the cowardly joy of our troops it is fine to see the desolation expressed by the whole being of a sailor who goes by with his bundle under his arm.

People never stop talking about the incapacity of the government in general, or the stupidity of each member of the government individually. Charles Edmond was telling me about hearing this remarkable piece of ineptitude issue from the mouth of that old warhorse of journalism, Emmanuel Arago: "We're cooking up a pretty surprise for the Prussians, one they don't expect; they'll be nicely caught when they try to enter Paris." This man's intelligence being known to his hearers, they expected the use of Greek fire. It wasn't even that. After making them wait a moment for him to continue, Arago came out with this: "The Prussians will find no government with which to negotiate, for we shall have gone away!"

I go about in the bombarded areas. Everywhere holes, scars, cracks; but except for the destruction of one pillar of La Balayeuse store on the Place Mouffetard nothing very frightful. A population determined to live in cellars could very well and without great danger endure a month of heavy bombardment. In these districts you run into little handcarts bringing back furniture; traffic and life seem to be reborn there.

A man in a white overcoat hands a shell to the omnibus conductor: "Hold that while I get on, but be careful! For God's sake, be careful!"

Burty has confirmed the story of Trochu's mystical notice about which Berthelot told us at the Brébant dinner—an order for the holding of a novena to the Virgin, which was to be followed by a miracle. How ironic it is, if true, that the safety of France was placed in the hands of a man who belonged in an institution!

Sunday, January 29

The Mobiles return and pass under my windows to the jibes of National Guards scattered along the boulevard.

I go to see the naval battery at the Point du Jour. All of Gavarni's garden is cut up with trenches, pierced on either side by deep round holes, at the bottom of which unexploded shells are buried. A National Guard with a pick, escorted by his wife, who is bent over under the weight of a heavy sack, digs up a shell that had disappeared into the frozen ground. Poor Gavarni garden! The tripe merchant's chalet has had its roof pierced by a shell which seems to have made a shambles of the interior of the fragile structure. The last of the fir trees in the little green dell are lying on the ground; and a stovepipe sticks out of the ivy-garlanded roof of the *al fresco room*, which has been turned into a casemate.

I go on toward Versailles. In this area, I must admit, the bombardment was serious. All you see is houses full of shell holes, houses lashed by shell bursts, and the last ten on each side of the road nearest the ramparts are all open to the sky. At Number 222 a shell which went right through the shop of a certain Praisidial—a pretty name for a stage revolutionary—exploded in a room where they show you the spot where it cut off a man's head as with a knife. On the other side, in a house which has crumbled to the ground, the roof has fallen down just like a tarpaulin thrown over an entry hall under construction.

But there is nothing comparable to the destruction at the corner of the circular road known as Boulevard Murat. There are no houses left, only fragments of wall, pieces of façade holding up a bit of stairway, heaps of debris in which a window without glass remains standing, you can't see how; formless mounds of brick, stones, slate on which you see an eviscerated mattress, a jumble of debris, and in the middle a big bloodstain, the blood of a Mobile with the top of his head sliced off.

Indescribable disorder. Mobiles who have been waiting two or three hours leaning on their guns or lying in the openings of the wire entanglement; I finally see them break in the fronts of shops and the doors of houses in order to find shelter.

I would not want members of the government to be either hanged or shot; I would only ask that they be sentenced to make honorable amends in dunce caps on the former Place de Grève from sunup to sundown. Yet I read that they have had the incredible effrontery to offer themselves for reelection!

Monday, January 30

Oh, the hard consequence of surrender, which will turn the next Assembly into those twelve burghers of Calais, who, rope around their necks, had to submit to Edward VI's conditions! But what angers me most is the Jesuitry—never was word more accurate—the Jesuitry of these rulers, who, hav-

ing succeeded in placing the word *Agreement* instead of *Surrender* at the head of this dishonoring treaty, hope like sinister, cowardly deceivers to conceal from France the extent of
her misfortunes and her shame. Bourbaki excluded from the
armistice, which is supposed to be general! The agreement
about unsealed letters! And all the secret shame which the
negotiators still conceal and hide from us, which the future
will gradually unveil! Could French hands have signed that?
Truly, they are proud of having been made the jailers and
provisioners of their army; how worthy of them! Don't they
understand that the apparent mildness is a Bismarck trap? To
shut up in Paris 100,000 men, undisciplined and demoralized
by their defeat, during the period of famine before supplies
start coming in, isn't that equivalent to shutting up rebellion,
riot, and pillage? Isn't it a way of providing the Prussians with
an almost certain pretext for entering Paris?

In a newspaper which contains an account of the surrender,
I read about the enthronement of King William as Emperor
of Germany at Versailles in the Galerie des Glaces in sight of
the stone effigy of Louis XIV in the courtyard. There indeed
is the end of French glory.

Tuesday, January 31

This evening I was having dinner in a restaurant next to M.
Pouillet, a lawyer at the Court of Cassation. I told him I
thought it would be fine if the next Assembly were rationed
as to lawyers, merchants of verbiage and empty words, and I
added that as far as I was concerned, if France could do without eloquence for the next twenty years, she would be saved,
but that this was the indispensable condition of her well-
being.

Lawyer though he is, my interlocutor pretty much shared

my opinion and went on to tell me about the *scrounging*—
that's the word he used—the scrounging by all the lower elements in the Palais de Justice. He gave me an account of how
all the two-bit lawyers, all the briefless lawyers, all the lawyers without talent or honor, were being aided and pushed by
Crémieux in the scramble for posts in the top administration.
And at a time when the mind of France is concentrating on
the Prussians, at that very moment, I shall never forget the
picture he gave me of this office concerned exclusively with
removing people from their posts, this office where the door is
constantly being pushed open to give passage to an intruder
who, without a by-your-leave or good-day, shouts: "Crémieux, get rid of Robinet, of Chabouillot! We don't want any
more of them!" After this intruder another intruder, asking
for the dismissal of some other imperial public prosecutor,
which is at once granted by the senile good nature of the minister.

What a pretty piece of comedy is the one in which he told
me he took part! M. Pouillet has a brother-in-law who was
imperial public prosecutor at Blois. A complaint was made
against him. M. Pouillet's sister, who liked her husband's position, wrote asking him to use his influence, his connections
with men in government, so that her husband might keep his
post. He was against this step, thinking that the dismissal
would later on be to his brother-in-law's advantage; however,
on his sister's insistence he undertook to go to see Crémieux.

He explains the situation to the latter, tells him of his sister's
wishes, and appeals to the good nature which the minister has
always shown him. The minister, without letting him finish,
says to him: "My dear boy, you know how fond of you I
am!" And forthwith embraces him—during his time in office
Crémieux has always embraced everybody. He adds: "It's

enough for you to state your wishes; your brother-in-law will not be removed; you can rest assured." Then M. Pouillet reaches the door; Crémieux calls him back:

"You say your brother-in-law's name is Pelletier, that he is at Blois?"

"Exactly."

"Well, I promise you he will not be removed today. . . . Today it's all right; but I am not sure but that in a few days I shall have to put him out. Wait, perhaps we can fix this up. What would your brother-in-law like?"

"Well," answers M. Pouillet, "he has family and interests at Orléans; there is a counselor's post vacant there; I think that would make him very happy."

"Fine, fine, I'll kick him out at Blois," Crémieux replies, "and at the same time appoint him to Orléans. And since I shall have appointed him myself, you see, I won't be able to kick him out again."

He summons his chief secretary: "Prepare M. Pelletier's nomination to Orléans."

"But, sir, posts have already been reassigned."

"Oh, that's annoying, very annoying. . . . No matter, I have something else in mind. I shall arrange things so that you will both be happy. I'll write you tomorrow or the day after. Consider it done."

Then embraces all over again. The matter ended with the pure and simple dismissal of M. Pelletier with, however, a letter of regret from the minister, who had been obliged to bow to the wishes of the people of Blois.

Lack of discipline, which made the army perish, is on its way to killing French society. Is the republican regime capable of restoring the discipline without which societies cannot live? Yet it would be desirable to keep that label *Republic* and under its name bring together the able men of all parties, thereby submerging the infinite nothingness of the republican party in the whole.

Tuesday, February 7

A strange procession as all the people come back from the Neuilly bridge. Everybody is laden with bags, with toilet cases, with pockets swollen with something to eat. There are middle-class people carrying five or six chickens on one shoulder balanced by two or three rabbits on the other. I see an elegant little woman bringing back potatoes in a lace handkerchief. And nothing is more eloquent than the happiness, I might almost say the tenderness, with which people carry four-pound loaves of bread in their arms, that beautiful white bread which Paris has had to do without for so long.

This evening at Brébant's, conversation abandons politics for art, and Renan takes the occasion to say that he thinks the Piazza San Marco is horrible. When Gautier and the rest of us protest, Renan asserts that art ought to be judged by *the rational faculty*, that there is no need for anything else, and he goes on like that, raving in public. What a poor excuse for a man and what a stupid brain when he talks of things he knows nothing about! I interrupt him suddenly and ask him out of hand if he can tell us the color of his living room paper. The question throws him off, upsets him. He cannot answer. And we try to make him understand that in order to judge art we consider the eyes more important than *the rational faculty*.

Overcome by a kind of inner rage against my country and this government, for the last few days I have shut myself up, cloistered myself in my garden, trying to still my thoughts, my memories, and my apprehensions about the future by means of exhausting work, not reading the newspapers and avoiding people with information.

Paris is a disheartening spectacle with all the Mobiles displaying their laziness and uprootedness like the stupid and frightened cattle which you saw wandering in the Bois de Boulogne at the beginning of the war. Even more disheartening is the spectacle of strutting officers around the tables of boulevard cafés, preoccupied with the canes they have just bought in order to parade along the sidewalk. Their unheroic uniforms are too much in evidence. They lack tact.

Saturday, February 11

Parisians are now beginning to have meat and other things to eat; but they still completely lack coal and wood to cook with.

Sunday, February 12

I go up to see Gautier, who has taken refuge from Neuilly in Paris on the Rue de Beaune, fifth floor, in a workman's lodgings.

I go through a small room and find his two sisters seated on the window sill. Dressed in rags, wearing fichus and with their thin white hair in pigtails, they look like Fates from the Central Market.

The attic room where Théo lives, so little and low that he completely fills it with the smoke of his cigar, contains a bed with dirty sheets, an old oak armchair, and a cane chair; over these lean cats range and stretch themselves, famine cats, shadows of cats. Two or three sketches are hung crookedly on the wall and a few volumes are tumbled on plain wood shelves which have been set up in a hurry.

Théo is there in a red night cap with Venetian horns and a velvet coat made for informal affairs at Saint Gratien, but now so spotted, so greasy that it looks like a Neapolitan cook's coat. And the charming, opulent master of the written and spoken word looks like a ridiculous doge, like a ridiculous Marino Faliero on the stage of the Saint Marcel Theatre.

While he was talking as Rabelais must have talked, I mused upon the unjust remuneration of art. I thought of the sumptuous and abominable furnishings of Ponson du Terrail, which I saw being moved out from the Rue Vivienne this morning, now that the man who made 70,000 francs a year in some provincial hole or other during the Siege has died.

Thursday, February 23

Many months have passed since my fingers disturbed a book in its case in the stalls along the quays. The other day, for the first time, I bought a volume with the intention of reading it and, I think, with the ability to concentrate sufficiently to do so.

Friday, February 24

The taste for literature came back to me today. This morning I was bitten by the desire to write *La Fille Elisa*,[4] the book which he and I were to have written together after *Madame Gervaisais*. I scribbled four or five lines on a piece of paper. Perhaps they will become the first chapter.

Sunday, February 26

Why these agitated nights? Why without fail these painful nightmares? Why in my dreams does my brother's illness always begin again? Pitiless and murderous reenactment which in my dreams takes on all the horror of the *cases* we read together in medical treatises for use in our books.

There has been an announcement that the Prussian occupa-

[4] This novel, describing the life of a prostitute, was completed by Edmond and published in 1877.

tion will occur tomorrow; tomorrow we shall have the enemy among us. God protect France henceforth from diplomatic treaties drawn up by lawyers!

Monday, February 27

Something somber and upset on Parisian faces; you feel on them an anxious, painful concern over the occupation.

On the Place de l'Hôtel de Ville, at the back near the river, some tipsy National Guards are on parade, with a drum in the lead and immortelles in their buttonholes; they salute the ancient building with a shout of "Long live the Republic!" The Rue de Rivoli is a fair, with every imaginable product spread out on the sidewalks, while vehicles of death and provisions meet each other in the street—hearses and wagons full of dried cod.

There is a great, divine irony which seems to take pleasure in giving human progress the lie. In these times of universal suffrage, in these times when all the citizens carry on the government of the country, never, never will the will of one man, be it Favre or Thiers, have disposed more despotically of the destinies of France accompanied by a more complete ignorance on the part of its citizens concerning everything that goes on, everything that is done in their names. [See Illustration 4.]

Tuesday, February 28

Impossible to describe the atmosphere of sadness that surrounds you. Paris is weighed on by the most terrible apprehension, apprehension about the unknown.

My eyes see pale faces in the ambulances: they are the wounded from the Tuileries who are being moved in haste so that King William may have lunch at the palace. On the Place

Louis XV [5] the cities of France have their faces veiled in crepe; these women of stone, with night on their faces in the sunlight of bright day, make a strange, lugubrious, fantastically alarming protest.

Wednesday, March 1

Accursed Auteuil! This suburb, having been starved, cut off from the rest of Paris, sacked by the Mobiles, and finally bombarded, now is to have the misfortune of being occupied by the Prussians.

This morning we no longer hear the great humming voice of Paris, and the disquieting silence of the bad hours is such that we can hear eleven o'clock strike at the Boulogne church. On the horizon there is the silence of empty, dead places. So far we have seen only a few Uhlans, penetrating the Bois de Boulogne in the direction of the Auteuil gate with the utmost caution.

In this great silence of all space gradually there begins to rise dully the dead and distant sound of drums of the approaching Prussians. The thought of opening my door to let in these Germans, of having them masters of my hearth for a few days, makes me suffer as from a physical ailment. I feel a great disturbance within me, and my mouth tastes as though I had just taken a spoonful of castor oil.

Now the Prussian carriages and military vehicles are rolling on like thunder. Through the grille of my garden I see two gilded helmets stop before my house and babble away in German as they look at it for a moment. They go on.

Never have the hours seemed to me so long, hours during

---

[5] Actually the Place de la Concorde. The Strasbourg statue continued to be draped in black until the restoration of Alsace after World War I.

which it is impossible for me to keep my thoughts on anything, hours when it is impossible to remain in any one place for a moment. The Prussians have sounded retreat and no Prussian has yet appeared: no doubt we shall have some tomorrow.

I slip out into the darkness of Auteuil, where there is not a living soul on the street, not a light in the windows; in the strange and mournful streets I see some Bavarians pass by, walking four by four, anxious and ill-at-ease in this dead city.

Thursday, March 2

It is nine in the morning and nothing yet. I have a remarkable feeling of relief. Perhaps we will escape the Prussians. I go down to the garden. There is a fine spring sky, full of a young sun and vibrating with the chatter of birds. Nature, about which I have said so many harsh things, alas, takes cruel vengeance on me. I am caught, bound up, and tamed by her. My garden becomes my whole occupation, the whole goal of my thoughts.

I want to see whether it is possible to go to Paris, and in spite of my desire not to look at any Prussians, I push on as far as Passy. At La Muette, Bavarian sentinels at the area headquarters. On the street, calm groups, nonprovocative groups of soldiers, who stroll or foolishly look at carved umbrella handles. On the doorstep of every house a Bavarian in beret. In spite of the yellow poster inviting the shopkeepers to close, all the shops are open. Bourgeois and workingmen look at the foreigners with indifference. Among them a few old women's heightened feelings are betrayed by their angry eyes and the muttered insults which they spit out of their toothless mouths as they walk along.

Upon leaving home I heard that peace has been signed and

that they will depart at noon tomorrow. At Passy I hear that additional corps have arrived and that houses at Auteuil will be occupied. I go home. All day I wait, saying to myself each time the bell rings: "Here they come!" All day long suffering the cruel emotion of having my hearth occupied by these vanquishers in whose land my father and my uncles on both sides requisitioned quarters for so long.

Friday, March 3

I am awakened by music, their music. A magnificent morning with one of those bright suns that are indifferent to human catastrophes, whether they be called the victory at Austerlitz or the capture of Paris. Splendid weather, though the sky is full of the sound of crows, which are never heard here at this season but which follow along behind Them, the black escort of their armies. They are going away? They are leaving us at last! We cannot believe in our deliverance, and under the impact of a shattering stupefaction we can look at the dearly loved objects in our houses—which have not been carried off to Germany.

Deliverance appears to me in the form of two gendarmes taking possession of the Boulevard Montmorency at a gallop.

The people near me walk slowly, as happy as convalescents who are out for their first walk. The only trace of the occupation at Passy is chalk marks on porte-cochères and shop shutters indicating the number of soldiers quartered on the inhabitants.

The Champs Elysées is full of a lively and talkative crowd, who are taking the air without apparent notice of the vindictive destruction of a café that remained open for the Prussians during every night of the occupation.

Sunday, March 5

All along the road from Boulogne to Saint Cloud the mattresses which the Mobiles deigned to leave in possession of the householders are airing in the open windows. Saint Cloud, with its crumbled houses, its windows black from fire, has the grim grey look of a stone quarry.

The conditions of peace seem to me to be so heavy, so crushing, so mortal to France, that I am terrified lest war begin again before we are ready.

Friday, March 10

A scatological pamphleteer might produce a biting, witty book with this title: *Shit and the Prussians.* Those disgusting conquerors have *sullied* France with so many researches, inventions, and fantasies of this sort that there ought to be a psychological study made of that people's taste for things excremental. At Charles Edmond's house they took down his father's portrait, made a hole where the mouth was. . . . You can guess the rest.

Wednesday, March 15

I am lighting a cigaret at La Civette. A bank messenger comes in and hands a note to the cashier. She answers: "Prisoner in Germany."

Browsing at Beauvais' bookstore, I run into Bocher, the staff officer who with Mahérault did the Gavarni catalogue. He has just returned from Germany, where he has been a prisoner since the beginning of the war. He tells me the following, which he had from one of his relatives, who had it from the mouth of the Archbishop of Reims. The King-Emperor arrived in Reims, was housed by the Archbishop in the finest room in his palace, but at first the king did not consider it worthy of his greatness. The Archbishop informed him that it was the room where Charles X slept when he came for his coronation. On this assurance the king consented to occupy it. The next morning the Corporal-King took a crap in the window corner and wiped himself with the curtain.

Friday, March 17

Saint Cloud no longer exists. It is a field of stone, gravel, plaster, pieces of twisted iron; out of this there rise over the sunken cellars fragments of burned wall where you still see pieces of furniture at inaccessible heights. Here is the niche for the stove; there a daguerreotype portrait; farther on a framed statement of the rules of billiards and a scoring rack; farther still in a cupboard, the door of which flaps in the wind, is a bidet shattered by an exploding shell.

Everywhere houses with windows licked by flames, through the open holes of which you see the blue sky. On the site of the little Saint Nicholas Hotel, the hotel where my brother and I passed a happy week with Marie, a woman is seated in the despairing pose of a statue, weeping over the ruins. In the historic dining room where all Paris has eaten, there is scarcely anything left but a piece of wall on the ground floor where all you can read of the broken sign is . . . *of the Black Head.*

The main street of Saint Cloud is a pathway full of debris between two rows of houses with crumbling façades from which a stone tumbles down now and then. You would think you were walking along during an earthquake. Among these crumbling ruins, which still smell of fire, in the holes of doors and windows held up by big posts, a miserable commercial life

is starting up. Here a bar where you see a man in a red Garibaldi jersey seated at a table. There a poor little milk shop
where a huge shell stands on the window sill among the dried
herring. On charred shutters, where the trace of petrol is still
evident, you read, written in chalk: "Frenchmen, remember!
Vengeance!"

The hospital founded by Marie Antoinette has no roof.
Next door in a young ladies' boarding school the dormitory
beds, dislocated and twisted by fire, look like a junk heap.

At the very top of Saint Cloud next to the church a bareheaded old man, his white hair flying in the wind, his manner
excited and wild, shouts to the passers-by: "You can say it
was the Prussians who set the fire with petrol and torches.
You can't tell me different!"

The palace, with its poor female statues wounded in the
breast by Prussian bullets, is only the shattered façade of a
ruin. A ruin to be preserved, as Germany preserved Heidelberg, a ruin to cover with ivy and climbing vines which will
cling along its pilasters, its bas-reliefs, and its baked and shattered marble, a ruin of which the sight and legend will sustain
a just hatred and an enraged desire for vengeance, as does that
ruin in the Palatinate.

Saturday, March 18

This morning the bread woman says there is fighting in
Montmartre.

When I go out, I find only an astonishing indifference as to
what is going on over there. The Parisian population have
seen so much in the last six months that nothing seems to
move them any more.

I reach the Orléans station, where the body of Hugo's son

lies. Old Hugo is receiving in the station master's office. He says to me: "You have had a blow; so have I, but my case is not ordinary, two strokes of lightning in a single life!" [See Illustration 5.]

The procession sets out. A bizarre crowd, among whom I see scarcely two or three men of letters, but there are a great many men in soft hats and there is a gradual infiltration of drunkards, who stagger into line as we go forward through the carbaret district. Behind the coffin Hugo's white head in a hood dominates the mixed group like the head of a warrior monk in the time of the League. All around me people are talking of provocation and making fun of Thiers. Burty irritates me greatly with his whinny and his lack of understanding of the terrible revolution which is getting under way around us. I am very sad and full of the most painful forebodings.

Armed National Guards, through whose ranks the procession makes its way, present arms to Hugo, and we come to the cemetery.

The coffin won't go into the vault. Vacquerie takes advantage of this mishap to make a long speech telling us that young Hugo is a martyr, that he died from the labor of founding the Republic. He says this just at the moment that Busquet has finished whispering in my ear that he simply died of conjugal enjoyment and diarrhea. Vacquerie uses his speech as an occasion to proclaim the democratic social Republic. Disgusted at seeing politics always intrude on grief, I go and sit down on the stone of an honest bourgeois and wait for the end of the orations.

We retrace our steps. The triumphant revolution seems to be taking possession of Paris; National Guards are swarming and barricades are being put up everywhere; naughty chil-

VICTOR HUGO.

Et lui cèdre vivant par la hache insulté
tressaillant sous le spectre aux lugubres revanches
il regardait tomber autour de lui ses branches.

5. Victor Hugo, the stricken cedar

UN FÉDÉRÉ, RETOUR DU FORT

Dépôt central de l'Imagerie populaire, 65, Rue Galande. Propriété de l'Éditeur. (Déposé.) PARIS — IMP. J. HOR"

6. A drunken Federal

dren scramble on top of them. There is no traffic; shops are closing. My curiosity leads me to the Hôtel de Ville, where orators addressing groups scattered on the square are talking of putting the traitors to death. In the distance along the quays in a cloud of dust harmless charges by the Municipal Guards, while the National Guards load their rifles on the Rue de Rivoli, and some riffraff make an attack on the two barracks behind the Hôtel de Ville with shouts, howls, and stones. As I return, there are bands everywhere shouting "Long live the Republic!" Everywhere on the sidewalks loafers talking about the execution of Clément Thomas and Lecomte.

I have dinner at the Frères Provençaux to the deafening sound of patriotic shouts, and I am completely surprised when I leave the restaurant to bump into people standing in line for the Palais Royal Theatre.

Sunday, March 19

This morning's papers confirm the execution of Clément Thomas and General Lecomte.

A feeling of weariness at being a Frenchman; a vague desire to go look for a country where the artist's thoughts are tranquil and not constantly troubled by the stupid agitations, the stupid convulsions of a destructive mob.

People on the train say the army is in full retreat to Versailles and Paris is at the mercy of the insurrection. On the Rue Caumartin, when I ask Nefftzer who is in the new government, he answers, his warty face rejoicing strangely over our disasters: "You have Assi!"

There is stupefaction on Parisian faces; numerous groups, noses upraised, are looking at Montmartre and its cannons through the opening provided by the Rue Le Peletier and the

Rue Laffitte. I run into Hugo, who is holding Charles's son by the hand and saying to a friend: "I think it would be wise to think about laying in a few supplies!"

Finally on the Boulevard Montmartre, I see the names of the men in the new government posted, names so unknown that it seems like a joke. After Assi's name the least unknown is that of Lullier, who is notoriously mad. To me this notice marks the eternal extinction of the Republic in France. The experiment of 1870, made with people from the top of the basket, was deplorable; this one, made with men from the very bottom, will be the end of this form of government. Decidedly a Republic is a beautiful illusion of minds that think in grandiose terms and are generous and disinterested, but it is not practicable in view of the evil, petty passions of the French populace. To them *Liberty*, *Equality*, *Fraternity* mean only the enslavement or death of the upper classes.

I encounter Berthelot, whom current happenings have so beaten down that he looks almost humpbacked. He takes me into *Le Temps*, where with the staff absent and the noisy presses running we despair together over France in agony. In what is taking place, in the day's violence, we see an opportunity afforded to the extremists in the other direction, an opportunity for the Count of Chambord. Berthelot also fears famine. He has just crossed the Beauce, where lack of horses has forced farmers to sow barley.

I go on my way toward the Hôtel de Ville. A man with a pamphlet in his hand shouts: "Trochu exposed and shown up." A vendor of *L'Avenir National* is shouting: "Arrest of General Chanzy." The quay and the two main streets that lead to the Hôtel de Ville are closed by barricades with cordons of National Guards in front of them. You are overcome with disgust to see their stupid and abject faces, which triumph and drunkenness have imbued with a kind of radiant swinishness. You see them with their kepis awry constantly coming out of the wide-open doors of the wine shops, the only shops open today. Around the barricades a mixture of crossroads Diogenes and fat bourgeois of doubtful professions smoking earthen pipes, their wives on their arms.

A red flag on the Hôtel de Ville tower; below, the rumble of an armed populace behind three cannons.

As I return, on people's faces I see flustered indifference, sometimes sad irony, most often consternation, which causes old gentlemen to raise despairing arms to the sky, though they speak in low voices and look prudently around them.

Monday, March 20

Three in the morning. I am awakened by the alarm bell, the lugubrious tolling that I heard in the nights of June 1848. The deep plaintive lamentation of the great bell at Notre Dame rises over the sounds of all the bells in the city, giving the dominant note to the general alarm, then is submerged by human shouts, which seem to me to be a call to arms.

What a reversal of all human expectation! And how God seems to laugh in his great white beard of an aged sceptic and to make sport of our feats of logic here below! How does it happen that the battalions from Belleville, so craven before the enemy, so craven before the battalions of order on October 31, have been able to take control of Paris today? How is it that the middle-class National Guard, which was so determined to fight a few days ago, has melted away without firing a shot? These days everything seems to happen pat to show the nothingness of human wisdom and experience. The consequences of events and things are a lie! In short, for the moment France and Paris are under the control of workmen who have given us a government composed solely of their men. How long will it last? Who knows? The unbelievable rules.

What a repulsive paper *Le Rappel* is, a paper that soft-pedals the rifle shots that killed Clément Thomas and Lecomte, a paper whose editors make a play for low popularity —all, you feel, for the purpose of creating a claque for their ridiculous or infantile literary works, whether they be signed Meurice or Vacquerie.

At the station there are many people leaving for the provinces, and the Rue du Havre is full of baggage brought there by handcarts, since there are no horses. In spite of the snowfall of governmental notices on all the walls attesting to events, you feel that what is happening has not happened. And wide awake, you walk along feeling like a man asleep who is in the grip of a bad dream and knows that he is dreaming.

Now and then a fanciful staff officer of the new government goes by at a gallop in a red jersey, which makes the onlookers turn and stare. And the cohorts of Belleville throng our conquered boulevard opposite Tortoni's, going along in the midst of a somewhat mocking astonishment which seems to embarrass them and makes them turn their victors' eyes toward the toes of their shoes, worn mostly without socks.

Tuesday, March 21

The continuous and precipitate sound of the call to arms. The appearance of groups has changed. Irritation is fermenting. Words are getting heated, rifle shots are near. The Belleville troops are beginning to be jeered at on the boulevard. You are surrounded as if by the splashing waves of a great rising sea which is about to unloose itself in a wild rush. From Burty's windows I see a big demonstration go by preceded by a flag with the words: *Long Live the Republic! Men of Order.*

Dinner at Brébant's. Charles Edmond tells a very characteristic story about the new government. After destroying police dossiers, the first activity of these men was to wipe out the register of prostitutes. Because their mistresses, their wives, their sisters were on this list, do you suppose?

Saint-Victor recounts bits of a conversation with Ernest Picard. The lawyer said to him concerning Trochu: "He is honest and false!" He also told a pretty anecdote about Gambetta. The former habitué of the Café de Madrid was not satisfied to give *Pipe-en-Bois* and the others jobs in his immediate entourage; having surrounded himself with guzzlers, he was still not satisfied. The Café de Madrid had not in the dictator's opinion been altogether reconstituted in Bordeaux. So he sent for the waiter who used to serve his table and raised him to the dignity of doorkeeper to his office with a steel chain around his neck.

From these anecdotes the conversation rises to a higher plane. It is wonderful and sad what power anything said, written, or printed in Germany has over Renan's thought. Today I hear him adopt Bismarck's criminal formula: *Might makes right.* I hear him assert that nations and individuals who cannot defend their property do not deserve to keep it. When I rebel at this, he answers that such has always been Law and Justice. Only Christianity, he has to admit, has sought to mitigate this doctrine by protection of the weak. And he plunges into a verbose dissertation on the books of Job, Esther, Judith, and the Maccabees, on the Jewish race's capacity for assimilation, on Spinoza's philosophy, coming back to Christ, whom he declares a plagiarist with nothing original of his own except *feeling.* In support of his thesis he cites the words of

Isaiah written 800 years before Christ: "What do your sacrifices mean to me? Amend your ways!"—the themes paraphrased by Racine in *Athalie*.

I listen to all this somewhat abstractedly, with one ear to the noise in the street, which is getting louder, and not attending to these archaic controversies. Meanwhile the tumult doubles in volume, the crowd becomes more angry and more dangerous; the National Guards from the Drouot municipal offices are greeted with whistles and boos. Suddenly two rifle shots ring out. I am pushed about in a general flight which carries me along in its terror. And a shout of "To Arms!" resounds all along the boulevard.

Wednesday, March 22

All morning incessant and redoubled cannon fire. About one o'clock silence in the air, so that you can hear roosters crowing and the sound of iron foundries. I don't know what the cannonade was and I don't have the courage to go out for information. Indeed! I'm well paid for my expenditure of emotion. All that terrible cannonade was a Prussian anniversary celebration. I can breathe again.

At that moment Pélagie comes home from Paris to tell me that fighting is going on there. A call to arms, a frenzied call to arms during the entire late afternoon. In the evening no newspapers. I go to Passy for news. Passy looks like a little city a hundred miles from Paris in the throes of emotion over a revolution in the capital about which it doesn't know anything.

I push on to the Trocadéro. There a gentleman, pointing to three silhouettes in the darkness, tells me that one of these men had taken him by the hand and tried to drag him away.

"You understand," he adds, "they are wicked, disbanded soldiers; they know there are no more punishments; they are quite capable of knocking you out for what they can find on you."

I return to Passy, where the prolonged call to arms of bugles and the urgent beating out of the general alarm resound. A young man in one group is telling them that in the Place de la Concorde the Committee troops fired on an unarmed demonstration for peace and order and that there were half a score dead or wounded, that he himself rescued De Pène, who was wounded in the thigh. On the Boulevard Montmorency a dubious encounter with a dubious soldier. The street begins to be unsafe.

Thursday, March 23

A general alarm all morning. I find the whole Second Arrondissement in arms. Every street is guarded by men from the neighborhood. The leader of a strong reconnaissance force which is on its way to take up a position near the Bourse tosses out in passing: "We just disarmed a post."

I go into Burty's for a minute. A National Guard officer is examining the apartment and the balcony overlooking the boulevard. He orders that all the doors of the building be left open so that at the first appearance of Committee troops his men may be able to take up their positions. I look at my furniture, my bibelots, my books which I have moved there, and I think they may be destined to perish in an attack on the building.

At Saint Lazare station a frightened National Guard closes a wooden barrier in my face and shouts that the trains are no longer running.

Paris under Siege

Friday, March 24

In spite of the barricades which I see being constructed or completed in the Place Vendôme, there is a feeling of relaxation, of letdown. But only one rifle shot is needed to change everything. At the moment the situation loses some of its seriousness by the fact that the people on one side have not decided what they want to achieve, and those on the other have not determined how far to give in.

Monday, March 27

During the last few days I had a liver attack lasting fourteen hours, something I had thought I was forever rid of. Fourteen hours of writhing like a worm cut in two. I don't believe I have ever suffered so much in my life. I came out of it battered, with the empty-headedness and weakness of a man who has been ill for two weeks. It is the result of the ending of the siege and its aftermath. A strange thing, this liver complaint, which killed my brother and will no doubt kill me; it is in no sense hereditary, but is an acquisition from literature.

Tuesday, March 28

In the events taking place the newspapers see only a question of decentralization. Decentralization, indeed! What is happening is very simply the conquest of France by the workers and the enslavement under their despotism of the nobles, the middle class, and the peasants. The government is leaving the hands of those who have, to go into the hands of those who have not, going from those who have a material interest in conservation of society to those who are completely unconcerned about order, stability, or conservation. Is it possible that in the great law underlying changes here on earth the workers are for modern societies what the Barbarians were for ancient societies, convulsive agents of dissolution and destruction?

Wednesday, March 29

The atticism of Athens and the atticism of the Grand Siècle are very ironically revealed in two contemporary literary figures, in Aristophanes and in Molière. In Aristophanes Athenian laughter rejoiced in shit, farts, and play on words about the cunt, the penis, and balls. In Molière, whom Christian decorum deprived of jokes about the genitals, the delicate French smile took superlative delight in the perspective of an ass hole into which an apothecary introduced a syringe.

The disastrous triumphs of the Republic come back to this and this alone: on every occasion the Republic presents to a society which is rebellious and ready to come to blows a front of gentlemen more or less washed, combed, and honest. It is true that these reassuring gentlemen, these gentlemen newly endowed with power, keep that power only long enough to hand over society—which has been disarmed by their kindly faces, their soft words, and their white ties—to the stupidity and ferocity of the groups behind them. Then it happens that the very men for whom the gentlemen in front obtained stupid conciliation and humanitarian clemency out of religious respect for their dirty hides, those men who have been spared, pardoned, amnestied, talk only of execution by rifle squad or guillotine. Those gentlemen who lull us to sleep with their platonic programs, their philanthropic nonsense, their theses about ideal government, they are the great danger. It is not Assi and his gang who gained the victory in these last few days, but Louis Blanc and his defeatist mayors who, in the name of brotherhood. persuaded the forces of order to drop their rifles.

Paris under Siege

I have a tyrannical faculty within me: the continuous, perpetual giving birth to a conception that bears the seal of my personality. If, as at this moment, it is not a book that I roll around in my head, then my mind amuses itself day and night with the planting of a garden, the creation of a private corner of greenery and leaves. Or in default of a garden, my brain occupies itself with the creation of a room, with the arrangement and furnishing of a bedroom, carried out under ideal artistic conditions, something which other people buy from their interior decorator. And it has been like this all my life: I rested from writing a book by composing an original collection, piece of furniture, or binding.

Friday, March 31

Risum teneatis! Hold that laugh! Jules Vallès is Minister of Public Instruction. The bohemian of the beerhalls occupies Villemain's chair. Yet it must be admitted that of all Assi's crowd he is the man with the most talent and the least meanness. But France is so inveterately classical that the literary theories of this man of letters are already doing more harm to the new government than the social theories of his colleagues. A government, a member of which has dared to write that Homer ought to be put on the shelf or that Molière's *Le Misanthrope* lacks gaiety, appears to the bourgeoisie more frightening, more subversive, more antisocial than if this same government were to decree on the same day the abolition of inheritance and the replacement of marriage by *free love*.

Saturday, April 1

There is something revolting to me in this government of violence and every extreme: it is their debonair acceptance of the treaty of peace; it is their cowardly submission to its dis-honoring conditions; it is, shall I say, their near friendliness toward the Prussians. The preliminaries of peace are the only *fait accompli* that finds favor with these men, who are otherwise occupied in overturning everything—and that without a single protest.

God knows that I am not asking for it, but it does surprise and bewilder me at this time of effervescence, of boiling up of anger, that the excitement does not get out of hand and turn unreasonably, wildly against the Germans.

I sadly observe that in present-day revolutions the people no longer fight for some word, flag, principle, or faith which makes men's deaths a disinterested sacrifice. I observe that love of country is an outmoded sentiment. I observe that present generations revolt only for the satisfaction of crude material interests, and that today carousing and revelry are the only things that have the power to make men give their lives heroically. Today the French people fight in order to drink a glass of wine for nothing; tomorrow they will fight to get their hands on the *long green* of the bourgeoisie.

Sunday, April 2

Around ten o'clock a cannonade in the direction of Courbevoie. Thank God! The civil war has begun! When things have reached such a point, it is preferable to hypocritical mouthings. The cannonade dies down. Is Versailles beaten? Alas, if Versailles has the least setback, Versailles is lost! A caller tells me that from what he has overheard on the street he is afraid of a defeat.

I leave at once for Paris. I study people's faces, which are the barometer of events during revolutions; what I see is a sort of concealed satisfaction, a sly joy. Finally a newspaper informs me that the Belleville forces have been beaten. I savor my jubilation for a long time. Let tomorrow bring what it will.

Burty sees a *new era* in these events. For my part I have had enough of new eras directed and led by men with whom Burty would not want to have anything to do.

I hear a young Belleville fellow exclaim as he speaks to his comrades: "It's disgusting! In the companies all they care about is stuffing themselves with food and drinking even more!"

Monday, April 3

Bombardment like that when the Prussians were here. The cannonade beginning at dawn from Mont Valérien, then spreading in the course of the day all around Meudon, where the Versailles forces have set up cannons in the Prussian fortifications. Incessant fire, from which the smoke, falling back on the houses on the plain and turning them grey, makes the hillside in the vague indistinctness look like the staggered rows of a slate village, from which smoke, fires, and exploding craters erupt.

In the midst of this raging artillery fire people have become so accustomed to living to the sound of cannons and have acquired such insouciance that I see gardeners quietly laying turf alongside workmen who are resetting gates with all the calm of former springs.

It is unbearable, this uncertainty, this lack of knowledge about an action going on before your eyes, which you can follow with a pair of glasses but which you cannot understand.

Requisitioning is beginning to turn from public funds to the wealth of merchants. This began at Passy yesterday.

Outside on my street there is such happy abandon among the passers-by that you doubt that you hear cannon fire. In front of the Quartermaster's Depot I see the 181st battalion of the National Guard pass by. The faces of the men are yellow and serious.

Nothing is known in Paris about how things went during the day; street gatherings, newspapers, acquaintances are all without any late news. All of a sudden the boulevards ring with the sensational news shouted to all the echoes of Paris by the newsvendors selling *Le Journal de la Montagne:* "Capture of Mont Valérien by the National Guard." I smell a trick and a maneuver to bring the undecided to the point of going out and getting themselves killed.

Someone tells me this: After the execution of Clément Thomas two women began to piss on the corpse, which was still warm. A lieutenant from La Villette, who was on the spot, shouted: "For God's sake! Shit! I'd rather go back to prison than see a thing like that!" This terrible story was told me the very day of the execution, which removes the suspicion that it was made up by a newspaperman.

Tuesday, April 4

I wake up very sad. The horizon is mute! Can it be that Versailles has been defeated and we are at the mercy of the men of the Commune? Happily I soon hear the sound of machine guns,[6] a sound so distant and stifled that I am not sure but that it might be the rattle of the railroad tracks. The sound becomes more distinct and quickly becomes a homicidal discharge of lead.

[6] The word *mitrailleuse* here refers to a clumsy predecessor of the modern machine gun, consisting of a twenty-five-barrel monstrosity on the model of the six-barreled American Gatling gun.

On the boulevard the drunken National Guards, who feel a vague anxiety about the morrow, become aggressive toward the passers-by.

Why is it that in civil wars courage increases, and why do the people who would have fled from the Prussians heroically get themselves killed by their fellow citizens? Today we cannot berate that inept National Defense Government enough for not having been able to turn such valor to account.

All day noise of the death machines, which at times seem to show human anger. The omnibuses have their red lanterns turned inward so as not to be winged on the fly in the area near the Quartermaster's Depot.

Wednesday, April 5

According to the morning papers, the Committee Government is about at an end; however, the cannonade lasts all day around the Issy fortress, where a big red flag can be seen floating in the wind.

The threat of forcing the troops who are for the Assemblée Nationale to march against Versailles has made the few able-bodied bourgeois left around here try to escape.

Truly, if the Prussians were not in the wings it would be a good idea for the experiment by the Committee Government to go all the way. It would be desirable for them to have two or three months of victory during which to put into effect their secret program and carry out everything anarchistic and antisocial that they have stored in their minds. That is perhaps the price of France's well-being. That alone would give the present generation the hardihood to destroy universal suffrage and freedom of the press, two suppressions which the good sense of the mediocre declares impossible. Yes! freedom of the press, for I have no more respect for this sacred cow than Balzac and Gavarni had. To me the political paper is only an instrument of lies and excitation. To me the literary paper, the little paper, is only an instrument of moral dissolution and intellectual abasement, as I tried to show in *Les Hommes de Lettres*. I won't deny that I would be interested in seeing such a regime in action. I don't pretend that France would be forever saved from demagoguery; but my retrograde regime might well give society more years of peace than have been given it in the last seventy years in particular by impotent efforts to reconcile authority and liberty.

In the moonlight I read cannibalistic notices, still shining with paste, which speak of "assassination by the Versailles bandits" and proclaim a law of reprisal announced in these significant terms: "An eye for an eye and a tooth for a tooth." If Versailles does not hurry up, we shall see rage over defeat turn to massacre, executions, and other gentle acts on the part of these kind friends of humanity.

Thursday, April 6

A young National Guard goes by on our boulevard weeping, weeping like a child. Is it his father or his brother for whom he weeps?

All morning a cannonade around Issy and Neuilly; thundering fire of cannons, machine guns, and small arms, fire such as I never heard while the Prussians were here.

A dozen ambulances go up the Champs Elysées as I am walking in that direction. At the Etoile barrier an enormous crowd is looking at three Versailles batteries which have been set up above the Neuilly bridge and are firing on the barricade at the bridge and on the ramparts. Groups of workmen perched on the roofs of the two sentry boxes. Young girls balancing on the iron chains, with one hand on a friend's shoulder. Some Englishwomen standing up in victorias which have stopped in front of the barrier. A dark multitude, above whose heads there flashes the shining brass of a big telescope.

At bottom it is an indifferent curiosity on the part of everybody, bourgeois and workmen, women of society and women of the people. To ease her conscience and as if she were playing a role, one of the women exclaims: "It's so sad!" But almost as soon as the words are out, she laughs again, at nothing in particular.

Flights of crows pass cawing through the brilliant sky, having been routed from their accustomed haunts by cannon fire. Now and then part of the crowd rushes to an open carriage that is bringing back some slightly wounded man or some man with a bloody head.

Preceded by an officer with sword in hand, to cries of "Long live the Republic!" shouted by drunken artillerymen, three cannons, drawn by at a gallop, divert attention for a moment from the climbing road and the shattered barricade. Shells begin to fall on the ramparts and the crowd gives way slowly before the shell bursts, which leave a little motionless cloud floating for a long time in the blue sky. It is an artillery duel without apparent advantage to either side.

Versailles shows lack of judgment in not striking a heavy blow. The Parisians are not discouraged, for they have been kept in ignorance about the extent of their defeats by official and semi-official lies. It must be admitted that they even begin to be caught up by the amusing aspect of this war behind the ramparts as at Issy, or among the houses as at Neuilly.

The aberrations and fantasies of this rabble-at-arms exceed imagination. Here is an example: This morning a naive Communard said at my villa: "They are shooting all the National

Guards at Versailles. But today we are going to change our uniforms; we are to get army uniforms; then if the Versailles forces keep this up, foreign powers will intervene."

An interesting poster is the one which blames the present social system for the prostitution of women and the enrollment of men in the police. If there are whores and informers, it is the fault of the bourgeoisie!

Friday, April 7

The sixth day of fighting, bombardment, rifle fire, killing.

At the Arc de Triomphe de l'Etoile, always a crowd, ambulances, dispatch-riders lying against their horses' bellies, and battalions of National Guards replacing each other in the line. The cannonade is incessant. Mont Valérien is covering Neuilly with shells.

In a corner, groups of motionless, stupefied women say they are waiting for their husbands, who have been forced into service. Among all the lower orders an unreasoning feeling makes Versailles responsible for all the harm the Committee has done—a feeling that it is very difficult to destroy and one that makes these unhappy victims of the revolution look upon the Versailles forces in the same light as Prussians.

People surround individual National Guards as they come back. An irregular with an energetic, powder-blackened face tells with savage grief that Neuilly is untenable under the shells which are falling like hail. Through the open curtain of an ambulance window I see the living or dead head of a wounded man with a fixed stare. Four or five cannons arrive and the rampart begins to answer frenetically. In the sunshine on this avenue which in its sharp ascent looks like a stage set at the old Franconi Circus, beyond the upraised arms of the rampart gate, fog streaked with lightning immerses the trees on the avenue, the houses on either side, and the barricade in a blue and gold haze—a fog in which the buildings and columns on the horizon are heaped up like a vague Acropolis. A regular effect of apotheosis with the play of light, the luminous transfiguration of objects, the glory of the setting sun, and the gold sky crackling with fireworks.

My contemplation is shattered by a *pif, pan, crac!* A shell has struck the left cornice of the Arc de Triomphe above our heads. Immediately everybody falls flat on his face, while a bursting shell bounces near me with its ugly dull sound. At once everyone is up and away, and so am I.

A poster announces that any citizen not enrolling in the National Guard within twenty-four hours will be disarmed and arrested, if there is occasion. This decree along with the one concerning landowners seems to me to be a pretty preliminary to a reign of terror.

This evening Burty tells me casually: "It's quite likely they will shoot the Archbishop this evening!" [7] They are indeed capable of plagiarizing 1793 by beginning September all over again.

Saturday, April 8

At Voisin's I ask for the day's special: "There isn't one, nobody's left in Paris," a waiter answers. The only diner today is an old habituée whom I saw all during the siege.

As I leave the restaurant I am struck by how few people I meet. Paris seems like a plague-stricken city. There are really not enough men left to make little groups, and the few faces

[7] Monsignor Georges Darboy, Archbishop of Paris, was arrested on April 4, was offered in vain to the Versailles authorities in exchange for Blanqui, and was killed on May 24.

of young men that I see are those of foreigners. The only movement, the only life in Paris is the removal of small households' goods, at the hour of twilight, on handcarts pulled along by National Guards. The democratic tenants are hastening to take advantage of the Commune's decrees about housing.

No group under the Opéra lamp post. No group at the corner of the Rue Drouot. I only find a few people gathered together at the entrance of the Rue Montmartre. A curious thing: In the groups into which I make my way people are not talking about the day's events, and what I hear is only about the past, about the siege of Paris and events during the siege, and about the weakness and ineptitude of the defense. You get a very clear impression that the principal strength of the insurrection does not come from stupidity or maladroitness on the part of Versailles, but from what the Trochus and the Favres have failed to try or undertake. And Thiers' great mistake is to have taken into his cabinet men whose incapacity the people look upon as treason.

In the evening they are selling perfume on the boulevard at fifty centimes, to the shouts of newsvendors hawking *Le Soir, La Commune, La Sociale,* and even *La Montagne,* which this evening, to encourage sales, has announced a republic in Russia.

At Auteuil some people are now buying ropes so that friends can let them down along the fortifications in order to escape the national requisition.

Easter Sunday, April 9

Sleep constantly interrupted by cannon shots. Around six in the morning terrible cannon and rifle fire simultaneously around Neuilly and around the Vanves fortress. Soon the whole south and southwest horizon is thundering and crackling with artillery fire.

The concierge of the villa warns me that domiciliary visits are to be made at noon. He urges me to conceal any arms I may have. These gentlemen take everything—de luxe arms, collector's items, curiosities. He has seen them carry off primitive bows and arrows.

On my way to Paris I see a poor devil of a shoe repairer go by under the escort of five National Guards; I have often seen him working in a shop near the market. They have made him get up from his sick-bed. He is being taken to the front lines. His wife follows him, making terrible outcries of grief. Why was he arrested? Nobody knows.

On the way I hear it said that the Versailles forces were beaten back at the Rond Point in Courbevoie. At eleven I am alone, completely alone, in Peters' large dining room. Not a soul having lunch—a symptom of the prevalent terror. The waiters speak only in low tones.

At Burty's I meet Bracquemond, whose thirty-eight years have put him under the coverage of the National Guard law. He leaves to go ask a hospital friend of his to have him enrolled as an assistant and to let him sleep in his barracks so that he will not be picked up.

Burty and I go with him to the hospital, which is set up in the garden of the Musard concert hall. On the Place de la Concorde they are taking down picks and shovels from a wagon for the construction of a barricade. On the Seine gunboats are being armed.

On entering the hospital we see a spectacle of wounded men dragging along on crutches, looking like a figure X; wounded men being given rides in little carriages; wounded men, among them an adolescent with his arm in a sling who practices sword drill with a stick. We enter a room where the picturesqueness of war is mingled with the disorder of a student's room. Four or five gay young ambulance aides are eating out of mess tins among the books. Bracquemond's friend quickly takes us into a tent, with the red cross of the *International* visible through the grey canvas. We are given brandy in glasses used for cupping.

The conversation is naturally frightful, with the habitual gaiety of tone of internes: "The wounds are awful," says one of the young men, who has scissors and a clamp stuck in the first buttonhole of his smock. "We have eighteen abdominals in the little pavilion over there. Why, it's a regular human porridge. There are some with the whole front of their overcoats in their bellies. Others have shattered, swollen legs, which give them the shape of tulips. The other day they brought in one with his jaw down to the middle of his stomach, a hole, a regular antique mask! And the orderly insisted on asking him his name!"

Another tells of a wounded man whom they turned over and opened up from behind, like an armoire, in order to trace the curious course of a bullet. "Look at the strange old fellow going by over there in a black cap," M. Guichard, Bracquemond's friend, says; "he's the man who gets forty sous for undressing the dead. It's a real passion with him. He only sleeps in the pavilion when there are some there. You ought to see with what a loving eye he comes to look at, to spy on the ones that are going to croak. Oh, an ambulance. Here are some more wounded."

He disappears, but soon passes in front of us holding up a man whose head is swathed in bandages, whose face is covered with plaster like a plasterer's. "Now there's a lucky one!" says Guichard, when he comes back. "He was at the post on the Rue Maillot when a shell burst and knocked everything down. Well, he has contusions all over and not a single wound!" He adds that the Versailles troops are completely in control at Neuilly and that the rampart is becoming untenable. It would appear also that the Federals are beginning to run out of shells.

Bracquemond has gone to make a tour of the room where the wounded are. He is very pale when he comes back. He has just seen stumps of men whose life is no more than a flutter of the eyelids.

At this point four hearses decked with red flags appear and delegates of the Commune enter to claim some bodies as escort for the dead Bourgoin. They quickly shut the nearest at hand in coffins. The delegates are in a hurry. They don't take them all.

Guichard shows us one which has been left behind. A man, half of whose face and nearly all of whose neck have been carried away by a shell, with the white and blue of one of his eyes running down his cheek. His right hand, still black with powder, is upraised and clenched as if it clasped a gun.

With that we leave. As they open the barrier for us, a woman is saying to the gatekeeper in a slow voice: "Sir, is my husband among the dead?" "What is his name?" "Chevalier." "We don't know him here. Go to Beaujon, to Necker, etc."

I go into a café at the foot of the Champs Elysées; and while the shells are killing up the avenue at the Etoile, men and women with the most tranquil, happy air in the world drink their beer and listen to an old woman play songs by Thérésa on a violin.

Then, preceded by many National Guards, coffins covered with red flags go by, and behind them I recognize Vallès, fat and shining, yellow as a piece of rancid lard, in great boots, a black jersey, and an ox-blood-colored scarf.

Having returned to Auteuil for a while after the horrible spectacle of the day, I am thrown into profound sadness by the fury of the continuing cannon fire. I feel a sort of tenderness over the fate of these brutes.

This evening the beginnings of barricades on the Place de la Concorde. On the Rue Neuve du Luxembourg a National Guard says to a doorkeeper: "But if this man is under suspicion, he must be run in, and I'm going to do it!" On the boulevard a good many people, even some young people. It seems that the day's lack of success has brought part of Paris out of hiding.

Monday, April 10

During this drawn-out struggle, aware of the ease with which it might go either way, we go through terrible alternations of fear and hope in response to everything that is announced, spoken, printed, or lied about.

Toward five o'clock a dispatch-rider who, they say, has given the order to lower the siege pieces on the rampart, arrives at a gallop. At the same time a reinforcement of three hundred men arrives at the Auteuil gate.

Conciliation between Versailles and the Commune—a pretty idea of the simple-minded!

Tuesday, April 11

A National Guard from Passy whom I encounter on top of the omnibus starts up a conversation with me: "I went in full of confidence," he tells me, "but I'm getting out. There is no order. The officers are so inept. In fact, watching them, you wonder if they aren't being paid to foul things up. I got into this because I'm out of work and earn thirty sous, and can't bring myself to steal. But if I could find any kind of job tomorrow, even pulling a cart, I wouldn't stay in the National Guard."

From the Madeleine to the Opéra the boulevard is empty. People seem to have gone back into hiding; it is pitiful to see the sad solitude in which the prostitutes drink their beer as they maintain their stand in cafés near the Opéra. Bad news seems to hover over Paris. The papers announce a setback for the Versailles troops at Asnières. Only around the Passage Jouffroy is there a little life.

On my way home I see all the inhabitants of the quays at windows and doors, their eyes looking toward Issy. The cannon fire is frightful. A noise as if the sky were falling. From my brother's window I see a line of lightning from Bicêtre to the Châtillon plateau, as though there were the regular mechanical fire of a machine gun of cannons as wide as the horizon. That lasts almost two hours, mixed with the crackling of rifle fire and, toward the end, interrupted by frightening silences, when you can hear the wailing of a little dog in the house next door, terrified by the long thunder.

Wednesday, April 12

When I wake up this morning I see that the Issy fortress, which I thought had been taken, still has its red flag. The Versailles forces must have been pushed back.

Why this zeal, such as the Prussians never encountered? Because the idea of patriotism is dying. Because the formula "All men are brothers" has made headway even in these times of invasion and cruel defeat. Because the International's doctrine of indifference to nationality has infiltrated the masses.

Why this zeal? Because in this war the people themselves

make the war, lead it themselves, and are not under the yoke of militarism. This amuses and interests these men, and so nothing tires or discourages them, nothing disheartens them. You can get anything from them, even heroism.

Shells continually falling on the Champs Elysées as far up as the Avenue d'Alma; and as far as the obelisk there are crowds of curious people who continually give way to the gallop of a dispatch-rider bent over his horse just like a monkey at the circus. At the Place Vendôme, barricades, the coming and going of men in dirty maroon overcoats, some of whom have casseroles at the end of their rifles. These men seem to be carrying out duties in the area.

As we pass the Quartermaster's Depot, from which casks of wine are constantly being brought out, the omnibus conductor tells me of the frightful waste which occurs there; the officers demand double rations for their men, and the Belleville women carry off four or five loaves of bread every day in their aprons.

Thursday, April 13

We begin to hear the plaintive *hou-hou* of shells falling on the Trocadéro battery, which is carrying on a duel with Mont Valérien above our heads.

I pass by the Café du Helder, my eyes instinctively looking for someone in uniform. The café is empty. Two foreign women seated at the door are the only people there.

The human brain, truly, is off its track right now like everything else. It gets so-called good ideas which make the most intelligent people utter stupidities as big as houses. This evening Burty was upholding the position that everything should give way to the instinct of the masses. *The instinctive people,* as he calls them, without being aware of the feelings that lead them, ought to command an obedience that is not given to science, knowledge, study, or reflection. That is saying that the most stupid people are the most intelligent.

Friday, April 14

I am awakened to bursting shells and the following piece of news, given me by Pélagie. A notice commands all men of whatever age to march against the Versailles troops. And there is terrified talk at Auteuil of a house-to-house search for those evading service.

Basically I cannot conceal from myself the fact that things are going very slowly, if not badly. There have been two or three unsuccessful attacks on Vanves and Issy; and the Federals seem to be passing from the defensive to the offensive around Asnières.

A quiet day, only a few isolated cannon shots here and there.

Saturday, April 15

I was working in the garden this morning. I hear the whine of several shells. Two or three explosions very close. A shout from within the villa: "Everybody to the cellars." And there we are, like our neighbors, in the cellar. Terrible explosions all around the house. Mont Valérien is sending us a shell a minute. At every cannon burst you are caught up by a disagreeable feeling of anxiety, which lasts for the few seconds of the trajectory, fearing that it will fall on your house, on you.

Suddenly there is a terrible explosion. Pélagie, who, with one knee on the ground, is making bundles of kindling, is thrown over on her behind by the shaking of the house. We fearfully wait for a fall, a tumbling down of stones. Nothing!

We risk sticking our noses through the gaping door. Nothing!

The bombardment starts up again and goes on for almost two hours, all around us, enveloping us in shell bursts. Still another explosion, which rattles the zinc on the roof.

A feeling of cowardice such as I never felt while the Prussians were here. My physical being is at its lowest ebb. I had taken the precaution of having a mattress put on the floor, and, lying on it, I remain in a state of sleepy torpor, only vaguely aware of cannon fire and death. Soon a frightful storm mixes with the bombardment, and the ripping sounds of lightning and shells give me there in the depths of the cellar a feeling of cataclysm and the end of the world. At last, about three o'clock, the storm breaks up and the firing begins to be controlled and the shells to fall in front of me, on the ramparts and the moat, where the Federals are again setting up siege pieces.

During an interruption in the cannon fire I make a tour of the house. Yes, you might truly say that my house was Mont Valérien's target. Each of the three houses behind me on the Avenue des Sycomores, Numbers 12, 16, and 18, has been hit by a shell. The Courasse house, which was hit twice during the Prussian bombardment, has a hole from the top of the roof to the foundations. The explosion which sat poor Pélagie over on her rump cut the railway switch across from me and passed under a rail; a whole section of rock has fallen down; it was struck by shell bursts, a piece of rail, and a hunk of earth.

We foresee danger during the night and install ourselves in the cellar. We stop up the air vent with sod. We light a fire in a stove, and Pélagie sets up a bed for me under the stairs.

Sunday, April 16

Contrary to all expectations a quiet night. Nothing but a big artillery duel in rain and wind over toward Neuilly.

Yesterday provided me with a serious study of acoustics. I did not know what caused a sort of agonizing wail which I once took for a moaning man. I had read in the paper that it was the special sound of shells. I had heard it was a whistling in the grooves of the lead sheath. Now I know that this wail comes when a concave shell fragment is projected a very long distance. I have also noticed that in a cannon shot there is something like the sound of rebound of the carriage which is easily distinguished from the shell explosion, even when the latter is very flat.

A white poster calls on citizens to build barricades in the First and Twentieth Arrondissements. The white poster offers four francs a day as pay to the workers on the barricades. They always offer money to the patriots of 1871.

A pink poster urges the citizens to take possession of the forty billions belonging to men of the Empire. And as if the signatory of the notice felt this sum too small to satisfy the appetites of the populace, he points out that there is a group of 7,500,000 families who have only ten billions, while there is another group of 450,000 families of financiers and big industrialists who possess four hundred billions, obviously acquired in a dirty way. This notice is the focal point of the Commune's secret program! Don't I already see these men sitting with their wives on my boulevard and saying aloud as they look at our villas: "When the Commune is set up, we'll be very comfortable in there!"

A tragic episode of these times. A few evenings ago the bell rang at Charles Edmond's. He opened the door to a white-haired woman whom he did not recognize for a moment. It was Julie, his wife! She had left for Bellevue some days before the insurrection, taking with her her dying mother and a maid. There is fighting at Bas Meudon. Four gendarmes fall in front of her garden. There are wounded to bring in and take care of. The basement of the house becomes a hospital, and the old mother dies there. No municipal office and no way to get a burial permit. At last after two days a little girl runs clear to Meudon and brings back a permit, a coffin, and a priest. But no pallbearers or gravediggers. They set out at night—the priest and the two women carrying the coffin. A shell falls and explodes. The coffin is thrown to the ground and the three bearers fall flat. Another shell, and another; with each shell the same performance. At the cemetery they had expected to use the gravedigger's pick. No pick. The women have to put the coffin down in a corner and cover it scantily with earth scraped up by means of scissors and fingers. This went on in the midst of the terrible cannon fire and rifle fire of the last few days.

Going down from Charles Edmond's, I hear what sounds like a preacher's voice coming from a hole. I perceive a piece of painted stairway, go down a few stairs, and find myself in the Chapel of the Luxembourg Palace, where to the sound of the organ the voices of the little daughters of the employes blend with those of two or three hundred wounded men in grey coats, whose pale and languishing procession grips your heart.

In the whole district, in all the workrooms and reading rooms, ordinarily so full, today I see only one young forehead resting on a hand above a book.

Shells are beginning to be featured in the show windows of curiosity shops, and I hear a street Arab with a handkerchief full of iron on the ground beside him shout: "Ten centimes for a piece of shrapnel!" The closing of shops is on such a widespread scale that today even Guerre's pastry shop, the one at the Tuileries gate, is closed.

All around the Place Vendôme a confusion of marching troops and of dispatch-riders ready to mount their horses, and among them there passes a huge vehicle from which bayonets gleam forth.

These days life is lived in a state of extraordinary absent-mindedness and physical fatigue.

Monday, April 17

Although the bombardment is rather well-behaved and only three shells have fallen during the day near my house, I am so distracted that for a few days I need to live out of this danger, to have a few good nights' sleep, a few nights when I can sleep, and sleeping in a cellar is an abomination. However well-covered I am, I am always cold, and I feel as though air from a snowbank were blowing on my face. I leave for Paris. I take refuge in a big apartment on the Rue de l'Arcade, which one of my cousins has left empty.

Are things going badly for the Commune? I am astonished today to find that the population has come back to life. The boulevard is swarming. In front of the Passage Jouffroy I am astonished to hear shouts of "Down with the Commune!" National Guards intervene. A stentorian voice yells in their faces: "Long live the Republic and down with the Commune!" From Burty's balcony I vaguely see a convulsive movement accompanied by shouts of "Death!"—a convulsive movement from which, energetic and threatening, there emerges a man in a grey overcoat who goes on up the boulevard defying the angry rowdies and turning around to shout aloud his disdain for the Communards.

Madame Burty, who is with me, confirms a letdown on the part of the National Guards. At the hospital this morning Bracquemond is reported to have seen a wounded man who all the time they were removing his arm at the shoulder murmured as he died: "The National Guards have betrayed us, they've betrayed us!" Put at ease by the absence of her husband, she confirms with curious details that all the leaders are men of doubtful character and reputation, the dregs of society, people indeed whose first act was to arrest Claude, the chief of the Security Service, fearful of his memory and his terrible sleepy eyes.

Tuesday, April 18

The scaffolding for tearing down the column is being erected in the Place Vendôme. The square is the scene of a terrible uproar and a fantasia of impossible costumes. You see some extraordinary National Guards there. One of them looks like a Velásquez dwarf, swallowed up in a civilian greatcoat from beneath which twisted feet stick out.

Always a sidewalk market, to which today lilac branches have been brought. On the wall of Saint Roch with its tight-shut doors a death notice has been posted, announcing that the service will take place at the Petits Pères, since this church is closed.

A sign of the times. I see a man in a coupé blowing his nose through the door with his fingers.

Posters, posters, and more posters! White government paper is thick on the walls. The latest notice, the one of the last quarter of an hour, is about courts-martial. This notice spreads out for all eyes to see the penalties of death, forced labor, detention, imprisonment—the whole barbarous penal code which they are using to establish liberty.

A few groups around little gaming tables presided over by faces which you feel are Jewish. In front of the Gymnase a woman in a trance sitting on a chair, her eyes blindfolded; assisted by her hypnotizer, she is sibyllizing on the open boulevard.

On the Place de la Concorde at the head of the Rue de Rivoli workmen digging a ditch as wide as a rampart moat. Work of the same kind going on where the Rue Castiglione begins; as they are filled, sacks of earth are piled up under the arcades.

At every streetcorner you meet people, both men and women, carrying overnight bags, traveling bags, and small bundles, which are all it is possible to escape from Paris with.

It seems that the Louvre employes are very anxious. Guess where the *Venus de Milo* is hidden? At the Prefecture of Police. It is deeply and doubly hidden, for it is concealed behind a first hiding-place that is full of dossiers and police records, which are enough to stop searchers from looking further. They are afraid, though, that Courbet may be on the scent, and the stupid employes fear the worst from that ferocious modernist against the classical masterpiece.

Renan, who tells us this at Brébant's, where there are only four diners today, complains of the Paris deputies' lack of courage. He says they should have gone about Paris rallying a spirit of resistance by talking to groups of people. He says that if he had been honored by his fellow-citizens' mandate, he would not have failed in what he calls a duty: "I would have wanted," he adds, "to make myself seen carrying on my back something that spoke to the eyes, which would be a sign, a symbol, something like the yoke the Prophets Isaiah or Ezekiel bore on their shoulders!"

Then by those zigzags peculiar to roving conversations,

Renan goes on to talk of Prince Napoleon and his voyage to northern waters. He tells us of accosting him gaily on the morning the ship was getting ready to leave for Spitsbergen, accosting him with the remark, "Fine weather, your Highness!" "Yes, fine weather for returning to France!" the Prince replied. During the night the Prince had received a dispatch apprising him of the declaration of war against Prussia and recalling him to France. The Prince added: "One more piece of madness, but the last one they will commit!"

Thereupon Renan expatiates at length on the accuracy of the Prince's foresight, on his Cassandra-like perspicacity, and he tells us of listening for a whole night at the London embassy to the Prince predicting to La Vallette and Tissot everything that has happened.

Wednesday, April 19

Charles Edmond told me yesterday that it is estimated that 700,000 people have left Paris since the elections.

Heavy movement of National Guards all day. Returning battalions are garlanded with lilacs, but they look pretty sheepish.

On the Quai Voltaire the smell of powder carried by the wind goes up the Seine over the water. For a long while I stop to listen to the cannonade at the end of the terrace along the river behind the statue of Fame astride her stone horse, which is upreared whitely against a showery, smoky sky where great violet clouds rush by.

Thursday, April 20

At eleven in the morning the boulevard from the Rue Montmartre to the Bastille looks like the main street of a sleepy provincial town where people used to take a turn in former days as they waited for a change of horses for the stagecoach.

Calm and emptiness on the Place de la Bastille. At the top of the column, the Spirit of Liberty brandishes a red flag. At its feet merchants sell fried potatoes and café au lait in the midst of a display of iron scrap. Beginnings of barricades, old style, at the head of the Rue Saint Antoine, where the entire left-hand sidewalk is an outdoor market for everything under the sun. In that street you see National Guards returning the worse for wear or departing with their provisions in handkerchiefs attached to their bayonets. Companies full of old men with white hair and young men who look like children. One of them carrying a long rifle has a boyish face which makes the passers-by turn their heads in a gesture of pity. In front of the Hôtel de Ville the shining new brass of thirty cannons or so.

Always lies and reports of victories, signed by all those foreign names who to me are as suspect as would be Prussian generals given to France so that we might tear ourselves to pieces and finish ourselves off.

Men coming up to you mysteriously with something hidden under their coats and offering you *Le Bien Public,* which has been sold surreptitiously for the last two days.

This evening I hear about the original enterprise of a sexagenarian who belonged to a company of sharpshooters during the Siege. He wasn't concerned about saving France; the scholarly fellow merely wished to study the cryptogams which come out on corpses. This personal activity provided him with some very interesting observations of French and Prussian cryptogams.

Friday, April 21

At the top of the Champs Elysées, groups of workmen

conversing and looking in the direction of the cannonade. All the talk is about the high cost of living; and the orator in the group says of his father, who turned a millstone: "He only got fifty sous a day; yet he could feed three children, while I earned five francs under the Empire and it was all I could do to feed two." The rise in wages does not equal the increased cost of living, that is basically the big complaint of the workingman against society today. I then remember that somewhere my brother and I wrote that the gap between wages and the cost of living would kill the Empire. The workman adds: "What good does it do me for there to be monuments, operas, café-concerts where I have never set foot because I don't have the money?" And he rejoices that henceforth there will be no more rich people in Paris, so convinced is he that the gathering of rich people into one place raises prices. This workman is at once stupid and full of good sense.

La Vérité announces that tomorrow or the day after a decree will be printed in *L'Officiel* by virtue of which every man from nineteen to fifty-five, married or single, will be compelled to sign up and march against the Versailles forces. Here am I under the threat of that law! Here am I under the necessity in a few days of hiding away as if in the time of the Terror! It is still possible to get out if need be, but I don't have the will to leave.

What partisanship by men of party! Burty declares that he would prefer a Prussian occupation to one by the Versailles forces! Where is justice? He is the same man who was indignant against the émigrés. Yet they had the mitigating circumstances of the confiscation of their property and the killing of their relatives as justification for seeking aid abroad.

Hearses going by to bring in the dead traverse the boulevard; their eight decorative flags float in the wind and their sinister folds envelop the macabre faces of the coachmen. At my brother's grave in Montmartre gun fire and cannon fire seem to be very close and right inside Paris. In the upper part of the cemetery, occupied by the Russian and Polish dead, women lying on the stones listen and, getting up, try to see what is going on.

When I am on the Tuileries terrace along the river, I hear the cannonade again—it is terrible today. Now and then a rentier, disturbed by the noise, climbs up from his seat in the sun and is promptly sent back down to *La Petite Provence* by the rude eloquence of a tipsy National Guard.

But you can't leave, for at times your friends the enemy seem to be coming so close that you wonder if they haven't entered the city, and you half expect to see the heads of the Versailles columns appear under the Arc de Triomphe in a confused rout of National Guards and bursts of rifle fire. But after all the awful noise nothing comes, and you go away saying to yourself: "Well, it will be tomorrow!" And that tomorrow never comes.

Saturday, April 22

Here in Paris I feel as though I were living, as if on a journey, in a great foreign city where I have been held up by some mishap or other. I pass here the empty, boring hours of a fly-by-night existence.

A few miserable little pots of greenery in the Flower Market, which workmen take away with them as they eat their bread.

I go to the Zoo with the idea of reconnoitering the place. I want to see if there isn't a deer or gazelle hut vacant and if I can't bribe a keeper to allow me to go there at night to sleep in case the draft or the enmity of the all-powerful *Pipe-en-Bois* pursues and tracks me down on the Rue de l'Arcade.

The Zoo has the sadness of Paris. The animals are silent. The boredom of the fierce ones is evident in their relaxed poses. A dozen National Guards stroll along the dug-up paths; one of them makes tender remarks about a mother kangeroo, contrasting the ever-open pouch of the animal with the neglect women of the *aristocracy* show their children. Abandoned by his public, the elephant, indolently leaning against a wall, eats his hay like a man suddenly condemned to dine alone.

I go up the cedar walk to the belvedere, the walk my brother and I followed several times when we were writing the first and last chapters of *Manette Salomon.* Ah, if I had been told then: "In a few years you will come along this walk alone, alone for ever; and the cannon shots you hear there will be ones that will destroy your home!"

The only things I see around me are does fleeing in fright or buffalo in their astonished immobility listening to this storm and thunder which never, never stop.

The whole length of the Rue de Rivoli there is a procession of the baggage of the last bourgeois making their way to the Lyon railroad station.

In the Place de l'Hôtel de Ville they are hawking Jules Vallès' biography, and I buy the broadsheet in which my colleague is represented as the type and paragon of the man born "between the *Orleanist-Clerical-Legitimist-Bonapartist* reaction and the restoration of the Empire, between a shady deal and a crime so bad it cannot be described."

Sunday, April 23

I pass part of the day at *Le Temps.* Nefftzer does not want to write there any more. Scherer is putting a paper together at Saint Germain with Hébrard. During this confusion, Charles Edmond discourages one man who wants to move to

Saint Germain, tones down another who has Communard tendencies, clamps down on another who has Versailles principles. I hear all this through the open glass partition of a large office where, lying on a divan to the shaking of the building by the rolling presses, I have the feeling and vague discomfort of being on a wave-tossed ship.

As he comes out, Charles Edmond is accosted by a sort of mulatto. It is Clemenceau the doctor. You would say he was one of those wild doctors invented by Eugène Sue in his novels.

This evening in the Luxembourg district a general alarm at every street corner.

I go into a tobacconist's. Some National Guards declare with great vigor that they will go without rifles. One of them, raising his hands threateningly in the air, adds: "I'll always have the strength of my arms!" I ask the proprietress of the shop what is going on. She answers: "There have been riots at the municipal offices; some National Guards want to disarm others." And the woman bursts into tears. Poor France!

A pretty scene under the Rue de Rivoli arcades. A prostitute, being rather intimately fondled by the two hands of a National Guard officer, slips away from him with the bodily twists and turns of a soubrette defending her honor from a noble lord. When the National Guard is safely a few feet away, with a charming and mocking strut, she hisses out with untranslatable disdain: "*Such dirrt!*"

Monday, April 24

How much is wine responsible for whetting patriotic, liberal, Communard feelings in this uprising? What strange statistics might be gathered about all the wine drunk during this period and the part it plays in national heroism. All you see is

National Guards rolling barrels to their posts, and the troops
as they go out to seek glory are always accompanied by carts
sagging under the weight of casks. [See Illustration 6.]

The Théâtre Français is playing *Le Malade Imaginaire.* It
is exactly the delicate kind of comedy needed at this moment.

This evening I once more run through *La Confession d'un
Enfant du Siècle,* of which I have found a first edition. I already have the first edition of *Volupté.* I would like to have
those of *Mademoiselle de Maupin* and *Lélia.* To me these
books are very strange; they are analyses of Insatiability, the
intellectual malady of our times.

Tuesday, April 25

Today there is a truce to permit evacuation of the inhabitants of Neuilly. I push on as far as the ramparts.

Up to the Etoile barrier nothing but broken street lights
and a few scars on the stone houses. Beyond, it's something
else again. The Etoile barrier is marked all over with blackened, rayed bursts; in the bas-relief of *Invasion,* a shell has
taken off an arm of the child carried on his mother's shoulder.
Below, there are blocks of granite broken into fragments the
size of a lump of sugar.

The real devastation begins on the Avenue de la Grande
Armée and follows it clear to the ramparts on the Rue Pres-
bourg, Rue Rude, and Rue Pergolèse side. There is nothing
but gaping holes where destruction has burst out—broken
angles of windows, broken pilasters, balconies torn away,
drain pipes cut in five or six places, shop windows with
twisted, torn ironwork. You see nothing but glassless windows, with shreds of tulle curtains floating out. Beside the
twisted urinals you walk on the dust of bricks, glass, and slate
covering the sidewalk. When you go into a building you pass

the concierge's lodge protected by mattresses piled on ladders, and you find the fourth story lying in the courtyard.

I see two frightful examples of the destruction a shell can cause inside a building. One is at a hairdresser's; all that is left of the furniture of the shop is a piece of molten stove-metal and half a clockface without hands. The other is at a bakery; a shell which hit a wood partition made it into a sort of matting with broken fibers.

Everyone is running away. Everyone is moving. A distracted woman is throwing drawers from some shop or other on a cart; and the porte-cochère steps are covered with brides' bouquets under glass ready for transport into Paris. Survivors of the bombardment and continuous threat of death seem stupefied, asleep. Many seem to have a fatalistic resignation.

The crowd roaming this destruction is angry. And before this spectacle of devastation a little old man with eyes like gas jets talks of frightful torture to inflict on Thiers, using his assassin hands to make strangling motions in front of him.

At the moment Voisin's café is the place where the headquarters personnel from the Place Vendôme come to have coffee with their *brothers and friends*. It is curious to hear these gentlemen and to be present in one's shadowy corner at such a savage parley.

Today the destruction of the Vendôme Column leads them to talk about the Cluny Museum. One of them, bursting out against *false antique stuff*, emits the idea that the money devoted to such stupid purchases is diverted from ends that are useful and profitable to the people, and he urges sale of these knick-knacks for the profit of the nation.

Towards four o'clock a continuous procession of ambulances, today converted into moving vans for Neuilly. All around the Palace of Industry, seated on the curbs, pale women with red eyes are surrounded by bundles of linen and by nibbling children. Bit by bit the upper part of the Champs Elysées becomes empty and the crowd is massed at the top of the square awaiting renewal of the bombardment, which is late.

Burty, who passed the day with members of the League, confirms the stunned feeling, the resigned fatalism of the people he has seen, many of whom did not want to come back into Paris. He tells me that as he was passing in an ambulance by a group of women huddled under a porte-cochère, he shouted to ask if they wanted to go back into Paris and was greeted by laughter, a refusal at once sad and mocking.

Wednesday, April 26

Yes, I continue to believe that the Commune will perish because it has not given satisfaction to the feelings which are the basis of its incontestable power. Municipal rights, autonomy of the Commune, etc., all the metaphysical cloud-cuckoo-land in which it floats may be good for satisfying a few cabaret ideologues, but this is not what gives it a hold on the masses. Its strength comes absolutely from the awareness of the people that they were inadequately and incapably defended by the National Defense Government, from their belief, in a word, that this one is a government with balls.

Therefore if the Commune, instead of showing itself more complaisant toward Prussian demands than Versailles itself, had broken the treaty for which it reproaches the Assembly, had declared war on Prussia in a wild fury of heroism, M. Thiers would have found it impossible to begin his attack and would have been unable to work toward the subjugation of Paris with the help of the foreigner. Now if resistance had been vigorous, if the attempt had been begun by two or three unimportant successes—impossible you will say—do you know what would have happened? Neither M. Thiers nor his generals would have controlled this movement and the whole country would have been swept along to a full-scale renewal of the war. And with the German army's weariness and reluctance to take up fighting again, who knows what might have happened at such a moment? At any rate the death of the Commune would have been a total death, a death which would have made it hard going for the ideas it had been sheltering under its banner.

I find Madame Burty alone, nervously polishing the Japanese bronzes in the little show case. She tells me sadly about the harmful overstimulation that politics provides for her husband, and the sharp discomfort this brings into the household. She deplores a sort of mania which kills any sentiment of justice or injustice in him. She cites his incomprehensible partisanship which permits him enthusiastically to accept no matter what on the part of this government, which has nothing in common with his instincts or his tastes.

She tells me of a terrible scene she had with him this morning, because she had allowed herself to tell him that Madame Bracquemond, a teacher in a school of drawing, had had to endure before her students in the classroom the stupid and brutal observations made by a man and a woman delegate from the Commune. Now this delegate was a house painter and the woman was his wife.

I promise to try to hold him down a bit, to keep him from compromising himself in *Le Rappel*, where I have the impression that those acrobats, Meurice and Vacquerie, are receding into the background and pushing him to the front. She feels the way I do and tells me that on the night of October 31 three different editions of *Le Rappel* were put together, depending on the successive news that these seekers after big money and low popularity received about the battle between the Communard National Guards and the National Defense Government.

In the café the remaining dandies are this evening teaching the streetwalkers to calculate the distance of the cannons being fired by the number of seconds elapsing between the flash and the detonation.

"A Thiers dispatch for eight francs!" A workman seated on a boulevard bench is selling an enormous shell which is placed on the ground in front of him.

Thursday, April 27

While visiting Duplessis in the Print Room I am admiring the tiny drawings made by Gabriel de Saint Aubin on the margin of five or six catalogues which just turned up in the printed books section, when Lavoix comes to sit next to me.

At once we start talking about the Princess and soon about Popelin. We deplore the fact that in a nature so elevated, so generous, so highly distinguished, there should be a bit of the woman responsive to overtones of gallantry, to badly rhymed and stupid little amorous verses; with deep sadness we both speak of this ending, this compromise of what is left of a life that could have been so fine. We feel sorry for ourselves in that the installation of this man at the Princess's makes it impossible for us to go and pass the long months of exile with her, makes it impossible for us to take turns in bringing to her a bit of the Paris which she loves so much. The man so lacks tact that he can't help being embarrassing, irritating; and

Lavoix tells me that on his last visit to Brussels, the fellow said to him concerning his letters to the Princess: "We received your letters." A *we* where there seemed to be a very capital *W!*

Friday, April 28

Rereading *La Confession d'un Enfant du Siècle*, I am struck by the effect certain books have on certain men, and how such men, whose fathers have left no imprint on them, emerge fully formed from the entrails of a book. All the confused naughtiness of that book I had felt and touched in Scholl, but more ripened, more developed, put into splenetic action by a provincial nature and low birth. I wondered, then, whether my friend got all that from within himself. Today I recognize that he was merely a plagiarist, a literary plagiarist, who finally, with the aid of his detestable instincts, became a temperament. With the result that the Octave of the story really created, as if in a human womb, an Octave of flesh and blood.

Yesterday Lavoix and I admitted that we had exactly the same feeling, an almost painful feeling of anxiety, when the cannons stopped firing.

Weary of the spectacle of the street, of dirty drunken National Guards, of toughs in full flower, I take refuge in the Zoo! I need to see the animals and flowers. The assistant gardener who takes me into the hothouses says: "You come to see our sick ones." He alludes to all the delicate trees which have been killed by the cold, let in by the Prussian shells.

Saturday, April 29

I read a poster appealing to the population to furnish a corps of scouts for the National Guard. In this proclamation the salient phrase, the one that leaps to the eye, is this: *You*

will be paid as soon as you enroll. Always pay to assure patriotism in 1871! I always find simple mercenaries underneath
these so-called soldiers of an idea. After reading the notice,
my eyes fall on the backs of three National Guards, who have
three pairs of new shoes slung over them. Paid, fed, clothed,
shod, and made drunk on top of all that, these liberators of
humanity may well sing: "It's the sweetest fate . . ."

Two true stories about the hospital on the Champs Elysées.
A wounded National Guard is brought in. He has an odd
wound. A piece of shell, a piece of lead the size of a forty-sou
piece, entering at the top of the femur, has gone the length of
his thigh and around the calf, and has lodged near the ankle.
After three days he is dying. His wife has been notified. She is
there wordlessly watching him die. A charity worker passing
by attempts to comfort her: "My poor woman." The wife interrupts: "We lived together for eighteen years and we
couldn't stand each other!" And she begins a recital of her
complaints against the dying man. The charity worker slips
away. The end hurries on. Not fifteen minutes has passed before the orderly says to the woman: "Your husband is dead."
"The doctor must say so," she replies. They go to find the interne, who listens to the corpse and says: "Yes, he's really
dead." To which the widow comes back at once with: "Well,
then, my pension!" "I don't have it on me," the interne replies, sending her to Chenu, who sends her to a member of the
Commune.

Another story. A young man dies of an almost impercepti-
ble wound in the chest, one which must, however, have done
great internal damage. The doctors are very eager to study
the case. The father, who had been at his son's bedside, disappears; they don't know what has happened to him. The
corpse is carried into a little room at the back; three doctors

slip in. The autopsy is beginning when suddenly the father rushes into the room with an outcry such as to stir up a mob. The operating-room orderly only has time to shut the doctors up in another room; he has barely turned the key when he finds the father bending over the body of his son, which has been opened up. The man shouts, he threatens to start a riot: "Do you want twenty francs!" the orderly asks coldly. "Twenty francs! An only son!" the father replies. You can visualize the scene. "Well, come now, twenty-five francs." The father calms down, holds out his hand, and leaves. It has been learned since that the father was a former operating-room orderly who had sensed the doctors' desire to perform an autopsy, had hidden in the hospital, had watched his colleague's movements, had given the doctors time to begin, and then had rushed out of ambush.

Sunday, April 30

In refusing conciliation Thiers and Dufaure are perfectly logical. What is to be said for journalists who in one column demand conciliation with the people against whom, in another column, they are clamoring for the application of such and such an article of the penal code?

At *Le Temps* today I see Clemenceau again. He looks less satanic to me than he did. He is only a gastralgic with intelligent, even animated, conversation, and a somewhat nervous comic manner in the style of the Palais Royal. At his side is Floquet, who resembles a loquacious druggist. He is the typical vulgar merchant of words of the courtroom—a hollow windbag.

This evening Paris-on-a-Sunday without any suburbs, with no open-air café-concerts, passes its evening at the foot of the Champs Elysées watching the bombardment as though it were fireworks.

Otherwise the civil war goes on at a great rate. This evening cannons and machine guns never stop. In the rainy sky above the not-yet-green skeletons of the elms along the Champs Elysées on the Ternes side there unfolds a great red cloud colored by three new fires which are devouring houses. In this lugubrious setting women in the shadowy groups curse the *Prussians of Versailles!* Orators speak with frogs and tears in their hoarse voices about the *exploitation of the workers.* And drunkards shout: *"Down with the robbers!"* as they look the bourgeois straight in the face.

Monday, May 1

Troops coming back from Issy and crossing the boulevard preceded by a joyous music and a merry din in sharp contrast with the pitiful appearance of the men and the exhaustion of their march. A woman with a rifle on her shoulder keeps step in their midst. Two wagons full of rifles follow behind. People in the crowd say that they are rifles belonging to the dead and wounded.

Tuesday, May 2

Since March 18 I have not seen a banknote, a goldpiece, or a piece of silver in a single moneychanger's window. This is perhaps the most curious indication of the confidence Money has in the Commune.

A woman who sells prints along the quays tells me that at the school on the Rue Boudry, near the Rue Saint Jacques, where her cousin is a teacher, the little girls are forbidden to say their prayers. The *Marseillaise* has been substituted for the *Pater Noster.*

Wednesday, May 3

There are still barbers' wives in Paris; of male barbers only a few, and of apprentice barbers not a one; with the result that you have to go to five or six shops before you can get a haircut.

A frail scaffolding is beginning to rise to the top of the Vendôme Column and to enclose its glorious bronze.

A War Ministry circular informs the National Guards that since the sending of a negotiator may be a ruse, they must continue their fire even when the enemy has stopped. A notice signed by Citizen Rossel, in reply to a demand for surrender of the Issy fortress, threatens on the pretext of insolence—it is very difficult in a demand not to be a bit insolent —threatens to shoot the first negotiator who brings another demand. That seems to me to be suppression of communication between the two armies.

Eight o'clock. Cannonade. On the Champs Elysées a pale gold sky touched with rose; the trees violet with black silhouettes beneath them which advance or draw back depending on the nearness of the exploding shells. Groups in angry conversation, in which any man who discusses the actions of the Commune is treated as an informer—a word which could excite the crowd to kill him. Among the orators a workman with the raging face of Gavarni's politickers. After a terrible outburst against Versailles, he ends with this significant statement: "And then ten years from now on the pretext of revenge they might make us march against the Prussians. That must not happen!" Three sailors draw away from the group, one of them saying to his comrades: "Shit on these *liberalistic* speeches. The important thing is to have eight liters of wine in our canteens, a lot of bread, and a big piece of . . . ," of something which I do not catch. This workman and these sailors well attest the attitude of the present revolution: Shit on the country and long live grub!

Thursday, May 4

Bad news from Auteuil and the Boulevard Montmorency. Shells are falling all around my house. The grille of the villa gate has been torn away.

Burty takes me along with him to the Hôtel de Ville, where he is going to try to get hold of a blank pass for a poor devil who wants to get away. He has to find the poet Verlaine, who has been appointed chief of the Press Bureau. The concierge doesn't know the number of the Press Bureau; the employes are completely unacquainted with one another. In a drawing room the National Guards are worrying the cloth enclosing the chandeliers with their bayonets. In a corridor a soldier is furiously jawing his officer. On the stairs the open doors of the toilets bang back and forth, and it smells very bad everywhere.

After wandering around the palace, where the bronze statues of François I and Louis XIV clash with all the *National Guardishness* of the building in its present state, after being sent to right and left, we present ourselves to the Committee. Four or five mattresses lie across the door; several dirty frantic people wander about in the large empty room. You would say it was an insurrectionaries' camp. It is not a seat of power but a badly kept guardroom.

From the Hôtel de Ville we go into an out-of-the-way district to see Jongkind. I was one of the first to appreciate the painter, but I was not acquainted with the good man.

Imagine a tall blond fellow with blue eyes—the blue of Delft pottery—and a turned-down mouth, painting in a knitted vest and a Dutch sailor's cap.

On his easel is a picture of the Paris suburbs with a clayey bank of delicious texture. He shows us some sketches of Paris streets, of the Mouffetard district, of the area around Saint

Médard, in which the apotheosis of the grey and muddy colors of plaster of Paris seems to have been caught by a magician in a radiant aqueous atmosphere. Then there are cartoons, smears on paper, fantasmagories of sky and water, the fireworks of ethereal color.

He shows us all those things good-naturedly, talking in a Dutch-French jargon which reveals at times the bitterness of a man of great talent who needs 3,000 francs a year to live on and has not always received that much, even in years when a Bonington sold for 80,000 francs. But softening at once, he speaks with a note of sadness about his art, his struggle, his researches, which make him, he says, "the most unhappy of men."

During all this talk there hovers around him, with the caresses and words that mothers have for children, a woman who has saved him from hunger and madness—a short, silver-haired woman with thick moustaches, an angel of devotion, who looks like a madam in a brothel.

It is a long session, for we look at drawings for several hours. Jongkind talks about and becomes animated over the Commune's politics. Suddenly his language becomes confused and Dutchified, his words bizarre and incoherent. It is a matter of agents of Louis XVI, of horrible things which the painter has apparently witnessed. He jumps up like a spring: "See, some electricity just passed by, there, right beside me." And with his mouth he imitates the whine of a bullet. He sits down again and speaks once more about the secret police, about people who want to make him disappear, etc. I witness the painful, horrible spectacle of this fine talent, which has been rescued from the abyss once already, wavering and ready to fall back as the result of any conversation that goes on too long, after the slightest nervous excitement, after the tiniest labor of the brain.

At Burty's this evening Verlaine confesses something unbelievable. He declares that he has had to fight against a proposal that has been put forward to destroy Notre Dame.

Friday, May 5

I see a shop on the Rue Saint Honoré which is beginning to cover its glass with strips of gummed paper. The reason is the nearness of two cannons emplaced at the Rue Castiglione barricade. I think I can see that part of the grille around the Vendôme Column has already been destroyed.

The cowardice and indifference of this population living in the midst of this terrible situation, under the power of this triumphant rabble, exasperates me. I can't watch them tranquilly continuing their aimless lives without getting angry. To think that from this vile herd of men and women there issues no anger, no indignation to attest to the upside-downness of things human and divine! No, Paris merely looks like Paris in August of a very hot year. Oh! these Parisians of today, you could violate their wives in their arms; you could do worse and take their purses from their pockets, and they would remain what they are, the most abominable moral cowards I have ever seen!

This evening the Communards among the groups of people are full of irony on the subject of charity. They disdainfully reject charitable organizations. One man proclaims that society owes an income to all men by virtue of the aphorism: "I live, therefore I ought to exist." And the general refrain is, "We want no more rich people!"

Thereupon a woman comes to the front of the group, her

paws in the air making wild gestures, and says: "The cowards! Men who look on while others fight! I'd just like to get my hands on a reactionary, on a royalist, I'd claw his face for him!" And she probes the crowd with an eye avid for the guillotine, then draws away, staggering in a sort of drunken anger.

Saturday, May 6

Decidedly, Burty's friends are swine and nothing but swine! While I was in a pastry shop on the Rue Saint Honoré, a hospital orderly drew out of his wallet a paper in which one Lehideux, arrested by the revolutionary authorities —at the Opéra Comique post, I think—and then released, asked restitution of a gold repeating watch, keys, and a purse containing some fifty francs which had been taken from him temporarily. The orderly said he had been to headquarters three times and could get nowhere. He added: "I'm English and I'm here because I'm a Republican. But this disgusts me and I'm going back to London!"

Sunday, May 7

During these sad days I go back over my sad life and the days of sorrow which make it up.

I think of the time in school, harder for me than for others because of a feeling of independence which during that whole time made me fight with those who were stronger than I or made me live in a sort of quarantine which the tyranny of embryo tyrants imposes on the cowardice of the child-man.

I think of my vocation as painter, my vocation as student at the Ecole des Chartes, broken off later at my mother's insistence. I see myself again leading a student's life as a penniless lawyer's clerk, condemned to sordid love affairs, ill at ease in an environment of low, vulgar, bourgeois comrades and friends, who understood nothing of the literary and artistic aspirations that tormented me and who teased me about them with the ripe reason of aged relatives.

Then there I was, I, who have never known exactly how much two and two are and have always been afraid of figures, there I was at the Caisse du Trésor, condemned to add up numbers from morning to night—two years during which the temptation to commit suicide was very familiar to me.

Did I finally win independence? Did I achieve a free life, able to concern myself with the things I love? Did I begin that sweet existence in common with my brother? Not six months had gone by when, on my return from Africa, dysentery put me on the verge of death for almost two years and left me in a state of health where there has never been a completely good day.

I had the great joy of being able to devote my life completely to the work for which I was born. But it was to the accompaniment of attacks, of furious hatred, I may say, such as no other writer of our time has endured. Several years pass in such a struggle, and then my brother is stricken by a serious liver ailment, while I have a dangerous illness of the eyes. Then my brother falls ill, very ill, is ill for a whole year of the most frightful ailment that can beset a heart and intelligence bound to the heart and mind of a sick man. He dies.

And after his death, for me, overwhelmed and without resilience, comes the war, the invasion, the siege, the famine, the bombardment, the civil war, all of it hitting Auteuil harder than any other part of Paris.

I have not been really happy up to this day! Today I wonder if this is the end of it. I wonder if I have much longer to see, if I am not condemned to become blind soon, to be deprived of the only sense which has given and continues to give me the sole joys of my life.

There is undoubtedly a *feeling of rage* among the Parisian population. Today I see a woman who is not of the people, who is of venerable age, in short a mature bourgeoise, I see her without provocation slap a man who took the liberty of telling her to leave the Versailles forces alone.

They are hawking a new paper of M. de Girardin's: *La Réunion Libérale*, whose motto is *conciliation without transaction*. The French must be a people of gulls to have swallowed this man of ideas who has no ideas, this inflater of antitheses!

This evening I go to Saint Eustache, where a club is having its initial meeting. On a workbench between two lamps and a glass of sugared water five or six silhouettes of lawyers. Down front, standing or sitting on chairs, an audience of curious people brought there by the novelty of the spectacle. Nothing profane in the attitude of the men, many of whom on entering automatically raise their hands to their caps, which they leave on only when they see hats on other heads. This is nothing like the profanation of Notre Dame in '93. It has not yet come to grilled herring on patens; there is merely a strong odor of garlic rising under the sacred vault.

The bell, the silvery, tinkling bell of the mass, announces the opening of the meeting.

Then a white beard stands up in the pulpit, and after gargling a few puritanical remarks, he asks the assembly to approve the following proposition: "The members of the National Assembly—Louis Blanc, Schoelcher, and others—the members of the National Assembly as well as all the other officials are declared liable in their private fortunes for all the misfortunes of this war, just as much for those who die on the Versailles side as for those on the side of Paris." To the effect, he says, as he begins an explanation, that a provincial deputy will be very disagreeably surprised when the peasant to whose home they have brought the body of a son comes to force him to pay the pension due out of his own fortune. The proposition, when brought to a vote, is not carried; I don't know for what reason.

Next comes a man in pearl-grey trousers who in a raging voice declares that Terror is the only way to insure victory. He seeks the establishment of a third power, the Revolutionary Tribunal, so that heads of traitors may roll immediately on the square. The proposal receives frenzied applause from a claque who are grouped on chairs around the pulpit.

A third civilian preacher, with all the turns of phrase of '93, informs us that 10,060 bottles of wine were found in possession of the priests at Saint Sulpice seminary and demands that searches be made in bourgeois houses, where great quantities of provisions are certainly hidden. He ends with a criticism of the pawn-shop decree, which he considers not sufficiently revolutionary.

Now—I want to be impartial—there climbs to the pulpit a member of the Commune in National Guard uniform who speaks amiably and in a forthright manner. First he makes plain his disdain for "rolling phrases by which one wins an easy popularity" and says that the pawn-shop decree was not applied to objects worth more than twenty francs since there is no intention to confiscate without payment. He adds that the pawn shop is a private enterprise, that there must be assurance of reimbursing it for what has been taken, that the Commune is not a government of expropriation, that it is impor-

tant for this to be known and that it is the maladresses of orators like the one who preceded him which have spread among
the public the idea that the men of the Commune believe in
sharing wealth and that everybody with four sous will have
to give up two of them.

Then, speaking of the men of '93, who, as he put it, "are
always being thrown up to us," he declared with a certain
pride that they had only *military action* to contend with, but
that if they had had to resolve the enormous and difficult
problems of the present day, these famous men of '93 would
perhaps not have been any more adroit than the men of 1871.
Then he threw out a rather fine and brave question: "What
do I care whether we are successful against Versailles if we
don't find solutions for social problems, if workingmen remain in the same condition as before?"

Next, very harshly criticizing the *bumblers*, he declared
categorically to the crowd which had just applauded the motion for a Revolutionary Tribunal that in setting up a Committee of Public Safety there had been no idea, no intention,
of a Terror and that the Committee's existence was due entirely to a need for concentration and simplification of labor.

And, believe me, if he hadn't ended by saying that Versailles fought only with baseness and treason, it was a speech
to make an impression on impartial minds. People around me
said the orator was Jacques Durand.

Monday, May 8

When I go into Burty's this morning, I see a magnificent
bouquet of tamarisk, lilacs, and wild roses on his mantel. He
tells me that he gathered it yesterday under the shells from
Courbevoie. Little by little there rises and forms for me from

his account, from his recollection of the day, a very original and charming landscape to use in a war novel.

Since the walls were broken down, the gardens of Neuilly and Clichy today form a single expanse full of white, pink, and mauve masses of lilacs and double roses, a garden in which you would think the paths had been macadamized by shell fragments, so many have fallen there, so many fall every day.

In the young verdure and flower of spring shrubs, here you see National Guards lying beside their weapons, which shine in the sun; there you see a blonde canteen woman pouring a drink for a soldier with Parisian grace; and in every nook, filtered through the sheltering leaves, there are colored stripes à la Diaz on the uniforms.

Constantly above our heads the fine noise of grape shot, at once resonant and flat, and at the same time in the sunny blue sky the bursting out, the formation, the slow enlargement of clouds like those fairy-tale clouds from which a genie or a fairy dressed in gilt paper emerges; only today they are spitting out pieces of lead.

Horror is mingled with this: a corpse being hoisted up into a baggage wagon, while one man uses his two hands to hold back the brains which are ready to spill out of the opened skull.

Tuesday, May 9

National Guards, National Guards, National Guards! Brand-new red flags. Canteen women in full costume; hospital nurses with bedding on their backs and bag of dressings at their waists. A multitude in arms massing on the Place Louis XV.

For a moment I thought all that soldiery was leaving for the ramparts. It is only a review, in which the number of armed street urchins is somehow hateful and disquieting.

Wednesday, May 10

Thiers' proclamation is as doddering as the man. On such a theme, not a fine phrase or a simple or eloquent or outraged one.

Recently, at the Commune Lefrançais asked that the secretaries be so good as to correct the French of the members of the Government. Their answer was that they did not have time.

Thursday, May 11

All the shops on streets near the Place Vendôme have their windows crisscrossed with strips of paper.

It is strange how historical documents must be rooted in the past if they are to move me. How I have envied the good fortune Manuel had in putting his hands on the papers on which he based his *La Bastille Dévoilée!* Perhaps if I had been his contemporary, the discovery would have left me cold. I feel this as I pass my time every evening next to Burty, who is surrounded and barricaded by papers, notes, notebooks, and dispatches found at the Tuileries and who reads me fragments from them which bore me. In his enthusiasm and jubilation over his discoveries he even wants me to touch the precious autographs with my fingers, but my hands mechanically push them away. Can it be that my lack of curiosity is due to the abundance of telegrams, which gives the imperial outpourings too rudimentary a style?

In the evenings I often encounter Asselineau at Burty's. I know of no loquacity that produces a boredom more like that of rain than does Asselineau's. To avoid being boring, in default of anything else, you must simply have a bit of passion. In his case you have the mellifluous and cold expansiveness of an old bachelor's egoism, reinforced by the repetitiousness of a bibliophile.

Friday, May 12

The Tuileries terrace is covered with bales of rags which are to be used to barricade the garden along the whole Place de la Concorde side.

Thiers' house is not yet demolished, but already the red flag flies above the little blue frame enclosing the famous Number 27. The square is occupied in military fashion by the *Avengers of the Country,* a collection of pale hooligans and the crapulous youngsters of Paris whose trade is to open carriage doors in front of the theaters on the Boulevard du Crime.

As I exclaim "the devil!" while reading an evening paper which informs me that the Versailles troops have opened the trench at the Mortemart battery, a man next to me in the café asks if there is something serious in the latest news. I show him the line and say that my outburst is due to the fact that I have a house at Auteuil situated opposite the battery. "So do I!" he says; "I have one, too," and we chat together.

Two bits of information drawn from his conversation. At present his child, who was operated on for croup, is being nursed by a nun. The sister is forced to come dressed in ordinary clothes in order not to be insulted on the street. The surgeon who operated on the child is surgeon at the Necker hospital. He told my friend that day before yesterday a wounded man on whom he was to do an amputation in the morning was still so drunk from the night before that he had to wait until four o'clock.

Paris under Siege

Saturday, May 13

This morning I happen to witness the mass dismissal of the employes of the Bibliothèque as well as the flight of those under forty—a debacle that would be grotesque if it were not lugubrious.

The demolition of Thiers' house has begun, and the roof, which has been laid bare, shows its bare scantlings. Basically this attack on property, the most striking that anyone could have thought up, is having an excellent bad effect.

A lamentable spectacle here in this district, as they track down draft-evaders and you see the national police rush, bayonet in hand, in pursuit of a fleeing adolescent who tries to escape them on his young legs.

Sunday, May 14

. . . . .

What is left of the Parisian population is at the foot of the Champs Elysées under the first trees, where the pretty, noisy laughter of children sitting in front of the Guignols sometimes rises above the voice of the distant cannonade.

National brutishness is coming to a pitch of fury. I see one of those ignoble National Guards taking on himself the role of policeman and trying to carry off by force a man who disagrees with him. He talks of nothing less than "carting him off to the Ecole Militaire and having him shot."

You have to hear the people in their conversation groups to have an idea of the immeasurable stupidity of the most intelligent people on earth. There is something even sadder than stupidity; it is that in all that is said, shouted, and mouthed you find only a stupid envy, a homicidal desire to tear things down.

288

Journal, 1871

Monday, May 15

Always waiting for the attack, for the deliverance that does not come.

You cannot imagine the suffering caused by the despotism exercised in the streets by the riffraff disguised as soldiers.

Tuesday, May 16

In the Tuileries on the path from which you can see the Place Vendôme there are chairs clear to the middle of the garden, and on the chairs men and women waiting for the Column of the Grande Armée to fall. I go away.

That National Guard! It really deserves no clemency or mercy. If today what is left of the Commune and the Committee of Public Safety were to be replaced by ten authentic convicts well known to it, it would servilely and unprotestingly carry out their prison-house decrees.

When I go back through the Tuileries at six o'clock, there is an empty place in the sky where once the record of our military glory was inscribed in bronze, and the plaster-covered pedestal shows four red fluttering rags where the eagles were.

People's faces look as though they had received good news. There is a rumor at the tobacconist's that the tricolor flag flies over the Maillot gate. In the gaslight I look at magnificent photographs showing the ruined houses at Saint Cloud, and I wonder if my own will not appear in the next installment of this gallery.

Wednesday, May 17

I am awakened by a neighborwoman from Auteuil, who has come to tell me that a shell demolished one of the windows of my house yesterday. The bombardment has redoubled in violence.

Odd details on Hugo's most recent stay in Paris, details which come from Madame Meurice. Hugo is one of those sexagenarians attacked by acute priapism, a regular Balzacian Hulot. Every evening around ten he would leave the Hôtel Rohan, where he had shut Juliette up on the pretext that she must look after his grandchildren, and would go back to the Meurice house, where one, two, three women were waiting for him and frightening the tenants who ran into them on the stairs. These women were of every sort, from the most distinguished to the most sordid. And through the ground-floor windows of Hugo's room Madame Meurice's maid, strolling in the garden, would witness naked bits of strange sexual rites. This seems to have been Hugo's chief occupation during the siege.

As the shells come still closer, the Guignols, which had taken refuge at the foot of the Champs Elysées, have left the field, taking away with Polichinelle the pretty childish laughter which distracted you from the cannonade.

Today heavy traffic of artillery and of wine vans, which indicates a forthcoming action. Shops close one after the other; and through the panes of the unshuttered doors of those that are not entirely closed, you can see the weariness and the sadly relaxed arms of the idle storekeeper as he sits on a chair.

I wander along the quays. Suddenly there is a vigorous and continuous explosion behind me. It is like the growling of a crater or the crackling of fireworks bursting in the air. I turn around; above the buildings a dense white cloud looking as solid as sculptured marble. People are yelling around me: "It's at Saint Thomas d'Acquin, at the Artillery Museum." I dash into the Rue du Bac: "It's the Issy fortress that has blown up," I hear someone say to the shopkeepers, who are still terrified by the shaking of their show windows.

I go back down the Rue du Bac and bump into Bracquemond, who says to me as he points in the direction of the smoke: "It's either the tobacco factory or the Ecole Militaire," and we go back up the Champs Elysées. An old woman with a bandaged hand shouts in a frenzy: "It's the cartridge works at the Champ de Mars, but don't go there; it isn't over; there's going to be a second explosion!"

We are in front of the hospital, and Guichard says to us as he opens the door: "If you have strong stomachs, come on in. But if you don't, go away. Some houses have collapsed. You are going to see pieces of women and of babies crushed while they were being given suck." We go away.

Thursday, May 18

Great tragic events give courage to women, to the women who lack it most; and in a dramatic situation their devotion rises to a point worthy of admiration. I was thinking thus as I listened to an account of the heroism of the maid in moving the possessions of a home near mine and also as I thought of my poor Pélagie risking death every minute as she sought to save me from fire or pillage.

From the moment that *L'Officiel* writes with such revolutionary badness: "A frightful retrogression into all the orgies of royalism," we can be sure that we are lost. This bit of literature tells us that we are on the verge of massacres!

The crowd carries me along to the spectacle of the day, to the powder magazine at the Champ de Mars. The streets along which I pass have no window panes; I walk on powdered glass, and I see a woman merchant of broken glass fill her carriage in a moment with glass that she has gathered up by the shovelful.

The shock was so violent that there are store fronts and porte-cochères thrown completely out of line; and I have never seen anything like the mishmash produced in a colonial products store. The walls are all scratched with the scars of shells. The tiles of the Gros Caillou hospital seem to have been set to dance by an earthquake.

The Champ de Mars, the site of the disaster, from which the National Guard is keeping people at a distance, shows a vague and confused heap of plaster and charred debris. At the barracks door women are poking about in the debris with the ends of umbrellas, looking for bullets, which yesterday were so numerous that, as an onlooker says, the ground at the Champ de Mars looked like a field "where sheep had grazed."

As if we had not suffered enough, the newspapers hint at the possibility of Prussian occupation.

Friday, May 19

Interminable days when I walk here and there, since anxiety and my fatigued eyes do not allow me the distraction of a book.

All the people you meet on the street talk to themselves aloud like crazy people—people from whose mouths come words like *desolation, misfortune, death, ruin*—all the syllables of despair.

Sunday, May 21

In my lack of occupation I allow myself to be taken by Burty to the Champs Elysées hospital.

The hospital has taken over the whole Musard concert hall building; the orchestra has become a linen room, and the winding path has disappeared under tents where you see haggard faces in beds. Many sick and dying have been taken into the open air of the garden. In the sun and under the greenery yellow hands flutter and wide eyes question the passer-by. There is a woman at the side of nearly every bed of suffering, and sometimes little children play on the bed clothes.

Guichard puts a dressing on a young man whose thigh has been shot away by an exploding shell. I mechanically ask the youth where he was wounded: at his house in Auteuil, where his mother had kept him in. This reply throws me into mortal anxiety. I reproach myself for my fierce egoism and vow on the morrow to go find that poor girl who has remained in my house, deciding to leave everything to the grace of God.

I pass the whole day in fear of a setback for the Versailles troops, tortured by a remark that Burty repeated two or three times: "The Versailles forces have been repulsed seven times."

With these various impressions of sadness and anxiety I go this evening to my usual observation post, the Place de la Concorde. When I reach the square there is an enormous crowd surrounding a hack that is being escorted by National Guards. "What's all this?" A woman answers: "That is a gentleman whom they have just arrested. He was shouting out the door that the Versailles forces had entered the city." I recall the little groups of National Guards whom I have just encountered on the Rue Saint Florentin, filing along in disorder. But we have been deceived so often, so often disappointed, that I have no faith in the good news; however, I am moved to the depths and stirred with that sickly state that doctors call anxiety.

I walk for a long time in search of information and clarification. Nothing, nothing, nothing. The people still on the street look like the people yesterday. They are just as calm or just as upset. Nobody seems to have heard about the shout in the Place de la Concorde. Probably another hoax.

I finally go home and to bed in despair. I cannot sleep. I seem to hear a distant noise through my hermetically closed curtains. I get up. I open the window. On distant pavements there is the regular tramp of marching men who are going in to replace others, as happens every night. Come now! It is the effect of my imagination. I go back to bed, but this time it really is the drums, it really is the bugles! I hurry back to the window. The call to arms sounds all over Paris; and soon above the drums, above the bugles, above the clamor, above the shouts of "To Arms!" rise in great waves the tragically sonorous notes of the tocsin, which has begun to ring in all the churches—a sinister sound which fills me with joy and marks the beginning of the end of hateful tyranny for Paris.

Monday, May 22

I can't stay home. I need to see, to know.

When I go out, I find everybody assembled under porte-cochères, an excited, grumbling, hopeful crowd, already steeling themselves to boo the dispatch-riders.

Suddenly a shell burst over the Madeleine, and all the residents immediately go back indoors. Far off by the new opera house, I see a National Guard being carried away with a broken leg. In scattered groups on the square people are saying that the Versailles forces are at the Palace of Industry. Demoralization and discouragement are visible among the National Guards, who return in little bands, exhausted and shamefaced.

I go up to Burty's, and we go out again at once in order to see what Paris looks like.

In the Place de la Bourse there is a gathering before a pastry-shop window which has just been shattered by a shell. On the boulevard in front of the new opera house there is a barricade made of barrels full of earth, a barricade defended by a few unenergetic-looking men. In a moment a young man arrives on the run and announces that the Versailles troops are at La Pépinière Barracks. He escaped as men fell all around him at the Saint Lazare station.

We go back up the boulevard. Sketchy barricades before the old Opéra, before the Saint Martin gate, where a woman in a red sash is pulling up paving stones. Everywhere there are altercations between bourgeois and National Guards. A small squad of National Guards returns from the firing line, among them a youngster with soft eyes who has a rag stuck on his bayonet—a gendarme's hat.

Always in groups the sad procession of grave National Guards abandoning the battle. Complete confusion. Not a senior officer giving orders. All along the boulevards not a member of the Commune in his sash. All by himself an out-of-breath artilleryman pushes a big brass cannon, without knowing where to take it. From time to time a column of white smoke from a cannon firing to the left of Montmartre.

Suddenly in the midst of the disorder and alarm, in the midst of the hostility of the crowd there passes by on horseback, with unbuttoned tunic, shirt tails out, face apoplectic with anger, striking the neck of his horse with his closed fist, a big common man, superb in his heroic disarray.

We go back. From the boulevard loud noises continually reach us, disputes and altercations on the part of bourgeois who are beginning to rebel against the National Guards, who end by arresting them to a hail of boos.

We climb up to the glass belvedere at the top of the building. A big cloud of white smoke covers the whole sky in the direction of the Louvre. Something frightening and mysterious in this battle that surrounds us, in these occupation forces which come closer and closer without noise and apparently without fighting.

I have come to make a call at Burty's and here I am a prisoner—until when? I don't know. You can't go out any more. The people whom the National Guards find on the streets are being pressed into service or made to work on the barricades. Burty gets to work copying extracts from *La Correspondance Trouvée aux Tuileries,* and I plunge into his *Oeuvre de Delacroix* to the sound of approaching shells.

Soon there are explosions all around and very close by. The building on the Rue Vivienne, on the other side of the street, has its kiosk broken. Another shell breaks the street light in front of us. Finally a last one during dinner explodes at the base of the building and shakes us in our chairs.

They have made me a bed and I lie down fully clothed. Under the windows the sound of the voices of drunken National Guards addressing a "Who goes there?" in hoarse tones to everyone who passes. At dawn I fall into a sleep broken by nightmares and explosions.

Tuesday, May 23

When I wake up no certain news. Nobody knows anything positive. Then imagination creates chimeras in the void. At last an unhoped-for newspaper, taken from the kiosk at the foot of the building, tells us that the Versailles forces have occupied a part of the Faubourg Saint Germain, Monceau, and Batignolles.

We climb up to the belvedere, where in the bright sunlight

which illuminates the immense battle and in the smoke from cannons, machine guns, muskets, we can see a series of engagements extending from the Jardin des Plantes to Montmartre. At the moment the major part of the action seems to be concentrated on Montmartre. In the midst of the distant rumbling of artillery and fire arms, rifle shots crackling near by make us suppose that there is fighting on the Rue Lafayette and the Rue Saint Lazare.

The deserted boulevard has a sinister air with its closed shops, with the big motionless shadows of its trees and kiosks, with its silence of death, broken from time to time by a dull shattering detonation.

Somebody thinks he can see the tricolored flag floating on Montmartre through his opera glasses. At that moment we are chased from our glass observatory by the whistling shells passing close to us, making a sound in the air like the meowing of kittens.

When we come down again and look out from the balcony, an ambulance is standing under our windows. They are putting in a wounded man who struggles as he repeats: "I don't want to go to the hospital!" A brusque voice answers: "You're going just the same." And we watch the wounded man raise himself up, gather his failing forces, struggle for a second with two or three men, and fall back in the vehicle, shouting in a despairing and expiring voice: "It's enough to make you blow your brains out!"

The ambulance leaves. The boulevard becomes empty again and for a long time you hear a cannonade coming near, with explosions apparently in the vicinity of the new opera.

Then the heavy gallop of an omnibus, the upper deck full of National Guards leaning on their rifles.

Then the galloping of staff officers who toss out to the National Guards gathered under our windows the recommendation to be careful they are not surrounded.

Then cannons start going by.

Then the stretcher-bearers arrive, going up the boulevard in the direction of the Madeleine.

Meanwhile little Renée is weeping because they won't let her go out to play in the courtyard. Madeleine, serious and pale, jumps at each explosion, and Madame Burty, feverishly moving frames, pictures, books, seeks and seeks again for an out-of-the-way corner of the apartment where her two children may be sheltered from bullets and shells.

The firing gets closer and closer. We are distinctly aware of rifle shots on the Rue Drouot. At that moment there appears a squad of workmen who have received an order to block the boulevard at the Rue Vivienne and to build a barricade under our windows. They do not put much heart into it. Some move two or three paving stones; others, to satisfy their consciences, give two or three blows at the asphalt with their picks. But almost at once in the face of the bullets which enfilade the boulevard and pass over their heads, they leave their work. Burty and I see them disappear down the Rue Vivienne with a sigh of relief. We both thought of the National Guards who were going to come up into the building and fire out of the windows with our collections all mixed up in a confused mass under their feet.

Then a large troop of National Guards appear, falling back with their officers slowly and in good order. Others come after them, marching at a more hasty step. Then still others bumping into each other in disorder; among them we see a dead man with a bloody head whom four men carry by his arms and legs like a bundle of dirty linen. They take him from door to door, but no one opens up.

In spite of this retreat, these abandonments, these flights, the resistance at the Drouot barricade is long-drawn-out. The fusillade does not cease. Little by little, however, the fire decreases in intensity. Soon there are only isolated shots. Finally two or three last cracklings; and almost at once we see the last defenders of the barricade flee—four or five young boys of fourteen, one of whom I hear say: "I shall be one of the last to get back!"

The barricade is taken. It is about six o'clock. The Versailles troops come out of the Rue Drouot, spread out in a line, and open a terrible fire in the direction of the Saint Denis gate. In the enclosure of the two high stone façades along the boulevard the rifles thunder like cannons. The bullets graze the house, but at the windows we hear only a whistling sound resembling the tearing of silk.

We had retired into the back room for a moment. I come back into the dining room. There, kneeling down and protected as well as possible, this is what I see through the open curtain of the window.

On the other side of the boulevard a man is stretched out on the ground; I see only the soles of his boots and a bit of gold braid. Two men, a National Guard and a lieutenant, stand near the corpse. Bullets make the leaves of a little tree spreading over their heads rain on them. One dramatic detail which I forgot. Behind them in a recess in front of a closed porte-cochère a woman is lying flat for her whole length on the sidewalk, holding a kepi in one of her hands.

The National Guard, with angry violent gestures, shouting to someone off stage, indicates by signs that he wants to pick up the dead man. The bullets continue to make leaves fall on the two men. Then the National Guard, whose face I see red with anger, throws his rifle on his shoulder, butt in the air, and walks toward the rifle shots, insults on his tongue. Suddenly I see him stop, put his hand to his forehead, for a second lean his hand and forehead against a little tree, then half turn around and fall on his back, arms outspread.

The lieutenant had remained motionless by the side of the first dead man, calm as a man meditating in his garden. One bullet, which made a little branch fall on him close to his head, which he tossed off with a flick of the hand, did not rouse him from his immobility. He looked for a moment at his fallen comrade. Then, without rushing, he pushed his sword behind him with disdainful deliberation, then bent down and attempted to lift up the body. The dead man was tall and heavy, and like an inert thing evaded the lieutenant's efforts and slipped out of his arms to one side or the other. Finally the lieutenant lifted him up and, holding him tight against his chest, he was carrying him off when a bullet, breaking his thigh, made them turn together in a hideous pirouette, the dead man and the living man, and fall on top of each other. I doubt that many people have been privileged to witness so heroic and simple a disdain for death. They told me this evening that the woman lying on the ground was the wife of one of those three men.

Our boulevard is once more in the hands of the Versailles forces. We are risking a look at them from the balcony when a bullet strikes above our heads. Some imbecile of a resident has decided to light his pipe at a window.

The shells begin again—shells this time shot by the Federals against the positions captured by Versailles. We camp in the anteroom. Renée's little iron bed is dragged into a protected corner. Madeleine stretches out on a sofa near her father, her fair face standing out on its white pillow under the lamplight, her long little body lost in the folds and shadows of a shawl. Madame Burty sinks into an armchair. And for a long time there sounds in my ears the harrowing moan of a wounded infantryman who has dragged himself to our door and whom the portress will not let in because of a base fear of compromising herself.

Now and then I go to look through the windows on the boulevard at the dark Paris night without a glimmer of gas, without the glimmer of a lamp in the houses, where thick and redoubtable shadows guard the day's dead, who have not been picked up.

Wednesday, May 24

When I wake up, I again see the corpse of the National Guard who was killed yesterday. He has not been taken away. He has simply been covered a bit with the branches of the tree under which he was killed.

Burning Paris makes this seem like the day of an eclipse.

A brief interruption in the bombardment. I take advantage of it to leave Burty's and get back to the Rue de l'Arcade. I find Pélagie there; she had the temerity to come through the whole battle yesterday with a big bouquet of Gloire de Dijon roses from my rosebush; she was aided and protected by officers who admired this woman going ahead fearlessly with her flowers in the middle of rifle and machine gun fire; they let her go through the area near the Expiatory Chapel, where a passage had been cut open and linked up by the engineers.

We set out for Auteuil, curious to see what it is like near the Tuileries. A shell bursting almost at our feet in the Place de la Madeleine forces us to fall back into the Faubourg Saint

Honoré, where we are pursued by bursts that strike above our heads on either side.

The shells continue no further than the Etoile barrier. From there you see a cloud of smoke over Paris like the cloud over a gasworks chimney. All around, like a black rain, little pieces of charred paper fall from the sky. The accounts and records of France. I don't know what the analogy is that comes to my mind between this rain of charred paper and the rain of ashes which buried Pompeii.

Passy has not suffered. But the ruins begin at the Boulevard Montmorency, where there are houses with nothing left but four blackened walls, and houses which have collapsed and are lying on the ground.

Mine is still standing, though with a hole in the roof! But how many shell bursts have buffeted it. Bits of rubble cover the sidewalk. In the stone there are hollows the size of a child's head. The door is pierced with twenty little bullet holes, and one big hole made by a larger-caliber shell; a big piece of wood has been torn out by the pickaxe of a Federal soldier who attempted to force his way in.

Inside the house we walk on plaster and broken glass mixed with shrapnel and bullets twisted like leeches that have been forced to disgorge with salt. On the first floor a musket ball— I consider this extraordinary—enfiladed the house, going through a blind, a mattress, a partition, a curtain, and a door covered with Chinese matting. But the real damage is on the second floor. A shell, a tiny little shell, one of the last fired by the Versailles forces—it was on Sunday night when they had already captured the Point du Jour—went through the roof, shattered a corner beam, went by the foot of Pélagie's bed and through the door, then exploded on the floor of the landing, splintering all the doors on the second floor.

Well, it might have been worse. Everything I value has been spared and the disasters of my neighbors are such as to reconcile me to my losses!

Poor garden, with its lawn looking like the overgrown grass of an abandoned cemetery, with the shining leaves of its shrubs covered by plaster dust and black with charred paper, with big branches broken off so that the brownish foliage of a dead tree is mingled with the green foliage of a living tree, with a big hole in the very middle of the lawn made by a shell —a hole big enough to bury three men in.

While we make a tour of the house and while Pélagie serves me my dinner, she tells me that my neighbor César, who had no cellar of his own with a stone vault, took shelter in one of mine. She and César's woman servant took possession of the other cellar, and since they had nothing else to do the two of them passed the days playing cards, their eyes becoming accustomed to seeing in the darkness.

She tells me, when the shell fell in the garden, how afraid the people in the cellar were that the house would cave in because such a heavy torrent of earth was sent up to the roof. She tells me of angry exchanges with the Federal troops who were trying to get into the house on the pretext of looking for men and weapons. One day after a terrible dispute, when stones were even thrown, a dialogue took place between her and these men, who gave her the bread she needed and said: "You can eat it; it isn't stolen!" She tells me that during the last day bullets were passing through the house so frequently that when the inmates wanted a drink, they climbed the stairs on all fours, put the watering can under the kitchen tap, and, without worrying about the water that overflowed, waited for a letup in the rifle fire before picking the watering can up again.

She tells me that she went to bed with her clothes on the whole time. In anticipation that the house might catch fire she made a bundle of her most precious possessions, arranged the household silver in such a way that she could put it in her pockets, and provided herself with a mattress to put on her back to protect herself from all that was falling outside from overhead.

All evening through a gap in the trees we could see the fire in Paris, a fire which under the night sky resembled those Neapolitan gouaches of an eruption of Vesuvius on a piece of black paper.

Thursday, May 25

All day cannon fire and the rattle of machine guns. I spend the day walking among the ruins of Auteuil. There is confusion and destruction such as a cyclone might make.

You see enormous broken trees whose shattered trunks look like a bundle of kindling; pieces of rail weighing a hundred pounds that have been thrown on the boulevard; manhole covers, lead plaques four inches thick, reduced to fragments the size of a cube of sugar; bars of grillework twisted and knotted around each other like the handle of a wicker basket.

At times in the midst of this devastation you are surprised to see, attached to a half-fallen building, a big climbing rosebush which persists in covering the gaping cracks and hanging debris with its roses.

Number 75, a brand-new five-story building, has lost its façade and you can see all the furniture in the house as though it were a stage set showing two rooms—furniture which is continually falling down as the floors gradually subside into the street.

The entrance to the main street of Auteuil rivals Saint

Cloud. The two rows of houses are nothing but smoking heaps of rubble or large pieces of wall with the broad cracks of ancient ruins.

The outline of the viaduct arcades has disappeared. The broken bridge sags in the middle and you can get under it only by bending down. Some iron pillars and some pieces of zinc scattered on the ground here and there are all there is to indicate the location of the railroad station. The guard's house —a heap of bricks, iron, and charred wood. Under foot there are unexploded shells, pieces of gun carriages, pieces of cannons, broken boxes with *4 de M* written on them, debris and slag of every kind; in the middle of all this, water from the broken water mains gurgles like springs.

A man points out a casemate to me on the lopped-off line of fortifications. It is there, he tells me, that the Belleville leader was installed with his men and his mistresses. There every day pushcarts, emptying the nearby houses, brought linen, furniture, and clothing, which the latter-day Sultan shared among his women.

As I watch, fire breaks out again in an Auteuil house without anybody's attempting to put it out.

Vehicles making the trip from Saint Denis to Versailles pass by, bringing back to Paris on their benches people whom residence in the provinces has made archaic. You would say they were the old-time lumbering coaches coming back from Coblenz.

Paris is certainly accursed! At the end of this month-long dry spell, now there is a wind like a hurricane blowing on burning Paris.

Friday, May 26

I am going along the railroad line near the Passy station when I see some men and women escorted by soldiers. I go through the broken barrier and am on the edge of a path where the prisoners are waiting to set out for Versailles. There are a lot of them, for I hear an officer say in a low voice as he gives a paper to the colonel: "Four hundred and seven, of whom sixty-six are women."

The men have been put in rows of eight and are tied to each other with a cord around their wrists. They are as they were when caught, most without hats or caps, their hair plastered on their foreheads and faces by the fine rain which has been falling since morning. There are men of the common people who have made a covering for their heads with blue-checked handkerchiefs. Others, thoroughly soaked by the rain, draw thin overcoats around their chests under which a piece of bread makes a hump. It is a crowd from every social level, workmen with hard faces, artisans in loose-fitting jackets, bourgeois with socialist hats, National Guards who have had no time to change their trousers, two infantrymen pale as corpses—stupid, ferocious, indifferent, mute faces.

Among the women there is the same variety. Some women in silk dresses are next to a woman with a kerchief on her head. You see middle-class women, working women, streetwalkers, one of whom wears a National Guard uniform. Among all these faces there stands out the bestial head of a creature, half of whose face is one big bruise. None of these women have the apathetic resignation of the men. There is anger and irony on their faces. Many of them have the eyes of mad women.

Among these women there is one who is especially beautiful, beautiful with the implacable fury of a young Fate. She is a brunette with wiry hair that sticks out, with eyes of steel, with cheeks reddened by dried tears. She is *planted* in an attitude of defiance, spewing out insults at the officers from a throat and lips so contracted by anger that they cannot form sounds and words. Her furious, mute mouth chews the insults without being able to make them heard. "She is like the one who killed Barbier with a dagger!" a young officer says to one of his friends.

The least courageous ones show their feebleness only by a slight sideways tilt of the head, such as women have after they have prayed in church for a long time. One or two were concealed behind their veils when a noncommissioned officer touched one of the veils with a cruel and brutal flick of his whip: "Come on, off with your veils. Let's see your ugly faces!"

The rain increases in force. Some of the women pull up their skirts to cover their heads. A line of horsemen in white coats has reinforced the line of foot soldiers. The colonel, with an olive face like those in Ferri-Pisani's pictures, shouts: "Attention!" and the African riflemen load their guns. At this moment the women think they are going to be shot and one of them collapses with an attack of nerves. But the terror only lasts a moment; at once they renew their irony, and some their coquetry with the soldiers. The riflemen have slung their loaded carbines over their backs and have drawn their swords.

The colonel has taken his place on the flank of the column, announcing in a loud voice with a brutality which I think put on to induce fear: "Any man who lets go of his neighbor's arm *will be killed!*" And that terrible *will be killed!* is repeated four or five times in his short speech while you hear the dull sound of rifles being loaded by the infantry escort.

Everything is ready for their departure when pity, which never entirely abandons man, impels some infantrymen to pass their canteens among the women, who turn their thirsty mouths in graceful movements, at the same time keeping an apprehensive eye on the grim face of an old gendarme, which they think augurs no good. The signal for departure is given, and the pitiable column gets under way for Versailles in the pouring rain.

The collapsing Ministry of Finance building fills the Rue de Rivoli with rubble, in the midst of which ridiculous companies of firemen from the provinces bestir themselves, looking like Clodoche types.

Returning to Passy, I meet a band of frightful street urchins and incendiary hooligans who have been put inside the station, which has been turned into a prison and is already full of prisoners sitting on the rails.

From Auteuil this evening all Paris appears to be on fire, with continual tongues of flame such as the bellows of a forge makes in a white-hot fire.

Sunday, May 28

I go by carriage into the Champs Elysées. In the distance legs and more legs running in the direction of the broad avenue. I lean out of the door. The whole avenue is filled by a confused crowd between two lines of horsemen. I get out and join the running people. The attraction is the prisoners who have just been taken at the Buttes Chaumont marching in fives, with an occasional woman among them. "There are six thousand of them," one of the escorting cavalrymen tells me. "Five hundred were shot at once." At the head of this haggard multitude marches a nonagenarian on trembling legs.

In spite of the horror you feel toward these men, the sight of the lugubrious procession is painful; among them you see soldiers, deserters, wearing their tunics inside out with grey canvas pockets bulging around them. They seem already half undressed for execution.

I meet Burty on the Place de la Madeleine. We stroll along the streets and boulevards which have suddenly been inundated by people emerging from their cellars and hideaways, thirsty for light and sun, their faces showing their joy at their deliverance. We go up to get Madame Burty, whom we talk into taking a walk. While Burty, who is suddenly accosted by Madame Verlaine, is talking to her about ways of hiding her husband, Madame Burty tells me a secret which Burty had kept from me. One of his friends on the Committee of Public Safety, whom she does not name, told Burty four or five days ago that the government no longer had control over anything and that there was a plan to make raids on private houses, clean them out, and shoot all the owners.

I leave the couple and go for a look at burned Paris. The Palais Royal has been set fire to, but the pretty façade of the two pavilions on the square is intact; it is just a matter of money and rebuilding the interior. The Tuileries will have to be rebuilt on the garden and Rue de Rivoli sides.

You walk in smoke; you breathe air that smells at the same time of burned wood and apartment varnish, and everywhere you hear the *pscht* of the pumps. In many places there are still the traces and the horrible debris of battle. Here, a dead horse; there near the paving stones of a half-demolished barricade, kepis swimming in a pool of blood.

The large-scale destruction begins at Le Châtelet and is continuous from there on. Behind the burned-down theatre, costumes are spread out on the pavement: charred silk, from which here and there the gold and silver spangles strike your eye.

On the other side of the quay the roof of the round tower of the Palais de Justice has been sliced off. Only the iron skeletons of the roofs remain on the new buildings. The Prefecture of Police is a burning heap of stones; through its bluish smoke there shines the bright new gold of the Sainte Chapelle.

By little paths made through the still undemolished barricades I reach the Hôtel de Ville.

The ruins are splendid, magnificent. In their rose, ashgreen, and white-hot-iron coloration, in the brilliant agatization of stone cooked by petrol, the ruins look like those of an Italian palace colored by the sun of several centuries, or, better, the ruins of a magic palace bathed in a play of electric lights and reflections. With the empty niches, the smashed or broken statuettes, the remnant of the clock, the outline of high windows and chimneys which by some strange power of equilibrium still remain standing in the void, with its eroded silhouette against the sky, the building is a marvel of the picturesque, to be kept as it is if only the country were not condemned without appeal to M. Viollet-le-Duc's restorations. Irony of Chance! In the degradation of the whole monument there shines out on an intact marble plaque in bright new gilt the lying legend: *Liberty, Equality, Fraternity.*

I go back to Le Châtelet by the quay. Suddenly I see the crowd head over heels in flight like a mob being charged on a day of riot. Horsemen appear, threatening, swords in hand, rearing up their horses and forcing the promenaders from the street to the sidewalks. In their midst advances a group of men at whose head is an individual with a black beard, his forehead bound with a handkerchief. I see another whom his two neighbors hold up under the arms as if he did not have the strength to walk. These men have a special pallor and a vague look which remains in my memory. I hear a woman shout as she takes herself off: "How sorry I am I came this far!" Next to me a placid bourgeois is counting: "One, two, three . . ." There are twenty-six of them.

The escort makes the men march on the double to the Lobau Barracks, where the gate closes after them with strange violence and precipitation.

I still do not understand, but I feel an indefinable anxiety. My bourgeois companion, who had just been counting them, then says to a neighbor:

"It won't be long, you'll soon hear the first volley."

"What volley?"

"Why, they're going to shoot them!"

Almost at that instant there is an explosion like a violent sound enclosed behind doors and walls, a fusillade having something of the mechanical regularity of a machine gun. There is a first, a second, a third, a fourth, a fifth murderous *rrarra*—then a long interval—and then a sixth, and still two more volleys, one right after the other.

This noise seems never to end. Finally it stops. Everybody feels relieved and is beginning to breathe when there is a shattering sound which makes the sprung door of the barracks move on its hinges; then another; then finally the last. These are the coups de grâce given by a policeman to those who are not yet dead.

At that moment, like a band of drunken men, the execution squad come out of the door with blood on the end of some of their bayonets. And while two closed vans go into the courtyard a priest slips out, and for a long time you see his thin back, his umbrella, his legs walking unsteadily along the outer wall of the barracks.

Monday, May 29

Posted on every wall is MacMahon's proclamation announcing that it was all over yesterday at four o'clock.

This evening you begin to hear the movement of Parisian life which is being reborn, and its murmur is like that of a distant high tide. The clocks no longer strike in the silence of a desert.

Tuesday, May 30

From time to time frightening noises: fusillades and collapsing houses.

Wednesday, May 31

Tricolor flags at every window; tricolor flags on every vehicle. Air vents in the basements of all the buildings closed and covered over. On the paving stones which have been replaced a swarm of Parisians in traveling clothes taking possession of their city once again.

It is good that there was neither conciliation nor bargain. The solution was brutal. It was by pure force. The solution has held people back from cowardly compromises. The solution has restored confidence to the army, which learned in the blood of the Communards that it was still able to fight. Finally, the bloodletting was a bleeding white; such a purge, by killing off the combative part of the population, defers the next revolution by a whole generation. The old society has twenty years of quiet ahead of it, if the powers that be dare all that they may dare at this time.

Thursday, June 1

A tremendous carriage ride with Marin.

The Rue de Rivoli still smoking. The Rue Saint Antoine with no traces of the fighting except on the outskirts of the Place de la Bastille. The boulevard with a few buildings burned down here and there. Limited devastation around the Château d'Eau. The barracks, the Magasins Réunis, collapsed; the Château d'Eau a shambles with one lion still standing—a bullet which passed through his jaws has made him into a roaring lion.

We go up to Belleville. At the foot of the main street traces of a hot fight which thin out and disappear farther up, where only now and then do you see a white scar on a wall. But all the way up, the remains of barricades over which our coupé passes and which give us a good shaking up. Empty streets. People drinking in cabarets with faces of ugly silence. The appearance of a vanquished but unsubjugated district. Little groups of infantrymen walk along, rifles on their shoulders, leaning on canes made from the ramrods of the insurgents' rifles. At almost every turning of these suburban streets you encounter an encampment of red trousers underneath the little trees which are scorched by bullets and hold in their branches a picturesque accumulation of knapsacks and cartridge pouches.

We go through Charonne, the Avenue du Trône. We go in front of the Grenier d'Abondance, which imparts the smell of a refinery to the whole area. We push on clear to Bercy, where Marin shows me, near the Austerlitz bridge, the burned houses, the overturned restaurant, the trees hacked to pieces by Bourbonne, whom we go to see on his gunboat. His cannons are still at the place from which they silenced seven cannons and two machine guns. Out of thirty men he had three killed and seven wounded; all had contusions. He believes that if he had not taken the precaution to protect the bow with sand bags, nobody would have survived. He has a very low opinion of the land army and tells us that there was a constant demand during the battle for forty sailors to stir up a fighting spirit. The very odd thing he told us was that three days before the entry of the troops, the Montretout batteries, where he was in command, told the Versailles forces to come in. Their glasses showed them that the Point du Jour had been completely abandoned. And if it had not been for Captain Trèves the entry would have been even longer delayed.

Marin had told me of a raid and a large-scale execution carried out during the night in the Gennevilliers peninsula. I had confirmation of this from a cavalry colonel who was eating dinner next to us at the Café du Pont d'Orsay. He criticized the fusillade as a bit summary.

In the wind this evening the Commune's notices, which have been pulled off the walls, make a sound like dead leaves chased by an autumn whirlwind on the pavement; and you hear the stiff flapping of brand-new tricolor flags.

Friday, June 2

A speculator on a grand scale comes to my house to buy shell fragments. He has just bought 1,000 kilograms of them at one stroke from my neighbor.

Saturday, June 3

In Saint Jacques square some ditch-diggers moving earth near a frightful jumble of military equipment mixed with wool tricots.

When I get home, I find a letter telling me of the death of my cousin Philippe de Courmont, who was killed at the Trocadéro on May 22.

Monday, June 5

I am struck by the provincialism of all these Parisians returning to the capital with their little handbags. I would never have believed that eight months' absence from the center of things *chic* would have taken from people the character and the mark, considered indelible, of *Parisianism.*

Tuesday, June 6

Crowds reappear on the Boulevard des Italiens, on the pavement which was deserted a few days ago. This evening for the first time it begins to be difficult to make your way through the lounging of the men and the solicitation of the women.

Saturday, June 10

I go to Philippe de Courmont's funeral; he was the only cavalry officer killed during the May days. A few years ago we had a gay dinner with him at the Fontainebleau mess; and family ties, which had become loose, were renewed. Poor fellow! A few hours before a shell took off a leg and part of his head, he had handed his watch and papers over to his orderly.

Dinner this evening with Flaubert, whom I had not seen since my brother's death. He has come to Paris to get some information for his *Temptation of Saint Anthony.* He is unchanged, a man of letters before everything else. The cataclysm seems to have passed over him without in any way detaching him from his impassive writing of his book.

Monday, June 12

This evening Burty shows me some fragments gathered up at the Hôtel de Ville, some shards, some pieces of calcined material which look like the scoria of precious stones. From the bell, the historic bell, which melted drop by drop like a candle, there is a bit of metal that looks like those undulant bronze surfaces with which the Japanese represent waves. He also shows me a piece of molten glazed earthenware: "It takes 1,500 degrees of heat in a potter's furnace to do that!" he tells me.

Wednesday, June 14

Burty comes out to my house for the whole day in order to rest up from Paris.

We speak of the sad state of things and we see no resurrection for France except through her admirable capacity for hard work, through the ability to work day and night which other countries do not have—not even England, where it is almost impossible to get people to work at night. An ability due perhaps to the superior nervous energy of the French, as attested by Dumont d'Urville's labors.

Thursday, June 15

Edouard Lefebvre, who is on leave, talks to me about Versailles with great discouragement. He adds: "It's always lies, as it was under the Empire, as it was under the September 4 Government."

Tuesday, June 20

A sad anniversary. He died a year ago today. I pass the day in gathering together the obituary articles devoted to him.

Chronology and
Biographical Notes

Chronology

1870

19 July	French declare war on Prussia.
20 August	News comes to Paris that Marshal Bazaine is trapped at Metz.
31 August–1 September	Marshal MacMahon is defeated at Sedan; Napoleon III taken prisoner.
18 September	A republic is proclaimed in Paris; Government of National Defense is formed.
18 September	Germans form siege lines around Paris.
7 October	Gambetta leaves Paris by balloon.
10 October	Gambetta arrives at Tours, on the Loire, to head Delegation of Tours and organize armies.
27 October	Marshal Bazaine surrenders Metz.
30 October	Thiers reaches Paris via safe-conduct from Russian Foreign Office to report on peace efforts.
31 October	Thiers goes to Versailles to discuss possible armistice terms with Bismarck. Insurrection led by Blanqui and other radicals takes temporary control of Hôtel de Ville; defeated.

5 November	Thiers reports failure of talks with Bismarck.
	Mayors are elected in Paris arrondissements.
10 November	French Army of the Loire takes Orléans.
30 November	Sortie from Paris, to the east, toward Champigny, fails.
4 December	French lose Orléans.
8 December	Delegation of Tours retreats to Bordeaux.

1871

5 January	Prussians bombard Paris.
18 January	King William I of Prussia is crowned German Emperor in Hall of Mirrors at Versailles.
19–20 January	Sortie from Paris, to the west, toward Buzenval, fails.
21–22 January	Insurgent National Guard units in Paris release prisoners, attack Hôtel de Ville, call for "Commune"; defeated.
28 January	Paris is surrendered as Jules Favre accepts Bismarck's terms for armistice and election of National Assembly to vote on question of making peace for all France.
8 February	Elections for National Assembly to meet in Bordeaux take place.
15 February	National Guard units in Paris form Federation and elect provisional Central Committee.
17 February	Thiers is elected Chief of the Executive Power of the French Republic by National Assembly at Bordeaux.

21–26 February	Thiers discusses preliminary peace terms with Bismarck at Versailles.
24–28 February	Demonstrations and disorders take place in Paris as *Fédérés* show displeasure at prospects of German victory and possible German entry into Paris; artillery belonging to National Guard is moved to Montmartre and other heights.
1 March	National Assembly at Bordeaux ratifies preliminaries of peace.
	Germans make triumphal entry into Paris, as agreed upon in peace preliminaries; quick French ratification forces evacuation after two days.
8 March	French regular troops under General Vinoy fail in effort to take National Guard artillery.
10 March	National Assembly at Bordeaux makes decision to move to Versailles and passes other measures distasteful to Parisians.
15 March	National Guard units in Paris choose definitive Central Committee.
18 March	Troops sent by Thiers to seize cannon at Montmartre and elsewhere fraternize with crowds; much of Paris joins insurrection; Thiers withdraws troops and officials from Paris; Central Committee of National Guard moves into Hôtel de Ville.
19–22 March	Mayors of Paris arrondissements fail in efforts to mediate between National Guard and National Assembly.

Chronology

20 March	First meeting of National Assembly is held at Versailles.
26 March	Municipal government (Commune) is elected in Paris without permission of National Assembly at Versailles.
28 March	Bismarck agrees to increase in number of French regular army units permitted north of Loire.
29 March	Paris Commune divides work among committees and forms Executive Committee.
3 April	Parisian sortie toward Versailles fails. Second siege of Paris begins.
6 April	General MacMahon is named commander of troops serving National Assembly.
10 May	Treaty of Frankfurt is signed.
21 May	Versailles forces enter Paris via Porte de Saint Cloud. "Bloody Week" begins.
27 May	Battle takes place in Père Lachaise cemetery.

Biographical Notes[*]

Abbatucci, Jacques-Charles, 1816–1885, a politician and ardent Bonapartist.

Alphand, Jean-Charles-Adolphe, 1817–1891, a lieutenant of Haussmann in the amelioration of Paris, head of the engineering corps of the National Guard and in charge of the fortification of Paris during the siege.

Arago, Emmanuel, 1812–1896, a journalist and politician, minister in the National Defense Government.

Asselineau, Charles, 1820–1874, the first biographer of Baudelaire, on the staff of the Bibliothèque Mazarine.

Assi, Adolphe-Alphonse, 1840–1886, of working-class origin, formerly a member of Garibaldi's army, a leader of the Commune, deported to Nouméa.

Barbès, Armand, 1809–1870, a revolutionary political figure, in exile after 1854.

Baroche, Ernest, 1829–1870, director of foreign trade in the Ministry of Agriculture.

Bauër, Henry, 1851–1915, an opposition journalist under the Empire, dramatic critic of *L'Echo de Paris*, deported after the Commune.

Bazaine, Achille-François, 1811–1888, at the head of Maximilian's

---

[*] A listing of *contemporary* figures whom it is possible to identify beyond the information provided in the text.

army in Mexico, commander of the Army of Lorraine, surrendered to the Germans at Metz, tried for treason and sentenced to death, but sentence commuted to life imprisonment.

Béhaine, Edouard de, 1829–1897, a diplomat and intimate friend of Edmond de Goncourt.

Berthelot, Marcelin, 1827–1907, a chemist, one of the great French scientists of the century, directed the Scientific Committee for Defense under the National Defense Government, active in the reform of secondary and higher education, named a senator for life under the Third Republic.

Bertrand, Joseph, 1822–1900, a mathematician, member of the Academy of Sciences and later of the Académie Française.

Bescherelle, Louis-Nicolas, 1802–1883, a grammarian and lexicographer, author of the *Dictionnaire Nationale* and other similar works.

Blanc, Charles, 1813–1882, an art historian and journalist, head of Beaux Arts after September 4.

Blanc, Louis, 1811–1882, one of the leaders of the Revolution of 1848, returned to France from exile in September 1870, opposed the Commune.

Blanqui, Auguste, 1805–1881, a socialist and revolutionary who participated in the Revolution of 1848, editor of *La Patrie en Danger*, elected a member of the Commune while in prison for his part in the October 31 uprising.

Bocher, Emmanuel, 1835–1919, an art critic.

Bourbaki, Charles, 1816–1897, the general in command of the Imperial Guard at Metz and of the Army of the East.

Bourbonne, a naval captain with the Versailles forces.

Bracquemond, Félix, 1833–1914, a distinguished painter, engraver, lithographer, and designer for the ceramics industry.

Burty, Philippe, 1830–1890, an art critic and connoisseur of Japanese art, a member of the commission to examine the documents at the Tuileries.

Busquet, Alfred, 1820–1883, a journalist and author.

Capoul, Victor, 1839–1924, a popular singer at the Opéra-Comique.

Chanzy, Alfred, 1823–1883, the general in command of the Second Army of the Loire, arrested by the Commune but escaped.

Charles Edmond (Edmond Chojecki), 1822–1899, a Polish refugee and man of letters, on the staff of *Le Temps*.

Chenavard, Paul, 1808–1895, a painter.

Chennevières, Philippe, Marquis de, 1820–1899, a man of letters, curator at the Louvre and Luxembourg, after 1873 director of Beaux Arts.

Chenu, Jean-Charles, 1808–1879, a military doctor, head of the military hospital service 1870–1871.

Chesneau, Ernest, 1833–1890, an art critic, inspector of Beaux Arts, 1869–1870.

Chevalier, Philippe, died in 1871.

Christophe, Ernest, 1830–1892, a sculptor.

Claude, 1807–1880, chief of police in Paris 1859–1875, arrested and imprisoned by the Commune.

Clemenceau, Georges, 1841–1929, a French politician of the Left in his early years, a doctor, mayor of Montmartre under the National Defense Government, took no part in the Commune, premier during World War I.

Clément de Ris, Athanase-Louis Torterat, Comte de, 1820–1882, an art critic, became curator of the Versailles museum in 1878.

Colet, Louise, 1810–1867, a romantic woman of letters, mistress of various important figures including Flaubert and Musset.

Courbet, Gustave, 1819–1877, the champion of realism in painting, went into exile in 1871 after his implication in the Commune.

Courmont, Philippe de, 1830–1871, a Goncourt cousin, died during the Commune.

Cousin, Victor, 1792–1867, a philosopher and politician of note.

Crémieux, Adolphe (Isaac-Moïse), 1796–1880, initially a sup-

Biographical Notes

porter, then an opponent of Napoleon III, Minister of Justice in the National Defense Government.

Dampierre, Anne-André-Marie Picot, Comte de, 1835–1870.

Decamps, Gabriel-Alexandre, 1803–1860, a painter of the romantic orientalist group.

Dorian, Pierre-Frédéric, 1814–1873, a deputy under the Empire, Minister of Public Works under the National Defense Government.

Ducrot, Auguste-Alexandre, 1817–1882, a general, Trochu's right arm, in command of various sorties during the siege.

Dudevant, Casimir, Baron, husband of George Sand, the novelist.

Dufaure, Armand-Jules-Stanislas, 1798–1881, a member of the government after the siege and the Commune.

Dumas, Alexandre, 1802–1870, the renowned author of historical romances.

Du Mesnil, Antoine-Jules, 1805–1891, a lawyer and later senator, also a writer on art.

Dumont d'Urville, Jules, 1790–1842, a famous navigator and naturalist.

Duplessis, Georges, 1834–1899, curator of the Print Room in the Bibliothèque Nationale.

Durand, Jacques, born about 1816, a shoemaker, member of the Commune.

Duvernois, Clément, 1836–1879, a member of the Palikao cabinet, in England during the siege and the Commune.

Favre, Jules, 1809–1880, a lawyer and politician, vice-president of the National Defense Government, negotiated the armistice with Germany, member of the Académie Française.

Ferri-Pisani-Jourdan (J. B. Félix, Comte de Saint-Anastase), 1836–1882, a general of brigade.

Ferry, Jules, 1832–1893, a politician who participated in the National Defense Government, later had an important role in education and in the conquest of Tunis and Tonkin, premier 1880–1881.

Feydeau, Ernest, 1821–1873, a man of letters, author of the novel *Fanny*.

Filon, Augustin, 1841–1916, a man of letters, tutor of the Prince Imperial, with whom he emigrated to England in 1870.

Flaubert, Gustave, 1821–1880, celebrated author of *Madame Bovary*, close friend of the Goncourt brothers, one of the intimates of Princess Mathilde's circle.

Floquet, Charles, 1828–1896, a lawyer, politician, and journalist in opposition to the Empire, adjoint mayor of Paris with Etienne Arago, attempted mediation between Versailles and the Communards.

Flourens, Gustave, 1838–1871, a revolutionary, one of the fomenters of the October 31 uprising, a leader of the Commune, died in the course of the latter.

Franchetti, Léon-Joseph, died in 1870, a cavalry officer, organized a group of irregulars.

Gagneur, Just-Wladimir, 1807–1880, a Fourierist, exiled under the Second Empire, a member of the National Defense Government.

Gambetta, Léon, 1838–1882, a lawyer and politician, proclaimed a republic at the Hotel de Ville on September 4, active in attempting to rally opposition to the Germans during the siege, escaped from Paris by balloon.

Gautier, Théophile, 1811–1872, one of the chief ornaments of the romantic movement in literature.

Gavarni, Pierre, born in 1846, son of the famous artist and himself a painter and sculptor.

Girardin, Emile de, 1806–1881, a journalist and politician.

Giraud, Eugène, 1806–1881, a painter.

Got, Edmond, 1822–1901, a comic actor at the Comédie Française.

Gudin, Théodore, 1802–1880, a painter of marine subjects.

Guizot, Guillaume, 1833–1892, a man of letters and scholar, son of the statesman.

Biographical Notes

Haussmann, Georges, Baron, 1809–1891, prefect of the Department of the Seine 1853–1869, famous for the physical transformation of Paris effected under his leadership.

Hébrard, Adrien, 1834–1914, director of *Le Temps*, a great political influence in behalf of the moderate republicans.

Hervilly, Ernest d', 1839–1911, a man of letters.

Hetzel, Jules, 1814–1886, a journalist and politician, in exile from December 2, 1851 until the amnesty of 1859, publisher of the works of Verne and Hugo.

Hirsch, Alphonse, 1843–1884, an artist celebrated for his portraits of men of letters.

Houssaye, Arsène, 1815–1896, a man of letters, director of the Comédie Française 1849–1856.

Hugo, Charles-Victor, 1826–1871, son of the poet, man of letters and one of the founders of *L'Evénement*, in exile with his father, editor of *Le Rappel*.

Hugo, Victor, 1802–1885, the celebrated poet, whose return from exile was an important event in the fall of 1870.

Jongkind, Johann Barthold, 1819–1891, a Dutch painter, one of the early Impressionists.

Kératry, Emile, Comte de, 1832–1905, prefect of police in Paris from September 4 to October 14, escaped from the city by balloon.

Knaus, Ludwig, 1829–1910, a German painter of sentimental scenes.

La Fontaine (Louis-Marie-Henri Thomas), 1826–1898, an actor at the Comédie Française.

Langlé, Aylic, 1829–1870, an author and politician, died of a stroke in 1870.

La Païva (Thérèse Lachman, Marquise de), 1819–1884, a courtesan à la mode in the Second Empire.

La Vallette, Félix, Marquis de, 1806–1881, a diplomat and minister under the July Monarchy and the Second Empire.

La Voix, Henri, 1820–1892, curator of medals at the Bibliothèque Nationale, a writer on Musulman art.

Lecomte, Claude-Martin, 1817–1871, a general shot at the outbreak of the Commune.

Ledru-Rollin, Alexandre-Auguste, 1807–1874, a lawyer and politician, a member of the provisional government of 1848, in exile under the Second Empire and not included in any of the amnesties, took no part in the Commune.

Le Flô, Charles, 1804–1887, a general, Minister of War during the siege and the Commune.

Lefrançais, Gustave, 1826–1901, in exile after December 2, 1851, a member of the Commune, took refuge in Geneva when the Commune was crushed.

Legouvé, Ernest, 1807–1903, a dramatic author and reader.

Lemud, François-Joseph-Aimé de, 1816–1886, an illustrator, engraver, and lithographer.

Lullier, Ernest-Charles, 1838–1891, a naval officer who committed himself to the Commune, general-in-chief of the National Guard, condemned to death after the Commune but sentence commuted.

MacMahon, Marie-Edmé-Patrice de, Duc de Magenta, 1808–1893, a marshal of France, defeated at Reichshoffen in 1870, later President of the Republic.

Mahérault, Marie-Joseph-François, 1795–1879, a public functionary and art historian.

Mahias, a member of the National Defense Government.

Marchal, Charles, 1826–1877, a painter of genre and historical subjects.

Marguerittes, Anne-Marie de Villedeuil, Comtesse de, born 1830, a Goncourt cousin cited for adultery in 1870.

Maria, a midwife, mistress of Jules and Edmond, supplied them with information about their servant Rose which they used in *Germinie Lacerteux*.

Biographical Notes

Marin (Eugène Labille), 1845–1930, a Goncourt cousin.

Masson, Frédéric, 1847–1923, a historian of the Bonapartes.

Mendès, Catulle, 1841–1909, a Parnassian poet.

Mérimée, Prosper, 1803–1870, a leader of the romantic school, a friend of the Emperor and Empress, a senator.

Meurice, Paul, 1818–1905, a novelist and dramatist, editor-in-chief of *L'Evénement*, editor-in-chief of *Le Rappel*.

Morny, Charles, Duc de, 1811–1865, bastard brother of Napoleon III, one of the chief figures in the coup d'état of December 2, 1851, and in the Second Empire.

Mottu, Jules Alexander, 1830–1907, banker and merchant, mayor of the Eleventh Arrondissement after September 4, 1870, until March 29, 1871; a supporter of Charles Delescluze; took no part in the Commune; was elected a municipal councillor in July 1871.

Nadar, pseudonym of Félix Tournachon, 1820–1910, a caricaturist and photographer of note, an enthusiast about airships, developed the first military balloons.

Nefftzer, Auguste, 1820–1876, a journalist, founded *Le Temps* in 1861, a powerful anti-imperial influence.

Nieuwerkerke, Alfred-Emilien, Comte de, 1811–1892, a sculptor, superintendent of Beaux Arts under the Empire, lover of Princess Mathilde.

Nubar-Pasha, 1825–1899, confidential advisor of the Egyptian Abbas-Pasha.

Ollivier, Emile, 1825–1913, a politician, briefly premier under the Empire in 1870.

Palikao, Charles-Guillaume-Antoine Cousin-Montauban, Comte de, 1796–1878, a general, premier at the fall of the Empire.

Parfait, Noël, 1813–1896, a man of letters, a deputy under the Third Republic.

Pélagie (Denis), born 1831, went into service with the Goncourt brothers in 1868 and remained with Edmond until his death.

Pelletan, Eugène, 1813–1884, a journalist and novelist, a member

Biographical Notes

of the National Defense Government, later a deputy and senator.

Pelletier, Edouard, died in 1900, a lawyer, counselor at Orléans.

Pène, Henri de, 1830–1888, a journalist with monarchist sympathies.

Picard, Ernest, 1821–1877, a lawyer and politician, a member of the National Defense Government, a supporter of Thiers.

Pipe-en-Bois, pseudonym of Georges Cavalier, 1841–1878, a Latin Quarter bohemian whom Goncourt considered responsible for the attack on the play *Henriette Maréchal,* a member of the Commune.

Ponson du Terrail, Pierre-Alexis, Vicomte de, 1829–1871, author of popular novels.

Popelin, Claudius, 1825–1892, a painter and man of letters, an intimate of Princess Mathilde's household.

Pouillet, Eugène, 1835–1905, a lawyer specializing in matters of intellectual property.

Pouthier, Alexandre, a painter, a childhood friend of Edmond de Goncourt.

Prince Imperial, Eugène-Louis Jean-Joseph Bonaparte, 1856–1879, killed in Zululand.

Prince Napoléon (Jérôme Bonaparte), 1822–1891, brother of Princess Mathilde.

Princess Mathilde, 1820–1904, daughter of King Jérôme Bonaparte, wife of Anatol Demidov, from whom she was divorced in 1846; her town house and her villa at Saint Gratien were meeting places of literary and artistic society.

Protais, Paul-Alexandre, 1825–1890, a painter of military subjects.

Proth, Mario, 1832–1891, a journalist.

Proudhon, Pierre-Joseph, 1790–1865, a philosopher and socialist theoretician.

Regnault, Henri, 1843–1871, a painter, killed at Buzenval on January 19.

Biographical Notes

Reiset, Marie-Frédéric de, 1815–1891, an art critic and collector, director-general of the national museums 1874–1879.

Renan, Ernest, 1823–1892, a historian and philosopher, involved in controversy by his *Vie de Jésus*, 1863; out of the soul-searching precipitated by the events of 1870–1871 came his *Réforme intellectuelle et morale*, 1872.

Révillon, Antoine (known as Tony), 1832–1898, a journalist, man of letters, and politician.

Richard, Maurice, 1832–1888, Minister of Beaux Arts in Ollivier's government.

Ricord, Philippe, 1800–1889, a doctor well known for his study of venereal disease.

Rochefort, Henri, 1831–1913, a political journalist, founder of *La Lanterne*, a weekly opposed to the Empire, a member of the National Defense Government until October 31, opposed both the Thiers government and the Commune.

Rose (Rosalie Malingre), in service with the Goncourt family 1837–1862, provided the basis of the portrait of Germinie Lacerteux.

Rossel, Louis-Nathaniel, 1844–1871, a general who participated in the Commune and was shot by the Versailles authorities.

Sainte-Beuve, Charles de, 1804–1869, the most authoritative literary critic of his time, his "Lundis" ran in *Le Constitutionnel* or *Le Moniteur* from October 1, 1849 on, a senator under the Empire.

Saint-Victor, Paul Bins, Comte de, 1827–1881, an art and literary critic, Lamartine's secretary in 1848.

Sand, George (Aurore Dupin, Baronne Dudevant), 1804–1876, a renowned novelist of the sentimental-romantic school.

Sarcey, Francisque, 1827–1899, the dominant dramatic critic of his time.

Sasse, Marie, 1838–1907, a singer at the Théâtre-Lyrique and at the Opéra.

Scherer, Edmond, 1815–1889, a politician and literary critic, attached to *Le Temps* from its inception in 1861.

Schoelcher, Victor, 1804–1893, a politician before and after the Second Empire, in exile in England from December 2, 1851, until 1870, elected to the National Assembly in 1871.

Scholl, Aurélien, 1833–1902, a journalist and famous wit.

Simon, Jules, 1814–1896, a politician, member of the National Defense Government, Minister of Public Instruction under Thiers, member of the Académie Française.

Soulié, Eudore, 1817–1876, curator of the Museum of Versailles.

Stoffel, Eugène, Baron, 1823–1880, former military attaché in Prussia, in command of the defense of the Avron plateau.

Strauss, David Friedrich, 1808–1874, a German theologian, author of *The Life of Jesus*.

Sue, Eugène, 1804–1857, the popular author of *Les Mystères de Paris* and *Le Juif errant*.

Tamisier, François, 1809–1880, a general, imprisoned after December 2, 1851; commander of the National Guard in Paris under Trochu; replaced by General Clément Thomas after the October 31 affair, resigning his command on November 9; elected a member of the National Assembly on February 8, 1871.

Thérésa (Emma Valadon), 1837–1913, a comic singer.

Thierry, Edouard, 1813–1894, a literary and dramatic critic, director of the Théâtre Français, later librarian of the Arsenal.

Thiers, Adolphe, 1797–1877, active in political life from the beginning of the July Monarchy on; he put down the Commune and was elected president of the Third Republic in 1871.

Thomas, Clément, 1809–1871, a general, commander of the National Guard during the siege, shot by the Communards on March 18, 1871, had been in exile from December 2, 1851, until September 4, 1870.

Tissot, Charles, 1828–1884, a diplomat and archeologist.

Trochu, Louis, 1815–1896, head of the National Defense Government and military governor of Paris.

Uchard, Mario, 1824–1893, a playwright and novelist.

Uhrich, Jean-Jacques-Alexis, 1802–1886, the general charged with defense of Strasbourg.

Vacquerie, Auguste, 1819–1895, a journalist and dramatist, Hugo's son-in-law, one of the founders of *Le Rappel*, for Paris against Versailles.

Vaillant, Jean Baptiste, 1790–1872, a marshal of France, held high office under the Empire, went into exile on October 22, 1870 after being threatened by a mob.

Vallès, Jules, 1832–1885, a journalist and novelist, founded *Le Cri du Peuple*, a member of the Commune, escaped to London.

Verlaine, Paul, 1844–1896, a major poet of the symbolist movement, compromised by his relations with the Commune, took refuge in London.

Véron, Louis-Désiré, 1798–1867, a publicist and politician, founder of *La Revue de Paris*, director of the Opéra, author of *Les Mémoires d'un bourgeois de Paris*.

Veuillot, Louis, 1813–1883, a Catholic man of letters.

Villedeuil, Pierre-Charles Laurens, Comte de, 1831 (or 1835)–1906, a cousin of the Goncourts, man of letters, founder of *L'Eclair* (1852) and *Paris* (1853).

Villemain, François, 1790–1870, a professor and literary historian, a member of the Académie Française.

Vinoy, Joseph, 1800–1880, replaced Trochu as commander in Paris during the last days of the siege, active in helping put down the Commune.

Viollet-le-Duc, Eugène, 1814–1879, the architect-restorer of Notre Dame de Paris, Carcassonne, Pierrefonds, etc.

Zeller, Jules, 1819–1900, a historian, professor at the Sorbonne, briefly rector of the University of Strasbourg.

Zola, Emile, 1840–1902, the celebrated author of the Rougon-Macquart novels and close friend of Edmond de Goncourt.